Elizabeth Gaskell

Elizabeth Gaskell

by

Angus Easson

Professor of English
University of Salford

Routledge & Kegan Paul
London, Boston and Henley

First published in 1979
by Routledge & Kegan Paul Ltd
39 Store Street,
London WC1E 7DD,
Broadway House,
Newtown Road,
Henley-on-Thames,
Oxon RG9 1EN and
9 Park Street,
Boston, Mass. 02108, USA
Set in 11 on 12pt Latinesque
Photoset, printed and bound in Great Britain by
Weatherby Woolnough
Wellingborough, Northants

British Library Cataloguing in Publication Data

Easson, Angus
Elizabeth Gaskell.
1. Gaskell, Elizabeth Cleghorn - Criticism
and interpretation
823'.8   PR4711   78-40967

ISBN 0-7100-0099-5   710 38093 - 3

Contents

Note on Texts

There is unfortunately no complete edition of Gaskell's works; even the fullest collected editions of Ward and Shorter (see Bibliography) have long been out of print. Some consistency of reference seems necessary, however, and I have used A. W. Ward's Knutsford edition for all page references, except where specifically mentioned in the notes or for uncollected items and *The Life of Charlotte Brontë* (which Ward did not reprint); for this latter my references are to the Penguin English Library edition (1975), edited by Alan Shelston. I have drawn very largely on the letters of Gaskell, edited by J. A. V. Chapple and Arthur Pollard (1966); a number in the text, without further indication – e.g. (106) – is a *page* reference to this edition. Other page references in the text – e.g. (p. 57) – are given when it is clear which work is being quoted from. All works are given a complete bibliographical reference either in the text or in the notes on their first occurrence in each chapter; thereafter, a short form is used in the notes by which they may be identified in the Bibliography.

Acknowledgments

My thanks to B. C. Southam, who invited me to write this volume, and to those who have taken an interest in its progress: Wendy Craik, Stephen Gill, George Powell, Rita Richards, Dennis Robinson, William Ruddick, Alan Shelston, and Deirdre Toomey. For specific help with Fanny Lewald's German, my thanks to W. J. Smith. My thanks to Phyllis Barry, who typed part of an early draft and to Mary Bryden and Lesley Scott, who typed the final version; to Peter Widdowson of Thames Polytechnic and to the Royal Holloway College History Society who invited me to give papers related to this study. I wish to thank J. A. V. Chapple and Arthur Pollard and Manchester University Press for generous permission to use and quote from their edition of Gaskell's letters; while Oxford University Press have generously allowed me to incorporate material from the introduction to my edition of *North and South*. The John Rylands University of Manchester Library have generously given permission to use and quote from the manuscripts of *The Life of Charlotte Brontë* and *Wives and Daughters*, while the staff of this Library (Deansgate Building) and the Manchester Public Library (Central Reference) have been helpful and courteous at all stages of my work.

1

Elizabeth Gaskell

The personal names, the personal presences, the personal
interests, beliefs, so queer and charming and touching, often,
the general mass of current history and current sensibility, that,
as a generation, we have moved away from. They are in short
the vanished society . . .

Henry James, *William Whetmore Story and His Friends*,
1903, i, 35

I

Many who attended the sale of the contents of 84 Plymouth Grove,
Manchester, in mid-February 1914, or viewed its contents the week
before, were drawn no doubt by natural curiosity to see the inside
of a house left by two sisters whose mother had died fifty years
before. Julia Bradford Gaskell died in 1908, and her elder sister
Margaret Emily – 'always called Meta' (81)[1] – in 1913. They had
kept house for their father, the Rev. William Gaskell, until his
death in 1884, and were well known themselves in the Manchester
community. But after fifty years, how to tell, amidst the growing
wrack and disorder of an auction, what was recent and what from
the high days of Elizabeth Gaskell's time – probably the handsome
pierced brass fender in the drawing room. But which amongst the
310 lots of china were survivors? Had the author of *Mary Barton*, of
Cranford, of *Wives and Daughters* used the set of Early English tea
ware (56 pieces) with red and gold butterflies? Or the breakfast set
(45 pieces) with flowers and trees in gold, red and green? Or the
willow-pattern dinner service (65 pieces)? There were association
items: two small sketches by Charlotte Brontë and a picture of

1

Florence Nightingale given to Elizabeth Gaskell by Florence's sister, Lady Verney; a painting of Silverdale, the family holiday spot in Lancashire, two busts of Gaskell and one of her husband. Amongst the books (662 lots in the catalogue) were survivors – William Gaskell's lecture notes on English Literature and Moral Philosophy, three manuscript music books of Elizabeth's (they fetched £5); mingling with Hardy and Kipling were copies of Gaskell's work – the first illustrated *Cranford* (1864), presented to Julia – and Thomas Gray's works, presented by William to E. C. Stevenson before their marriage.[2]

Whether those who attended the sale recognized the fact, it was the dispersal of the last and physical representations of a culture (an uneasy word in English, but necessary) that took its life from the Gaskell family and which in hospitality and artistic creation had peculiarly centred upon Elizabeth Gaskell. That culture drew on much that was best in the nineteenth century, and without its particular tone, Gaskell's own writings could not exist as they do. There are no dark secrets of the psyche to be delved for, but there is much evidence that can be pieced together, however patchy or intangible or liable to distorted emphasis, about the frame of mind, the sensibility that produced a body of work distinguished by range, sensitivity and observation, which while not amongst the top ranks of the Victorian novel none the less is guaranteed permanent interest and survival. This chapter will attempt to chart this culture.

Elizabeth Gaskell was born, Elizabeth Cleghorn Stevenson on 29 September 1810, at 93 Cheyne Walk, Chelsea, London, the second surviving child by her father's first wife, Elizabeth Holland; her elder brother John became a sailor and disappeared about 1827, perhaps contributing to figures like Frederick Hale in *North and South* and Peter in *Cranford*. Her father, William Stevenson (1772–1829), intended for the Dissenting ministry, became convinced, while supporting himself as classical tutor in Manchester and preaching as a Unitarian (1792), that a paid ministry was wrong. He turned to farming, tried his hand at editing, and in 1806 moved to London on appointment as Keeper of the Records of the Treasury. He wrote widely on technical subjects; refused a chair of technology in Russia; and lived in Chelsea until his death. A year after Elizabeth's birth her mother died – through her Gaskell had connections with the great intellectual families of the Darwins and the Wedgwoods[3] – and Elizabeth was taken to Knutsford in

Cheshire by her 'Aunt Lumb', Hannah Holland (c. 1768-1837), who had married Samuel Lumb and was living widowed with her invalid daughter. Gaskell was only to live occasionally with her father again, who remarried in 1814; she remembered those times as 'very, very unhappy' (797). To Aunt Lumb went all her primary affection; an etching of 'Mrs Lumb's House on the Heath' was in the Plymouth Grove sale, and she helped nurse 'my more than mother' in her last illness.[4] It was from Knutsford that she was married (at the parish church, as required by law until 1836) and in the graveyard of its Unitarian chapel (described in Ruth) she is buried with her husband. Though the Knutsford background of her work has been exaggerated, there is no doubt of its closeness to Gaskell's associations.

Gaskell was sent briefly to Avonbank school, Stratford upon Avon, run by the Byerley sisters, where, apart from general instruction, dancing, drawing, Italian, French and music were available. The Stratford countryside provided material for Gaskell's first published piece, a description of Clopton Hall (see Chapter 9). The school building she seems to have used for 'My Lady Ludlow' and it has been argued (rightly, I think) that Hollingford in Wives and Daughters is as much of Warwickshire as Knutsford.[5] One of the Byerley sisters (a redoubtable set), Frances, now Mrs William Parkes, had published Domestic Duties: or, Introduction to Young Married Ladies on the Management of their Households (1825), not unlike Mrs Beeton's later Book of Household Management. Formed into a dialogue between an experienced and a newly married wife, the work covers social relationships and moral and religious duties as well as common domestic cares. Whether Gaskell read it, we don't know, though it said nothing on wifely obedience unacceptable to her, Mrs Parkes not maintaining 'the doctrine of passive obedience in the married female to the will of the husband' (p. 3). Though Gaskell might half-jokingly feel 'sometimes coward enough to wish that we were back in the darkness where obedience was the only seen duty of women' (109), she neither expected nor wanted that subservience.

Leaving Avonbank in 1827, Gaskell went to London and then (1829) to stay with the Rev. William Turner in Newcastle upon Tyne, a typical example of the connections between Unitarian families. No details are known of her life in Newcastle, but we may presume a minimal constraint and cheerful home.[6] She was in

3

Edinburgh in 1831, where she was enough admired for a flourishing miniature to be painted of her;[7] that same year she met her husband. William Turner's daughter had married the co-minister at Cross Street Chapel, Manchester, James Gooch Robberds. Invited to stay, Elizabeth met Robberds's colleague, William Gaskell. An untitled page in one of her manuscript music books has a pencil note at its foot: 'May I go with you somewhere to have you to myself?'[8] Did William use it to ask a silent question as she played and he turned the pages? Or is it the plea of an earlier admirer?

In 1832 they were married and set up home at 14 Dover Street, where her first three children, Marianne, Meta and Florence Elizabeth were born; her only son, William, who died of scarlet fever at less than a year, and Julia Bradford, were born at 121 Upper Rumford Street. Then from early 1850 they lived at 42 (later renumbered 84) Plymouth Grove, the house of her years of fame, great centre of her domestic, religious, social and artistic activities. It was not quite her last house, for she was secretly buying one near Alton in Hampshire as a retirement home for herself and William; here she died on 12 November 1865, in the midst of a conversation, leaving her greatest novel, *Wives and Daughters*, not quite finished. Throughout her married life Gaskell made her home a vital centre, where William carried out his religious and educational duties, where Sunday-schools came, where famous people were welcomed, where she raised her children and where, amidst it all, from 1847, she was writing. This many-sided life revealed something of itself to the curious at that 1914 dispersion, as it still faintly does in the sale catalogue, if rawly and with the spirit gone.

II

The immediate fact in 1832 was that Elizabeth had become a Unitarian minister's wife, and religion is a constant factor in the life of the household, even when not directly brought into play. Unmentioned it may be, but never forgotten. Elizabeth Gaskell was a Unitarian. And while it is possible to read her works without becoming aware of that fact - sensitivity might make a reader suspect a connection with Dissent in some form - it was a fact intensely important to her personally and to her background. Her family and her husband were Unitarians and in that faith she found a rule of conduct, a way to the inner or ideal life that yet stressed the full play of reason, and a sympathy which sought to include all Christians and understand other creeds. Comprehension, an agreement on the minimum belief necessary to call oneself Christian, was constantly before advanced Unitarians of the nineteenth century. Other Churches enforced their identity by a body of necessary belief as the test of membership. The absence of this body of belief meant that Unitarianism was a peculiarly open church in the nineteenth century, where people might attend service and yet be communicants elsewhere.[9]

Unitarianism originates theologically in the rejection of two doctrines (others fall with them) – the Trinity and the Divinity of Christ. The first mystery was rejected by minds who saw only a paradox, justification being sought in Scripture for their denial of three persons who are yet one God. Their argument that certain passages are interpolated, or corrupt, or wrongly translated appealed to the Protestant right to individual enquiry and to reason. As Joseph Priestley argued in the eighteenth century, since religion and reason proceed from the same God, they cannot be contrary to one another. How but by reason can we judge of one religious scheme or another? The danger was to exalt reason; but Priestley urged the conjunction of reason and the Scriptures to guard against 'the gross delusions of Papists, who, after relinquishing reason, have been *made to believe a lie'*.[10] The rational basis of one God and him alone to be worshipped once established, the scriptural account of the ministry of Jesus and the promise of the Christ in the Old Testament had to be considered. What was the status of this being who could no longer be a second person of the Trinity? In turn he became god yet subsidiary to the one God (– the Arian position that Gaskell inclined to: 'more I suppose what would be called Arian than Humanitarian' (648)); then man yet god-like in power and authority; and eventually man, frail as we are, physically and morally, even though marked out by God. The Bible was still the essential basis, open for all men to read and interpret (how could any man fix the point beyond which his fellows might go no further in their enquiries?). Whatever Jesus's status, there was still no ultimate challenge to him or to scriptural authority: still no sense that Jesus was other than divinely appointed or the scriptures other than divinely inspired, however they might have suffered in transmission.

A vital outcome of this demolition (or re-establishment) of Jesus was that with his divinity went the Doctrine of Atonement. As God, Christ took on himself the sins of mankind, his suffering and death being in balance a sufficient atonement for man's offences against God: man's salvation, impossible through his own efforts, is obtained through the saving blood of Jesus, freely given. But if man, Jesus could not volunteer to take our sins on him nor his death atone for them - so the doctrine of salvation by grace alone through Jesus had to go and with it, almost inevitably, went all ideas of predestination. The relationship was between God and man, with Jesus not as mediator but as example: 'it is a great dishonour to God to suppose that this mercy and grace takes its rise from anything but his own essential goodness'.[11]

On two great principles, Unitarianism sticks: Unity of God, to whom all worship must be paid, and Jesus's mission as a man approved by God. The appeals are to reason and the Scriptures: every man's right to his own way to God, and the wrong of state establishment. In this openness of minimal belief, beyond which lay agnosticism and atheism, are the ideas of Christianity and a Church, though many in the nineteenth century found them too vague to be the Church they wanted.

Priestley had written enthusiastically of his own efforts, supporting Unitarianism's claim to be a restoration rather than an innovation, that 'we see the abuses gradually corrected, and Christianity recovering its primitive beauty and glory'.[12] The process of 'recovery' was a slow and uneven one.[13] Before the mid-seventeenth century heterodox opinions about the Trinity and the Nature of Christ were insignificant, except as indications of where independent study of the Bible might lead. The ideas of Socinus (1539-1604), that Jesus was not God, began to circulate in England early in the seventeenth century: Socinian (generally an abusive term) was the common label of Unitarians until the end of the eighteenth century. In 1662, after the Restoration, those ministers who refused to conform to the Church of England were expelled and the congregations established around these Nonconformists (Independents, Presbyterians and Baptists) were the main ancestors of modern Unitarians.[14] Through the late seventeenth and the eighteenth centuries these Dissenters moved in the direction of broader tolerance, simpler doctrine, and the test of reason in interpreting Scripture. A movement within the Church of England itself, questioning first the Trinity and then the Nature of Christ, largely died away, though with Theophilus Lindsey's resignation from his living (1774) and his establishment in a chapel at Essex Street, London, it seemed as though an Anglican tradition might be grafted onto Unitarianism. But few followed him, and when he retired his pulpit was filled by Thomas Belsham (1805), a former Dissenter, who might possess 'a scull that never reached in thought and thorough imagination two inches',[15] yet was an organizer and controversialist of great experience and skill. He was a worthy successor to Joseph Priestley, whose writings had formulated, as no one before had attempted, the tenets of the faith, and who came to be regarded as leader and spokesman for Unitarianism.[16] By 1810 England had twenty avowed Unitarian congregations.

Though young men were often attracted to Unitarianism at the end of the eighteenth century – Coleridge, Lamb and Hazlitt were early associated with it, partly because of Unitarianism's popular connection with political radicalism (Priestley's Birmingham house was destroyed in 1791 by 'King and Church' rioters hostile to the French Revolution) – many eventually moved away. Rejection was usually emotional rather than doctrinal: something seemed lacking in the reconciliation of religion and reason that Priestley offered. He himself was suspicious of mere feeling: since we are to form our life in following righteousness, mercy and truth, 'To judge of our love of God, or our love of Christ, directly, by what we *feel* when we think of them, especially when we are excluded from the world ... is to expose ourselves to the grossest and most dangerous delusions'.[17] Though a warning against superstition and 'enthusiasm', this idea of Unitarianism's coldness, light (reason) but no warmth (feeling), is in most adverse criticism.[18] In rejecting the divinity of Christ, the Unitarians had rejected the idea of a Redeemer, had denied 'that the Almighty had, in His own person, by some act of condescension and sacrifice, interfered to redress the evils and miseries of His creatures!' Where was the God who had shared in the world; wrestled with it; had known and therefore fully understood our humanity and had power to heal all its ill?[19] Priestley had prized reason and denied imagination. Yet human nature seemed so often to require mysteries. By 1799 Coleridge, who had thought of the Unitarian ministry, noted an opposition: 'Socinianism Moonlight – Methodism etc A Stove! O for some Sun that shall unite Light to Warmth'.[20] Methodism certainly offered that warmth of feeling, experienced by John Wesley at his conversion (1738): 'I felt my heart strangely warmed. I felt I did trust in Christ, Christ alone, for salvation',[21] but with the warmth went the doctrines, which Unitarians could not go back to. Yet unless the imagination was offered something to feed on it seemed Unitarianism would die. The rationalism of the eighteenth century, which had helped form Unitarianism, was being rejected in the Romantic movement; there was that new spirit afloat, characterized by Basil Willey as 'a sense that there were spiritual needs, and unseen realities, which had been unrecognized in the religious, ethical, political, and aesthetic teachings of the immediate past. The new demand was for an interpretation of the whole range of human experience which should be richer, more deeply satisfying, than the old, dry, superficial rationalism.'[22] Priestley's primitive Christianity, once 'recovered', brought on a crisis of religious response.

The revival of an emotional strain in Unitarianism, though part of a general current, finds its key figure in James Martineau. Born in Norwich in 1805, younger brother of the formidable Harriet whose progress into secularism was one path from Unitarianism, James came of Huguenot stock, long Unitarian.[23] Intended for an engineer, he experienced conversion, under which he found the chapels inadequate, 'too sober and too cold; and amid the broken lights of an immature judgment he thought there to be some stronger and more spiritual ministry, that should . . . take us off our feet, and fling us into a diviner life than that which prevailed among us.'[24] After Manchester New College (then at York), where William Gaskell was a fellow student, and ordination in Dublin (1828), he moved to Liverpool (1832-1857) – in an outwardly active life he never lost sight of the need for that 'stronger and more spiritual ministry'.

In 1856, writing about Coleridge, Martineau saw the Socinian moonlight in Coleridge's Unitarian associates and, understanding the poet's genius, understood why he rejected their religion, which Martineau himself was to revivify in spirit. He characterized those older Unitarians as a 'people eminently practical and prosaic, impatient of romance . . . scrupulous of the veracities but afraid of the fervours of devotion'.[25] These Unitarians, of course, survived; Gaskell recoiled from one school proposed for Marianne which offered 'the very worst style of dogmatic hard Unitarianism' (136), and 'Hampstead Unitarians' seems a touchstone for her of limited outlook (637). Martineau, in preaching and writing, showed the way to spiritual qualities, beginning from Jesus as man, yet proceeding by reason only though prompted first by the passional:

> 'A man,' says the apostle Paul, 'is the image and glory of
> God.' And truly, it is from our own human nature, from its
> deep experience, and earliest affections, that we form our
> conceptions of Deity . . . All that we believe within us, we first
> feel within us; and it is the one sufficient proof of the
> grandeur and awfulness of our nature, that we have faith in
> God; for no merely finite being can possibly believe the
> infinite.[26]

Any echo in this of Coleridge's 'I no sooner felt, than I sought to understand' may be coincidence so far as language is concerned, but the idea of feeling (faith) as necessary to our relationship with God is no coincidence, for Martineau has a Coleridgean sense of the One Life, uniting feeling and reason.

For someone like Gaskell's friend, Susanna Winkworth, who acknowledged the truth of Unitarianism, there was still the need for a personal Redeemer and a communion service that was the symbolic enactment of Christ's promise. It was feeling, the result of aesthetic experience, that led her to the Anglican communion: 'It is curious that my first glimpses and flashings of the idea of a *Church* came to me in hearing Mozart's Twelfth Mass the first time I was ever in a Roman Catholic Chapel.' Surveying her spiritual progress, she added, 'I see now that the fulness of my belief in the indwelling Spirit has all along rendered my inward religion something very different from that of Unitarians in general'.[27] Though Susanna finally followed her feelings rather than what reason bound her to, it was for such people that Martineau employed himself. Talking of 'The Spirit of Life in Jesus Christ', and presenting Christ as 'the representative and revealer' of both 'the human and the divine mind' (p. 2), Martineau deliberately uses a spectrum of language that includes intuitive, emotional and rational terms: 'we read in the gospel a divine allegory of humanity, symbolical of those profound and silent changes, of passion and speculation, of faith and love, through which a holy mind rises to its most godlike power' (p. 4).

Martineau helped open up the possibilities of mysteries in faith. He argued that to feel that God 'lives, as the percipient and determining agent, throughout the universe, conscious of all things actual and possible from the vivid centre to the desert margin of its sphere' is a 'sublimer, and therefore a truer mode of thought, than the conception of a remote and retired mechanism', which gives nothing 'for those affections which seek, not the finite, but the infinite'. The Psalms and Christ's prayers offer 'the living contact of the Divine Spirit with the human'.[28] He insisted upon the moral, not the physical, divinity of Christ: the moonlight began to glow.

There were other influences. Some Methodist congregations came over to Unitarianism, without abandoning their personal conviction in Jesus, and sects like the Christian Brethren, active between 1841 and 1848, may have contributed. Travers Madge, a strange, haunted figure, son of a Unitarian minister, who had worked in Manchester Sunday-schools, and who liked best to preach among the offshoots of Wesleyanism which were becoming Unitarian, with 'their love of vigorous, unconventional preaching, their capacity for being wrought up into fervour and enthusiasm', visited these Christian Brethren and found them congenial.[29] Though increasingly separated from formal Unitarianism, Madge undoubtedly played a part in cross-fertilization.

Unitarians' simplicity of doctrine and their tolerance (Gaskell's remark, 'But then you know I am not (Unitarianly) orthodox!' (784–5), is keenly aware of individual freedom in belief) allowed them to come, even if not passionately, to the Scriptures and the man Jesus without perpetual worry about dogmas. In William Gaskell's short study, 'The Person of Christ', Priestley's rationality mixes with Martineau's feeling. To Gaskell, Trinitarian belief meant that 'the simple narrative of Christ's life, instead of being as now a sweet solace and refreshment, would become filled with perplexing puzzles, and the most touching and beautiful passages deprived of their natural effect'. He cites Jesus at the well (John 4), where the orthodox must puzzle out Christ's two natures and how far one remains unaffected while the other is tired and thirsty, 'and in the midst of such questing the quiet charm of the holy narrative is gone'. William Gaskell leaves himself open to the sceptic's questions: why Jesus, if he is not God? was Jesus conscious of the divine will that expected him to suffer on the cross? Important to him, and we may be sure, to his wife, was that in Jesus, as a man tempted in all points as we are, 'we look up with unmingled admiration to the heights of moral glory which he attained'.[30]

Gaskell herself belonged to the newer tradition, though aware of the older that had received its character 'from the staid, quiet, formal, scholarly Dissent, which grew up in the old Presbyterian conversion',[31] and which receives its most sympathetic portrait in Mr Benson, the crippled, learned minister in *Ruth*. For herself, Gaskell needed the spirit rather than doctrine; in 1854 she commented: 'oh! for some really spiritual devotional preaching instead of controversy about doctrines, – about which I am more and more certain *we can never be certain* in this world' (537). Her chief statements of belief are called out by particular circumstances – by an encounter, holidaying at Heidelberg, with a young man, and by a crisis over Marianne, dangerously drawn to Roman Catholicism. Charles Bosanquet was an Evangelical, who fell in with them in Germany and assumed they were Anglicans (like most Unitarians, the Gaskells found no difficulty in attending services of other denominations). Meta got her mother to tell him what faith they were. This was some shock to him, though not as much as expected, and he in turn could explain the Low Church as more beautiful and true than Gaskell had realized (520, 648). The encounter with Bosanquet stresses the isolation of Unitarians – not because they shut people out, but because nineteenth-century sectarianism was often hostile to all other shades of opinion; Unitarians were particularly beyond the pale.[32] The Gaskells were the first Bosanquet had met and though his parents allowed the friendship to develop, they had always been hostile. Gaskell found Charlotte Brontë's husband, A. B. Nicholls, hostile from his high Anglican position (his wife's friends were 'heretics') and despite Gaskell's attempts at understanding (327) he seems to have conceded little during Charlotte's life. About 1860 an advertisement inserted in the *Norfolk Chronicle* declared Unitarians 'outcasts from the Christian hope';[33] but against hostile reactions it is equally important to stress that Charlotte Brontë was her special friend and that the first bishop of Manchester, James Prince Lee, took the initiative by calling on the Gaskells, invited them to his house, and talked with William about Unitarianism even in the midst of his 'cursing Evangelicals' (91, 112).[34] Gaskell's most explicit statement of faith (hedged around with implied attitudes and objections) is that to Marianne in 1854, some seven years before the Catholic crisis: she agrees about the aesthetic charm of worship in Church, but falls back on moral principle:

> I know it is wrong not to clear our minds as much as possible
> as to the nature of that God, and tender Saviour, whom we

can not love properly unless we try and define them clearly to ourselves. Do you understand me my darling! I have often wished to talk to you about this. Then the one thing I *am* clear and sure about is this that Jesus Christ was not equal to His father; that, however divine a being he was *not* God; and that worship as God addressed to Him is therefore wrong in me . . . (860).

Gaskell's religion was direct, scriptural and practical. It was above all doing the good that lay to hand. She wrote feelingly of a sermon by F. D. Maurice, in which 'he spoke of the falseness of that religious spirit which led people to disregard those nearest to them . . . in search of some new sphere of action' (47), and much though she admired Florence Nightingale she found it disquieting that Nightingale could do good in a general rather than a particular way: 'that text always jarred against me, that "Who is my mother and my brethren?" ' (319). The work to hand lay at the heart of 'the real earnest Christianity which seeks to do as much and as extensive good as it can' (117). The idea of duty done lies at the heart of her understanding of Charlotte Brontë, who like Gaskell neglected no household responsibility before turning to her writing. The spirit of this Christianity is in her favourite texts and her use of the Bible in writing, where a character's choice of quotation is often particularly indicative: the Book of Job is for sympathy and for contrast with the bustle of the world – in *North and South*, Hale thinks to read the bereaved Higgins the fourteenth chapter. Along with the human moments of the Old Testament (Ruth and Naomi, for instance), most citations are from the New Testament, almost all from the evangelists: Bessy Higgins's frequent recourse in *North and South* to Revelation suggests the heated, millennial fervour of her troubled life and soul. Against her hopes of crowns and visions of Apocalypse, Margaret Hale brings 'All beautiful scriptures', the refreshment they promise deliberately contrasted to Bessy's view of earth as the great battle of Armageddon and her hope of New Heaven and New Earth.

Unitarianism urged comprehension and tolerance upon its members and upon all fellow Christians: in *North and South*, 'Margaret the Churchwoman, her father the Dissenter, Higgins the Infidel, knelt down together. It did them no harm' (p. 233). If others cut themselves off, Gaskell herself was ready to meet those whose ideas and experience were very different from her own, which gave her something of that openness, even scepticism, of mind so necessary to the artist. Though F. D. Maurice, for instance, had passed from Unitarian to Anglican, and wrote his *Theological Essays* (1853) largely to controvert the Unitarian position, she wrote admiringly of him and vigorously defended him shortly after his dismissal from King's College, London, for unsoundness on Eternal Punishment.[35] Again, the close friendship of the Winkworths, particularly of Catherine and Susanna, survived without difficulty the latter's move to Anglicanism (Catherine always was Anglican, though much influenced by James Martineau). The Winkworths show the reciprocal tolerance possible from church people and acknowledged that

> Unitarians in Manchester were, as a body, far away superior to any other in intellect, culture, and refinement of manners, and certainly did not come behind any other in active philanthropy and earnest efforts for the social improvement of those around them.[36]

More extraordinary was Gaskell's fellowship with those passing beyond 'orthodox' Christianity or into its extreme forms. An amiable oddity was Francis William Newman, younger brother of John Henry, Professor of Classics in Manchester, 1840 to 1846, at the New College. A complete contrast to his brother, Francis moved through strict Calvinism to a spiritual faith in God free of all dogma, holding any fixed creed established as test of spiritual character as 'a most unjust, oppressive and mischievous superstition'.[37] Truth, however unpopular or difficult, was what he sought, often with the assiduity that produced the paradoxical 'A Defence of Carthage' and translations of Homer that led to a remarkable clash with Matthew Arnold. His appearance was striking: in 1847 he was described as 'a thin acute-looking man, oddly simple, almost quaint in his manner, but with a sweetness in his expression'. Another witness remarked on the North American Indian cast of his face, his smile rare but 'peculiarly sweet and engaging'.[38] Gaskell felt him holy, and wrote of how 'the face and voice at first sight told "He had been with Christ".... I long for the days back again when he came dropping in in the dusk and lost no time in pouring out what his heart was full of' (87-8). His dress was already shabby, including the famous bottle-green top-coat

13

(normally worn over two others) and possibly the trousers edged with a few inches of leather.[39]

Born in 1805, Newman had set out in 1830 with a small group of earnest Christians to convert the Móslems of Baghdad: a crazy expedition – one member, a recent widower, took his infant daughter and elderly mother.[40] Their originality was in trusting to convert by example, of 'a little colony, so animated by primitive faith, love, and disinterestedness, that the collective moral influence of all might interpret and enforce the words of the few who preached.'[41] They were also convinced that work could not hope to begin before thorough mastery of the language. Difficulties arose: gradually Newman came to see the problem of unintelligibility in a religion which was not external,[42] while personally he was moving to an Arian viewpoint and towards rejection of the New Testament as the law and basis of Christianity. Contact with other religions turned Newman increasingly to the basis of his own: it may not only have been Moslem resistance to conversion that determined his sudden return to England in 1833. He had borne much: while escaping from stoning in one village, he had his umbrella seized from his saddle, the assailant beating him with it as they galloped side by side until Newman wrested the umbrella back 'and then beat off his [assailant's] horse's head'.[43] At one point he had fever so badly he expected to die and was saddened by the failings of some companions; yet Newman learned much of language, of customs, and most important of the need to scrutinize his own beliefs. He always called himself a Christian, while rejecting all 'proofs' from the New Testament and rejecting the character of Jesus, so moving beyond any Unitarian: if Jesus was a man, for Newman he was sinful man like himself – a view different from Gaskell's Arianism and painful to friends like the Winkworths, whose chief intellectual intercourse, before they met the Gaskells, had been with Newman.[44]

Phases of Faith (1850) is a spiritual charting of rejection, though its main arguments are those of Newman's earlier book *The Soul* (1849): that religion, not a matter of revelation but of intuition, is essentially imaginative and spiritual. 'Religion', Newman felt, 'was created by the inward instincts of the soul: it had afterwards to be pruned and chastened by the sceptical understanding.'[45] *The Soul* has a Coleridgean stress on the importance of the imagination coupled with a recognition that since our language, however limited, is bound up with the expression and exploration of our feelings, figurative or poetic language used of our relationship to God, far from an avoidance, is the only vehicle for conveying truth. In such language Newman spoke of the soul as 'the mirror, in which alone God's face is to be seen', as 'that side of human nature upon which we are in contact with the Infinite, and with God, the Infinite Personality'.[46] Eccentric, often withdrawn, unorthodox, Newman was welcome still in the Gaskell house and opened up ideas, provided information and experience which, though never drawn on for the fiction, are part and measure of the largeness of the circle.[47]

Newman was eccentric, yet happily at terms with his eccentricity; moved radically in his religious position, yet by 1850 had worked out a way for himself; full of ideas, yet open to others' points of view. As such he offers a contrast as well as comparison to the unhappy but not untypical figure of Travers Madge, whose conscience and inner search allowed no rest in his short life – he died in 1866, aged 43. In a religious development as wide as Newman's (the son of a Unitarian minister, Madge was admitted a Methodist in 1853, and baptized an Anglican in 1864),[48] Madge always believed his own point of conviction to be the true one and therefore rejected (*not* scorned) those who could not go with him and who remained steady in belief. After study at Manchester College and work with the Lower Moseley Street Sunday-schools, he was drawn in the 1840s to those offshoots, already mentioned, of Methodism-turned-Unitarian and to the Christian Brethren; though intended for the Unitarian ministry he now rejected a paid ministry ('hireling shepherds'), as he had rejected the idea of prizes or competition in examinations. He never spared himself; a not untypical Sunday during 1848-50 found him walking to Oldham, visiting five Sunday-schools (three of them excluded from the Church for teaching writing), preaching twice, then back in Manchester preaching again and finishing with a Teetotal Meeting. During this time he founded the *Sunday School Penny Magazine*, to which Gaskell, 'always a willing helper of Travers', contributed 'Hand and Heart' and 'Bessy's Troubles at Home'. A breakdown in health in 1850 was coupled with a dark night of the soul, characterized by feelings of an overwhelming sense of sin and increasing rejection of the Unitarian position. He severed direct ties with the Unitarians, but as best he could continued in the early 1860s a Home Mission amongst the poor, he and Gaskell co-operating during the distress caused by failure in cotton supplies during the American Civil War. But he was, Gaskell could see, 'depressed by the constant sight of their misery' (677), and he finally left Manchester in 1863. For Madge and Gaskell their doctrinal differences were not important: charity, relief, the mission to the poor were. A genuine note of affection sounds in her comments on his illness (110, 833) for a man who gave all of himself.

Madge sought for the work of grace wrought by the sacrifice of Christ, Newman for the spirituality that lay beyond the word of the Bible, Susanna Winkworth for a Church; however involved with Unitarians and Unitarianism they felt dissatisfaction and this clearly was a problem in that belief, as Gaskell disturbingly found in her own daughter Marianne. All dogma removed, forms and trappings removed, Unitarianism might create only a void waiting to be filled by seven devils worse than before. The very openness of their society made this more likely, since they found themselves not only isolated religiously and often socially in a Trinitarian society, whose assumptions were contrary to their belief, but also, unlike say the Jews, in a society where they very deliberately did not themselves separate to keep their faith whole. In 1862 Gaskell was shocked that Marianne, returned from Italy, was drawn to Roman Catholicism, under the influence of Dr Manning. Bringing up her daughter, Gaskell had told in response to her questioning the simple truths of God's goodness and love, and when she was about four began 'to teach her a little prayer morning and night, merely a few words of thanksgiving and blessing'.[49] Elements in Marianne's education and artistic interests combined religious and aesthetic; she practised 'gorgeous Litanies to the Virgin', and sang mass music, while Gaskell provided a print of Raphael's 'Madonna della Sedia' for her room (91, 160, 218) – marginal influences, yet remember Susanna Winkworth's experience of Mozart's mass in a Roman Catholic chapel. Marianne on her return from Rome claimed she had never 'been a Unitarian in belief' (682). She undertook a course of study with her father, whose extreme dislike of Catholicism made her the more inclined to take up its defence (687), and things subsided, though the family, particularly Meta, were much upset.[50] It was a minor episode, heightened by Gaskell's parental love and solicitude, yet a reminder of the inadequacies as well as strengths of Unitarianism.

A breadth of experience, understanding, tolerance, and readiness of comprehension made Gaskell's religion; they also characterize religious concerns in her work. Usually she has the artist's chameleon ability to hide her own belief: Miss Matty's clergyman father in *Cranford* is referred to without comment, while in *Sylvia's Lovers* Dr Wilson, vicar of Monkshaven, though a Tory is also a philanthropist, a hater of Dissent who yet sends broth and vegetables to a rabid Independent. Nevertheless, there is sharper criticism of Wilson than George Eliot allows of a similar figure, Parson Irwine, in *Adam Bede*. Gaskell observes that Wilson, at the sailor's funeral, sees the discord between the laws of man and the laws of Christ, yet gives up the attempt to resolve that discord. For Gaskell the rebuke, even if not pursued, has a living importance, however far back the novel is set, since the dilemma is to be faced now; whereas George Eliot, uninvolved in Christianity, is free to use Irwine as commentator, whatever his spiritual failings. The clearest example of religious intrusion, an episode out of all proportion to what subsequently happens, is Mr Hale's resignation in *North and South:* his doubts are given prominence that seems unnecessary in moving him and family to Milton Northern. Despite commentators, Mr Hale's throwing up of his ministry is not linked directly to William Stevenson's relinquishing of his (he, like Travers Madge, objected to a paid ministry). Rather it is an Anglican's rejection of the Trinity, the 39 Articles, and a parliamentary religion.[51] The fullest portrait of a minister is Benson in *Ruth*, described only as a Dissenter, though his tolerance and doctrine are Unitarian. In the main, the Christian tenor of the works stresses the goodness of God, Jesus as example and God-sent,[52] free forgiveness for all and avoidance of Apocalyptic visions. With Gaskell's tolerance goes also an imaginative understanding that avoids faking: in 'Lois the Witch', for example, the consolation offered Nattee by Lois as they await execution is 'of One who died on the cross for us and for our sakes' (vii, 204), proper to Lois's belief, though the story as a whole is rational in its rejection of witchcraft and the power of the devil. In her works Gaskell's Unitarianism is a presence, rather than a force: she is not a religious novelist, yet there is an informing spirit, brought into fuller play when needed.

III

Closely linked with her religion is Gaskell's education. She was taught by Aunt Lumb and at Avonbank School but, moving in such families as the Newcastle Turners and having a lively mind and curiosity, she picked up much through conversation, observation and reading. The educated people she met are important, since the education available to Dissenters, though often limited, the more so for women, was none the less highly developed and broadminded. The English universities (Oxford and Cambridge) were closed in effect to all except Anglican men; hence William Gaskell went to Glasgow.

Many clergy excluded from Anglican livings at the Restoration set up as schoolmasters, and in the eighteenth century Dissenting Academies were founded to provide an education religiously acceptable and increasingly with a curriculum suited to business, mercantile and technical alike, the pursuits most open to nonconformists. These academies, like the famous one at Warrington, where Joseph Priestley tutored, were more like universities or sixth-form colleges than schools (the students would usually first attend school elsewhere). At Warrington Priestley set up the system sketched out in his *Essay on a course of Liberal Education for Civil and Active Life* (1765), which stressed languages, maths and history. A fellow tutor was Dr Aikin, whose daughter, Anna Laetitia Barbauld, of 'masculine understanding and gentle feminine character',[53] published much for children and on education, read enough by Gaskell for her to remember the moral of the little boy 'who asks all sorts of birds and beasts to come and play with him; and, in every case, receives the sober answer, that they are all too busy'.[54] These institutions were for boys only, but established a standard and kind of education (good, modern, practical) that affected the attitudes of those who educated and met women of the same cultural groups.

In a different way, though perhaps more vitally for Gaskell, there was the spread of Sunday-schools, established largely to educate those who would otherwise receive little or no education, where Gaskell and in due course her daughters taught. Most sects established their own schools, the Unitarians' having a high reputation, though Travers Madge felt rather bitterly that, having little zeal in the salvation of souls, '*education* rather than *conversion* had been their work'.[55] Still, education was important and Unitarians more open than many sects. The atheist George Jacob Holyoake preferred them amongst Christians because 'there was so much more to be learned among them than among any other religious body', and he 'could see that young men of any age trained in Unitarian schools were very superior to Evangelical youths, who had merely spiritual information'.[56] Many people objected to any study other than the Bible and any teaching beyond reading so that that one book might be studied. Although Gaskell got into a scrape through talking about Scott's novels to a group of Sunday-school girls (63, 64), Unitarian schools were prepared to teach on Sunday things that might be to secular advantage. The Lower Moseley Street Sunday-schools in the 1840s took people up to the age of 30 and classes, conducted in the evening as well as through the day (for Travers Madge, classes began at 7.30 a.m.), were not only in reading, writing and religion, but singing and natural history as well.[57]

Other efforts to bring education to the working classes, of which Gaskell would be aware, included individual efforts like that of Sir Benjamin Heywood at Miles Platting, whose agent there, David Winstanley, acted as master of a charity school founded for children of tenants, as well as being secretary of the Sunday-school.[58] More prominent were the Mechanics Institute (in which Winstanley was active), the Working Men's College founded in 1858, at which William Gaskell taught, later absorbed into a scheme of evening classes at Owens College.[59] At a higher level were the Manchester Literary and Philosophical Society, founded in 1781 for advancement of literature and science, which early on had used a room at the back of Cross Street Chapel, and the Portico Library, founded in 1806, of which William Gaskell was chairman (1849-84)[60] - his bust stands in the reading room - from which Gaskell herself so eagerly received current periodicals, though it was a bitter reflection that this was with 'a struggle and a fight' three months after publication, for 'till then they lie on the Portico table, for gentlemen to see' (567).

Advantage seemed to go to men, yet Gaskell's formal education at the Byerleys' was probably closer to that of men in her own religious and social group than that of, say, Church of England girls whose brothers went to public school and university. As in the academies, the emphasis was on modern subjects at Avonbank: literature, history, modern languages. Mrs Barbauld saw a great divide as fixed by the woman being 'excused from all professional knowledge', since her one department in active life was to be wife and mistress of a family. If this seems narrow (real enough given

19

most women's careers), she none the less expected a woman to learn French and Italian - even Latin if she liked, though not Greek; it was in the study of history that a woman would pursue 'manners and sentiments', and again in general literature attention should be engaged by works of sentiment and morals.[61] Mrs Barbauld's Dissenting background, with whatever limitations, is there in her openness to modern subjects, and many in Gaskell's circle went beyond this. Her friend Anna Jameson noted that Harriet Martineau, James's sister, 'talked of the use of classical literature to girls, of the delight she took in Horace; she said every woman who pretends to a commonly good education now reads Latin'; in *Ruth* the Bradshaw girls are taught Latin, and William Gaskell taught Emily and Catherine Winkworth Greek.[62] Gaskell herself seems to have had French and Italian, and at least a little German. It might need extraordinary effort, determination or character, but a liberal education was possible and not uncommon.

Gaskell's childhood reading clearly was extensive and imaginative. No doubt it was directed by those about her, who may have taken to heart Mrs Barbauld's warning that works of sentiment and morals 'often appear under the seducing form of novel and romance',[63] though Gaskell's own allusions to the works written by Barbauld and others to combat those seducing forms tend to be mildly ridiculing. She knew the improving children's literature of her youth: Mrs Barbauld's *Lessons for Children* and Mrs Trimmer's *Fabulous Histories, or The Story of the Robin* (to the pain of Molly Gibson in *Wives and Daughters* the Miss Brownings are irreverently called Flapsy and Pecksy, the names of the girl robins). Her tone suggests that Gaskell may have felt about these imaginative substitutes rather as Charles Lamb when he lamented that

> 'Goody Two Shoes' is almost out of print. Mrs. Barbauld's stuff
> has banished all the old classics of the nursery; and the
> shopman at Newbery's hardly deigned to reach them off an
> old exploded corner of a shelf, when Mary asked for them.
> Mrs. B's and Mrs. Trimmer's nonsense lay in piles about.[64]

Lamb's spirited defence of the imagination would have won Gaskell's whole-hearted approval (she was a child of the Romantics) and she seems to have had no difficulty in laying hands on the old nursery tales and rhymes. They cluster most thickly and amusingly in the short story 'Curious If True', but they spring to hand constantly in the novels: Cinderella, Sleeping Beauty – Mr Benson in *Ruth*, hunch-backed, is carelessly called Riquet-with-the-Tuft by Mr Bellingham, remembering some version of Perrault's *Mother Goose*. Then there are memories of those cheap, crudely produced pamphlets, the Chapbooks, with their popular versions of old stories and woodcut illustrations (the same blocks often doing service in book after book), tales of 'The Seven Champions of Christendom', which Philip of *Sylvia's Lovers* found at St Sepulchre Hospital (p. 491), or the story of Daniel O'Rourke who, drunkenly landing on the moon, clings to the handle of his sickle and responds to the Man in the Moon's command to be off, 'The more you ax us, the more we won't stir'.[65] Chapbooks might be versions of regular novels like *Robinson Crusoe* or the translation of Goethe's *Sorrows of Young Werther* that Philip in his love for Sylvia offers from his own fondness for reading and in hope to beguile her: a book so popular 'at that time that it had a place in all pedlars' baskets, with Law's *Serious Call*, the *Pilgrim's Progress*, Klopstock's *Messiah* and *Paradise Lost*' (p. 260).[66] Strange bed-fellows; but Sylvia put it aside after 'smiling a little at the picture of Charlotte cutting bread and butter in a left-handed manner'. This heritage of stories and tales and rhymes is usually and appropriately linked with children or the uneducated (not in 'Curious If True', but *that* is a very sophisticated collage), yet Gaskell always delights in these ranges of the imagination: even when she treats them playfully, she is never contemptuous.

Novels and belles-lettres she read in vast quantities. She 'was brought up by old uncles and aunts, who had all the old books, and very few new ones' (562), including works like Henry Brooke's *The Fool of Quality* (not everyone's childhood reading): Cervantes, Defoe, Fielding, Sterne, Smollett, Richardson and Goldsmith were obviously amongst these, and the Arabian Nights, and those oriental tales that ornament the *Spectator*, as that 'of the eastern king, who dipped his head into a basin of water, at the magician's command, and ere he instantly took it out went through the experience of a lifetime.'[67] Scott's novels were the new reading of her childhood: Molly Gibson reads *The Bride of Lammermoor* and to the Sunday-school class Gaskell illustrated Queen Elizabeth's character by that unlucky reference to *Kenilworth*. Still, Unitarians had nothing as such against novels and she eagerly read Dickens – snatching the first episode of *Little Dorrit* (1855) over the shoulder of a fellow bus passenger (373) – Thackeray, Charlotte Brontë and George Eliot – delighted by *Scenes of Clerical Life*, 'a discovery of my own' (493), and by *Adam Bede*, where she recognized the Warwickshire of Avonbank 'in every description of natural scenery' (533), though less happy about the author's moral character. She complained at the difficulty of getting books, yet the most recent works were obtained – *David Copperfield* or Ruskin's *Seven Lamps;* she shamelessly begged *Adam Bede* from the publisher, and after George Smith became a friend through publication of *The Life of Charlotte Brontë* he often sent books as loans or gifts.

Early in marriage Gaskell collaborated with her husband in a projected series of imitations of poets, illustrating modern life; only one was completed, in the manner of Crabbe, but she 'got up' the poets, reading Wordsworth, Coleridge, Byron, Dryden and Pope (7). This kind of intensive reading seems rather to have been an exception, yet poetry was of the first importance. Shakespeare, Milton and Chaucer are the great pillars, with Spenser and Fairfax's translation of Tasso, and, amongst the moderns, Wordsworth and Coleridge – strangely, perhaps, Keats and even Shelley seem of little importance, though she knew Keats's first biographer, Richard Monckton Milnes (Lord Houghton). The Romantic influence dominated the Victorian age, absorbed, accepted, and fruitful, and the supreme poetic figure is Wordsworth; his stress on feeling, on ordinary life, and language 'such as men do use', is vital. Gaskell quoted with fondness 'The Old Cumberland Beggar', the line 'we have all of us one human heart' being a key in her thinking on class reconciliation.[68] Her story 'Half a Lifetime Ago' is obviously, even consciously in the idiot brother, a prose Lyrical Ballad, emphasizing the lines of feeling kept open through love. And for her working-class characters Wordsworth's stand for everyday speech contributes their dialect (even when rather coyly glossed and justified in *Mary Barton* from Chaucer and such 'authorities'). The Wordsworth poems she knew centre on the earlier lyrical pieces and *The Excursion* (recommended to Bosanquet as companion on a Lakeland trip (569)): though she eagerly looked forward in 1850 to reading *The Prelude* (130), it appeared too late in her life to be a significant force – a fact difficult for us to realize, who have ditched *The Excursion* and discovered *The Prelude*. Of modern poets, Gaskell had no doubt about the giant – Tennyson; of the Brownings, Elizabeth

Barrett figured larger, and though she knew the Arnold family a. Matthew's poem on Haworth Churchyard, this poetry never penetrated her as did 'Oenone' and 'Mariana' and 'The Gardener's Daughter', poems that inspired Mr Holbrook of *Cranford* to walk seven miles to order a copy. We must recognize the sometimes patchy, inconsequential, or recherché nature of Gaskell's poetic reading: she read for pleasure, she read widely, she read anthologies like the eighteenth-century *Elegant Extracts*. There is also a host of minor poets and poems: the vapid Muse of Mrs Hemans, so popular in Gaskell's youth, remembered now only for 'The boy stood on the burning deck', is recalled in *Wives and Daughters* as someone startlingly forgotten, while a setting of one of her lyrics appears in Gaskell's manuscript music-books.[69] A personal favourite now forgotten was Gerald Griffin, whose bald lines, 'To turn and look back when thou hearest/The sound of my name', seem to have a special hold over Gaskell. Such minor figures are often brought to our notice in references or allusions.

Gaskell's use of her reading is complex: it may be of a tone – the Wordsworthian presence in 'Half a Lifetime Ago' or the Tennysonian mood that infuses the Hamley scenes of *Wives and Daughters*; she may use parallels to enforce a moment – Mr Holland's reference in *Cranford* to 'Locksley Hall', a poem of lost love, during Miss Matty's visit; or the oblique use of the Lucy poem, 'Strange fits of passion' in *Ruth*, where strength of feeling, in the mother on her return, rather than an exact relationship to the original, is invoked.[70] Often, indeed, to insist upon the full parallelism of an allusion can be misleading. In *Ruth*, old Sally comes to cut off the girl's hair, so she shall more convincingly pass for a widow: 'Queen Eleanor herself, when she presented the bowl to Fair Rosamund, had not a more relentless purpose stamped on her demeanour than had Sally at this moment' (p. 143). The moment and its expression is all important; the larger elements of jealous queen, poison, and king's mistress are scarcely relevant, except for a picture in which 'relentless purpose' is sternly marked: Sally offers no hostility or real threat. Gaskell has a vast range of reference to which she naturally turns for illustration, or to heighten emotion or control an incident, and we need to match her nimbleness with our own to recognize how the shared reference is used.

If much of Gaskell's literary context is fleeting, difficult to revive, even more tricksy is her command of history (she delights in its

the Queen of Spain has no legs; that Louis XIV's
heir faces in allusion to the Sun-King) and her
: and traditions. At Knutsford, amongst other
ie noted for Mary Howitt, was the strewing of
flowers and verses, white sand on red: when
married, 'nearly all the houses in the town were sanded'
(28-9). Presumably she knew the Manchester Whit Week Walks,
the children 'in their better-most best . . . pattering through the
streets singing with all their might',[71] and the May-day Bell-carts
of Old Trafford, adorned with flowers and branches to welcome in
spring.[72] While giving no credence, Gaskell notes with interest the
last fairy on the Isle of Man and is alive to the survival of beliefs:
Mr Benson knows that the foxglove recognizes spiritual beings who
pass by and 'bows in deference to them', while old Sally's beliefs
cling still, of the ill-luck to drop tears on an unweaned baby, of the
need to tell bees the news, and the truth of dreams (even if
interpreted somewhat awry).[73]

One area where, whatever her rational belief, imagination could
be aroused, was the ghost story, their telling long a pleasingly fearful
amusement. Gaskell and her circle enjoyed telling such stories:
Geraldine Jewsbury has a splendid one of a grey face, and though
Charlotte Brontë shrank from Gaskell relating 'some dismal ghost
story, just before bed-time', Dickens, who had some hankering after
them, paid Gaskell the compliment of stealing her 'lady haunted by
the face' for his 'To be Read at Dusk'.[74] References to ghosts
abound: the 'two odd eyes, seen through holes, as in the old tapestry
story', of Cranford (p. 86), and the headless lady wringing her hands
by the roadside (p. 100), while a ghost in Sylvia's Lovers helps save
his brother (p. 457). One of her best short stories, written indeed
for Dickens, is the ghostly 'Old Nurse's Story'.

Music clearly was one of Elizabeth's extras at Avonbank and it
remained a pleasure through life, though not much practised once
she left school. Three books of manuscript music (plus one of
printed songs) survive from her school days: only one is dated, 'June
12 - 1827', though in use earlier since two items are dated February
1826 and 7 March 1827. Each item is arranged for piano, many of
them traditional country dances, like 'La Triomphe' and 'L'Été', for
quadrilles, others with words original or adapted to the tune - the
range includes favourite operatic items like Gluck's 'Che farò',
'Batti, batti' from Don anni, piano pieces by Beethoven,

Hummel, Mayr, the so-called last waltz of Weber, national airs. Well represented are British popular songs like 'Caller Herrings', 'O weel may the boatie row', and modern songs like Haydn's canzonets ('While hollow burst the rushing winds'), Linley's 'O! bid your faithful Ariel fly', and Tom Moore's 'Oft in the stilly night'; a macabre item is the 'march played when the Queen of France was beheaded'. It is a mish-mash, heavily coloured by what was fashionable and geared to a demand for short pieces for dancing. One of the music-books shows that special pieces were copied from friends; a piece firmly marked 'not to be copied' has at its foot the mocking 'copied by' and the offender's name smudged out. The books were not entirely put away with school, for one volume has a group of nursery rhymes: 'Little Bo Peep' (a boy shepherd, surprisingly), 'Goosy Goosy Gander', and 'Merrily dance and sing', English words to Mozart's glockenspiel chorus of slaves in *The Magic Flute*, amongst others. These suggest Gaskell's use of the volume as her children were growing up and she played to them. The same volume was given over at one point for 'Sacred music copied by Marianne Gaskell', who got no further, having turned the book upside down to make a new beginning, than a piece that opens 'Thy will be done! In devious ways/Thy hurrying stream of time may run'.

The children were all instructed in music and Gaskell took what opportunity she could to go to concerts: in 1848 Charles Hallé came to Manchester, reformed music-making by dismissing the atrocious orchestra of the 'Gentlemen's Concerts', organizing amateur choirs and chamber music, giving opera and Gluck's works in concert performance. His greatest success came in 1857, when he determined to keep up the orchestra raised for the concerts associated with the Manchester Art Treasures Exhibition; after thirty concerts at his own risk in 1858, when he had made thirty pence profit, he decided he was justified (he had broken more than even) and the continuing series established the Hallé Orchestra.[75] The Gaskells certainly subscribed to their winter concerts of 1852-3 (213) and we find references to Mozart's *Requiem* and Mendelssohn's *Elijah* as special events (305; 685). It was at a concert that Gaskell was described by a German visitor in 1850:

Rather tall, full figure, robust, with black hair and a lively reddish-brown complexion. You would unquestionably take

25

> her for an Italian from the shape of her head, the cut of her
> features, and from her complexion ... There is in her
> appearance such a stamp of vigour and completeness that you
> do not find the healthy intellectual grasp of things and
> uniformity of talent exceptional in such a woman.[76]

Manchester musical life, though, was firmly based on amateur music-making and it is above all to songs that Gaskell returns and refers, the lyric expression most readily available and to which she seemingly responded most immediately and deeply.

Gaskell was competent enough at drawing to offer a sketch of Haworth to illustrate her *Life of Charlotte Brontë* (443) and Meta seriously thought of becoming a professional artist. Some teaching in drawing was a common educational extra, but Gaskell's own enthusiasm for art went beyond this. Before the éclat of *Mary Barton* took her into London society and access to private collections, she knew the older painters largely through engravings, singly or in books like that of Hogarth's mentioned in 'My Lady Ludlow' (v,45). For nineteenth-century visitors Italy was so overwhelming because, however well they knew its art from reproduction, they rarely had any sense of its colour. She ranked Raphael high, as taste generally did in her century: the circular 'Madonna della Sedia', hung in Marianne's room, its legend of being painted on a barrel-bottom well-known to her, no doubt appealed in its humanity, just as she was repelled by Bishop Lee's modern painting of a child burnt to death and drawn to Poussin's 'The Good Shepherd', who 'tenderly carried the lambs which had wearied themselves'.[77] The great Manchester Art Exhibition of 1857 ranged from a Roman tomb fresco to the modern day, 1,123 exhibits of the Ancient Masters alone,[78] yet despite entertaining and leading people round, despite having just returned from Italy, Gaskell found it 'really is beautiful', for 'I think Italy makes us enjoy the pictures of our old friends, the great Masters, all the more' (452). In London, she was invited to see collections of men like the banker-poet Samuel Rogers, and Richard Monckton Milnes. Rogers, famous for his literary breakfasts, showed Gaskell antique jewels (80) and probably engravings from his collection. This included Marc Antonio's series of Raphael, and was displayed in his house, where the walls and floor of pure crimson in the drawing-room set off pictures and vases and busts, while in the dining-room were the gems of his collection of paintings, amongst them Raphael's 'Madonna of the Tower', a Titian 'Noli Me Tangere', Giorgione's 'Knight in Armour', and the execrable 'Ecce Homo' of Guido Reni (all now in the National Gallery), where at night there were 'no candles on the table, but light thrown from shaded lamps on the pictures around the room, each a small but consummate gem of art'.[79] Monckton Milnes not only had pictures, but an important collection of manuscripts and drawings of William Blake. Gaskell was keenly aware of modern art – in *Mary Barton* she alludes to Paul Falconer Poole's sensational 1843 Royal Academy picture, 'Solomon Eagle Exhorting the People to Repentance during the Plague of London', as the fevered Davenport starts up 'in his naked madness, looking like the prophet of woe in the fearful plague-picture'.[80] She visited Rossetti and had a good deal of talk with him at evening parties, 'always excepting the times when ladies with beautiful hair came in when he was like the cat turned into a lady, who jumped out of bed and ran after a mouse';[81] and was instrumental in getting the young G. F. Watts to Manchester to paint her friend Wright the prison visitor as the Good Samaritan. She eagerly read Ruskin – *Modern Painters, The Stones of Venice,* and *The Seven Lamps of Architecture* – and was a friend of Anna Jameson whose writings on art are still of interest.

No doubt Gaskell's direct scientific training was restricted to arithmetic and the elementary geography of 'the use of the globes'. She may not have entered seriously into any subject, yet William's membership of the British Association for the Advancement of Science, her own observation and a good general reading meant she was aware of science, particularly botany and zoology. A gap left in the manuscript of *Wives and Daughters* shows she needed to look up the sundew's Latin name, but there need be no doubt she knew the plant. Growing up in the country, she was alive to the pattern of the seasons; living in Manchester, she was fond of gardens – at Malvern, Catherine Winkworth said, was a garden in the French style, full of roses, such 'as Mrs Gaskell would like', laid out in terraces with gravel walks and flowerbeds beside them,[82] while animal husbandry was essential in keeping hens, pigs and cows to supply the family. An important theme is the pride of Manchester and Lancashire in their men learned in science. The very basis of the city's prosperity and growth was a mechanical revolution – Gaskell's friends the Salis-Schwabes ran a famous calico-printing works; and through engineering and enterprise men rose to affluence and power, whether Thornton of *North and South* or Gaskell's friend Nasmyth (who perhaps provided hints for Thornton): he lived for two years on five shillings a week for food, five shillings for lodging and dress, so that when his wages were raised to fifteen shillings he began the 'butter' period 'and I laid by my first capital besides'.[83] Civic pride recognized the achievements in chemistry of John Dalton (1766-1844), who amongst other practical and theoretical work laid the basis of modern atomic theory. Henry Holland had known him 'in his rude laboratory of broken bottles and other uncouth apparatus', while Elizabeth Stone's novel, *William Langshawe, the Cotton Lord* (1842), at the end of a chapter violently justifying factory working hours and conditions suddenly has a pleasing vignette of Dalton at his night-time labours.[84] The dedicated amateur was also important: a visitor in 1835 found a collection of stuffed birds at the Natural History Museum prepared by a weaver, entirely self-taught.[85] Gaskell pays tribute to such men in Job Legh of *Mary Barton,* his introduction backed with evidence for the existence of a whole class of such men, including 'common hand-loom weavers, who throw the shuttle with unceasing sound, though Newton's "Principia" lie open on the loom to be snatched at in work hours' (p. 40). It is a world where the amateur still contributes, where the delight is in both personal and common gain. The English pursuit of the natural world, so happily found in Isaak Walton and Gilbert White, is alive in Lancashire men and in Elizabeth Gaskell.

Although the first foreign country she visited (1841), Germany did not make any special impression on Gaskell. She liked it when there, but it was never necessary to her. Her acquaintance with it was superficial because her teachers followed Mrs Barbauld's advice that, after French and Italian, the 'other modern languages you will hardly attempt, except led to them by some peculiar bent'.[86] From Germany came the early influences upon English Romanticism; in the nineteenth century it was the great centre of philosophical and religious thought: German was above all the language that the intellectual George Eliot strove to master. But philosophy as such did not engage Gaskell, nor was she concerned with the new approaches to Christianity, an indifference that may account for her lack of response to Carlyle, the English purveyor of German ideas – though paradoxically *Mary Barton* quotes Carlyle on its title page and overleaf a stanza in German from Uhland where an earthly traveller crosses the ferry with two spirit visitors: covert allusions to her son (his death the impulse to writing) and a still-born daughter. Gaskell's knowledge of German was limited (she claimed more than once not to know it), though her daughters were encouraged to learn it and she knew its literature in translation. She enjoyed her summer trip up the Rhine, the dancing as much as the cathedrals, and in 1858, at Heidelberg to get Meta away from a broken engagement, she hired piano and music, 'and laughed harder than I ever laughed before or ever shall again, the air clear delicious dry air, put one in such healths and spirits' (516; 531; 539). She knew Chevalier Neukomm, the musician, and Chevalier Bunsen, the scholar and Prussian ambassador to England, but more important would be the German community in Manchester, one attraction for Charles Hallé to the city, who by report remained German in showing keen interest in the fate of their Fatherland though they had adopted a completely English way of life.[87]

William Gaskell himself had a good command of German, teaching amongst others Catherine Winkworth, one of a remarkable family, who, 'led by a peculiar bent' – the desire to maintain herself without the fate of being a private governess – pursued German studies at Dresden and kept them up with William Gaskell.[88] Catherine Winkworth, encouraged by success with translations 'from German poetry that Mr. Gaskell required from his pupils', produced the *Lyra Germanica* in 1855, a large selection of hymns, which she followed with a survey of the *Christian Singers of Germany* (1869). The lyric spirit of German poetry was enjoyed by Gaskell as was the vigour of German life, though she only used her experience in a couple of short stories: in the unsatisfactory 'Six Weeks at Heppenheim' and more effectively in 'The Grey Woman'.

In a letter to Emil Souvestre of March 1854, Gaskell regretted not being able to write good and grammatical French and claimed her spoken command was imperfect (275); yet suddenly she bursts with great good humour into fluent French. Faced by natives, Gaskell may have doubted her ability, but clearly she was fluent in spoken and written French. The letter to Souvestre is doubly interesting, both for its amiable joke against herself and for its reference to Mme Mohl, establishing that she certainly knew this redoubtable 'character' by the spring of 1853. It was in her salon at the Rue du Bac in Paris that Gaskell wrote parts of *Wives and Daughters*, and on the famous Friday evenings heard the conversation of those admitted to a place where, as Mohl said herself of salon life, 'all outward conditions were subordinate to the pleasure given by the communion of one human being with another'.[89] Here De Tocqueville, the political commentator, was brought to meet Gaskell, as were admirers of her work like Prosper Merimée. Mary Mohl (née Clarke) lived most of her long life (1790-1883) in France, knew Mme Recamier and Chateaubriand, and married Julius Mohl the orientalist in 1847. She could be careless in dress and behaviour, wore her tangled curls until her death (fashion overtook curls in the 1850s and her appearance was increasingly eccentric) and regarded the crinoline as the downfall of society. With its coming she observed a shift from intelligence, ésprit and politics to dress, and for someone so involved in the cultivation of mind – so important were her salons that 'she hoped to die on a Saturday in order that she might have one Friday more' – this was the destruction of all she valued.[90] Perhaps it was Napoleon III rather than the crinoline that produced the change, and, though never claiming to keep a political salon, she hated him ('Brummagen Boney' was her contemptuous term).[91] Of her two drawing-rooms, one was for conversation, the other for the music in which she delighted, for dancing or blindman's buff or whatever.[92]

From such a milieu came the experience of 'French Life' embodied in Gaskell's charming chatty articles and a sense of an intellectual tradition going back into the seventeenth century. Above all other French writers, Gaskell was drawn to the great charmer, the best loved in England, Mme de Sévigné, whose society was still in some ways represented by that of Mme Mohl and whom Gaskell long had an unfulfilled ambition to write on. She did much serious reading in Paris for this book (in 1862) and visited Vitré in Brittany, where the Hôtel de Sévigné stood, and then 'we took a little market cart, and drove, shaking and laughing to Les Rochers', de Sévigné's country house.[93] The visit is preserved in 'French Life', but the account of de Sévigné herself is one of the great lost books, a tribute from one great woman letter-writer to the greatest of them all, paid in mind and spirit if never in print.

Mary Mohl's passionate admiration for Dante's Divine Comedy[94] was no doubt a link of understanding with Elizabeth Gaskell, whose command of Italian seems good and who read the great author who stood so central for the educated Victorian; to him Tennyson went for his 'Ulysses', rather than to Homer, and Lord Macaulay in the National Portrait Gallery poses with three great volumes of the *Commedia*. It is difficult nowadays to understand how usual a knowledge of Italian was: in *North and South* Margaret Hale reads 'the "Paradiso" of Dante, in the proper old Italian binding of white vellum and gold' (p. 23), even if like Ellinor in 'A Dark Night's Work' she needs to 'rummage up words in the dictionary' (vii, 457). While staying with Mary Mohl in 1855 Gaskell renewed acquaintance with William Whetmore Story, who was to be the host of her first Roman stay. She left England in mid-February 1857 and returned at the end of May; the sense we have is of unalloyed pleasure (even with a steam-ship accident on the way from Marseilles to Genoa),[95] heightened in contrast by troubles over the publication of *The Life of Charlotte Brontë* that met her on return. Through the accident of no letter from Italy surviving, the experience comes to us retrospectively, coloured by memory. Even so, it seems to have been overwhelming: 'It was in those charming Roman days that my life, at any rate, culminated. I shall never be so happy again' (477), she wrote that autumn, and even three years later she found she could 'sometimes think that I would almost rather never have been there than have this ache of yearning for the great witch who sits . . . upon her seven hills' (642). The Rome she visited was that of the old adventurers, as Henry James characterized it, the world before 1870, while all 'the discoveries now are made, and, with this, most of the feelings, the sweetest and strangest, have dropped. We know everything in relation to the objects that used to excite them – everything has been so felt for us'.[96]

Whether James was right, there is no doubt that Gaskell felt for herself: whether it was the Campagna with its expanse of view (514) or their lodging with the Storys in Via Sant' Isidoro with 'the amber sunlight streaming on the gold-grey Roman roofs and the Sabine hills on the one side and the Vatican on the other' (642) or gathering violets in the gardens of the Villa Borghese.[97] Story himself, a successful lawyer in the United States, had accepted a commission for a commemorative statue of his father, come to Italy to study the art (1847) and stayed virtually the rest of his life. In Story's studio she saw works like the Cleopatra, which Nathaniel Hawthorne was to appropriate for his sculptor Kenyon in *The Marble Faun*, a novel which delighted her, no doubt finding as did her American friend

31

Charles Eliot Norton that it 'fixed the vague delights of feeling, and turning them into intellectual possessions makes them serve as the ground work of new and more distinct enjoyment'.[98] There seems to have been none of that initial repulsion common amongst American and English travellers to Italy: none of Hawthorne's disgust with filthy habits, modern dilapidation, and 'degenerate' art – even in his gradual winning to the spell of Rome and Italy, so engagingly charted in the *Italian Notebooks,* Hawthorne was still not reconciled to the greatness of Bernini. Yet she probably agreed with Norton's strictures on late Renaissance art and modern Roman politics and society, so vehemently expressed in *Notes of Travel and Study in Italy* (1859), where only the religious spirit of Fra Angelico and of the builders of Orvieto cathedral wins praise. Drawn to Norton partly by his Unitarianism, partly by their share in Italy (which Norton, despite maledictions, obviously enjoyed), Gaskell maintained a correspondence with him to the end of her life, detailed, chatty, expressing in the early 1860s her full sympathy with the Northern cause in the Civil War, though needing to understand it fully when faced by the desperate condition of a Manchester deprived by blockade of its raw cotton supplies. There was an intensity in the Italian experience almost painful to contemplate: it only affected her work slightly, yet emotionally it may be seen as that culmination of which she spoke and may perhaps have played its part in the increasing emphasis upon memory and past happiness in the work after 1857; it had been 'a season the perfect felicity of which was to feed all her later time with fond memories, with renewed regrets and dreams'.[99]

IV

Central to life in Manchester and particularly to the house at Plymouth Grove was Gaskell's family. William Gaskell (1805-84) has been found enigmatic; there may be a certain reticence in his behaviour, emphasized by his destruction of letters received (not a single item to him from his wife is printed amongst Elizabeth's letters), but this destruction is part of that desire for privacy seen in Gaskell's own instructions to Marianne and others to burn letters (instructions not obeyed in every case). Gaskell spoke of William as a very shy man, not forthcoming until he knew people well (660) and certainly he never exposed his inner life by letters or diaries or poetry. In their early marriage Gaskell found it slightly distressing that he would not allow her to talk over anxieties about the children (45), perhaps as well to judge by her sometimes over-solicitous care, and often when visitors came he retreated to his study. Yet home was his office, he had his job to do, and he was an increasingly busy man. His not going on holiday with his wife and children has been much stressed; the evidence is that he objected not to family holidays but to himself and Elizabeth being away from home at the same time (129), if the children would have to be left. In 1852 Gaskell tactfully refused Marianne permission to invite a schoolfriend to their Silverdale holiday since 'Papa does not like the idea of having a *stranger* in the house in holiday time when you know he likes to play pranks, go cockling . . . and feel at liberty to say or do what he likes' (850). He delighted in puns, could sign himself at the end of a letter, apologizing for his sleepiness, 'Yours, in my dream, W. Goosequill'.[100] What is clearest is that he did not play the heavy paterfamilias, but expected Gaskell to get on with her side of things (even if she were an author as well), that he refused to go abroad except by himself because he disliked foreign food – perhaps because of a digestive disorder (506) – and that he was ready for his children to lead their own lives. Friends and acquaintances were much taken by him; William Whetmore Story, who met him holidaying in Switzerland, found him 'a sweet, broad character', and for his golden jubilee at Cross Street Chapel over 1,000 people attended a soirée in his honour, while donations of more than £2,000 established a memorial scholarship at Owens College (now the University).[101]

William Gaskell, educated at Glasgow University and Manchester New College (at York), was from 1828 joint pastor with John Gooch Robberds at Cross Street Chapel, where chapel and pastoral affairs demanded much of him. As a preacher he was aware of human frailty. The Sunday afternoon address, he told a friend substituting for him in 1860, 'need not be above 20 min. long and, as children are apt to be sleepy after dinner, (like their elders) the more conversational the style of the address the better. Last year, I made it little more than a story-telling with a few lessons thrown in.'[102] He was involved, like his family, in the Sunday-schools; took part in the larger concerns of the Manchester and Salford Sanitary Association, on its committee from the first (1853), lecturing on 'The Transgression of the Laws of Health', on the Tract Sub-

Committee from 1861; and apart from tuition for his children and friends, lectured constantly and tirelessly, above all in English Literature. He was Professor of English History and Literature in Manchester New College (1846-53), lectured at the Working Men's College from 1858, and helped set up the Unitarian Home Missionary College (1854), to train men for the ministry who coming from the working classes might be best fitted to proselytize amongst their own people – here William Gaskell taught English Literature and New Testament Greek, becoming Principal in 1874.[103] A pupil at the Working Men's College thought him 'the most beautiful reader I had ever heard. Prose or poetry seemed to acquire new lustre and elegance'.[104] He lectured on Lancashire dialect, recalling schoolboy memories of using wild hemlock stalks as pea-shooters and of 'Bragget' Sunday when the boys 'were indulged in a kind of sweet drink . . . composed, I believe, of ale, sugar, and nutmegs'.[105] He never published much, though his knowledge of literature was vast (a shared delight with his wife) and he seems to have provided some at least of the epigraphs for *Mary Barton* and *North and South*. Though he may have been slightly embarrassed even by his wife's sudden fame (people begin to feel sorry for 'Mr Mary Barton', noted Geraldine Jewsbury)[106] he encouraged Elizabeth in her writings, stood by her in the controversies over *Ruth* and *The Life of Charlotte Brontë*, overlooked what she wrote, corrected her punctuation and grammar, and read proofs – he also, as was his legal right, took her earnings (e.g. 113), though Gaskell kept a firmer hold later, whether to extend Continental holidays or to buy the house near Alton. William may have retreated to his study, but take all these activities, plus the British Association for the Advancement of Science, joint editorship from 1861 of the *Unitarian Herald*, presidency of the provincial assembly of Lancashire and Cheshire from 1865, and we see that the retreat was for work; Gaskell's letters show his constant presence in the life of the family, ready (as in Marianne's religious crisis) to take full and necessary responsibility. A man of learning, culture and industry, he was an essential part of that circle at Plymouth Grove.

Four children, all girls, survived infancy: Elizabeth Gaskell's first child, still-born (1833), she addressed in a rare poem, 'On Visiting the Grave of My Stillborn Little Girl', poignant in recalling 'thou/Whose eyes ne'er opened to my wistful gaze, /Whose suff'r-ings stamped with pain thy little brow' (i, xxvii), the death no doubt contributing to her anxiety in the early years of her first surviving child, Marianne (1834-1920): Meta (Margaret Emily, 1837-1913) may have been closer to her mother, and certainly the more reliable character, less indolent, less easily swayed. Marianne, as the first, seems the most precious, and the relationship with her mother is acutely charted in the long series of letters, which survives despite urgings of destruction, indication perhaps both of Marianne's less thoughtful side (no letter to Meta apparently survives, who presumably obeyed her mother's injuction) and of her impulsive loving nature. In a diary Gaskell kept during the first few years of Marianne's life, she noted details of the child and of her own concern with the difficulty of forming her daughter's character. She discovered how closely her record linked both lives: 'I had no idea the journal of my own disposition and feelings was so intimately connected with that of my little baby, whose regular breathing has been the music of my thoughts all the time I have been writing. God bless her!'[107] Her own besetting sin she sees as anger, yet both parents restrained themselves from physical punishment; an early slap on the hand had them both in tears after Marianne was in bed, though a slight hardening can be seen in occasional whippings when Marianne was obstinate in lessons. Meta showed greater independence, common in second children, apart from Gaskell's own confidence after dealing with one child already; though she could be made to sob violently by the tone of William's voice.[108] Gaskell felt this contrasting character of the young sisters clearly: Marianne's need for love, her dependence (no doubt partly why Catholicism, presented through the strength of Dr Manning, was so sympathetic) against Meta's independence, which Gaskell hoped would strengthen Marianne (46). Later, Marianne's education presented problems: faults of mental indolence and a talent only for music (135), yet she seemed a happy child ('as practical and humourous as ever' in 1859) and successfully married a second cousin, Edward Thurstan Holland, in 1866. Meta for a time seriously thought of being a professional artist, and Charles Eliot Norton praised her capacity.[109] She became engaged in 1857, breaking off when the fiancé, Captain Hill, was found untruthful. Not embittered, she cared for Plymouth Grove and her father after her mother's death, a highly regarded hostess and citizen.

The two eldest daughters seem the most important in Gaskell's life because they were grown up during her lifetime and, as her first children, gave her most worry. But the others were equally loved. The third daughter, Florence Elizabeth (1842–81), gave concern about her immaturity; she was sent to school in Knutsford rather than to London as Marianne or to Liverpool as Meta – the sisters' schools chosen carefully for particular capacities and needs. She married a young lawyer, Charles Crompton, in 1863, and though she had domestic problems they sound no more than the common ones of a young woman beginning to run a household.

Whatever part the children played in her writing – in remembering her own childhood for Molly Gibson in *Wives and Daughters,* Gaskell may have drawn also on her daughters' – only one seems responsible for starting her writing, and that, tragically, her only son, William ('Willie', to distinguish him from his father), who died in August 1845, within a year of birth, from scarlet fever, a virulent disease then. 'My laddie', she called him affectionately when alive, his red hair perhaps recalling the Northern side of her family. The house at Upper Rumford street remained full of 'feelings and recollections', of sitting 'reading by the fire, and watching my darling *darling* Willie, who now sleeps sounder still in the dull, dreary chapel-yard at Warrington' – in 1850, she still finds a 'precious perfume lingering' in the house and claimed the wound would 'never heal on earth, though hardly any one knows how it has changed me'.[110] Duty and love to the living helped her conceal the gap, but William Gaskell knew it and urged her to write: the result ultimately was her first major work, *Mary Barton,* the German verses prefixed to it remembering the major impulse to creation. Her last child, Julia Bradford (1846–1908), it has recently been suggested,[111] was a replacement for Willie – but it is quite likely she was a natural conception with the end of suckling and mourning. Julia is notable (as Florence also) for having won the heart of Charlotte Brontë, who found in her a sympathy that did not demand the embarrassment of words, Gaskell describing how the 'child would steal her little hand into Miss Brontë's scarcely larger one, and each took pleasure in this apparently unobserved caress'.[112]

The routine of household life was increasingly geared to the growing family, and Gaskell's letters, essential sources of information and interest, depict daily life at various periods, though above all in Plymouth Grove from 1850, the house of her years of fame. The chief servant, 'a dear good valuable *friend*' (760), was Hearn, nurse to all the children. By and large the servants seemed to have been faithful and efficient, a very different situation from Jane Welsh Carlyle's constant vexations in Chelsea,[113] though at one crisis Gaskell had to instruct Marianne by post to dismiss the cook. The household's even temper was a tribute to Hearn's watchfulness and Gaskell's efficiency and kindness. At Plymouth Grove, with its large garden and semi-rural aspect (now changed indeed, a hostel amidst the slum destruction of the University's growing campus), apart from pets – cats, including a kitten from Paris, and the dog Lion – the domestic economy was boosted by chickens, pigs and a cow, as well as vegetable stuffs. Here Gaskell might spend an afternoon spudding up dandelions (614) after writing all morning. Two letters of 1845 and 1857 give an idea of daily routine: Gaskell rising at 6 a.m. to set the household in motion, the tasks of the day linked in with the demands of young children (823-4); again, she sets the scene, writing at the round writing-table in the dining room, Marianne mending a pen for her, Meta gone to tell the gardener about next year's perennials; then a list of 'important questions' she has had to decide in the hour since breakfast: 'Boiled beef – how long to boil? What perennials will do in Manchester smoke, and what colours our garden wants? Length of skirt for a gown? Salary of a nursery governess' – and more still, that suggest the hurly-burly of her life (487, 489).

Early in marriage morning prayers had been established and a reading by William from Philip Doddridge's *Family Expositor* (1739), an arrangement of the gospels as a continuous narrative '*to render the reading of the* New Testament *more pleasant and improving*' (I, i-ii),[114] a practice that gave Bosanquet pleasure when he visited the Gaskells twenty-five years later. In the afternoon came visits or visitors, sometimes as an interruption when she had 'to do double duty and talk aesthetically (I dare say) all the time I was thinking of pickle for pork' (205). There were Sunday-school classes and parochial visiting, and periods of distress, when she took her part in relief work, notably during the cotton famine of the American Civil War, damaging her always uncertain health. It was this side of her life that brought her into contact with local men like Samuel Bamford and Thomas Wright, both commemorated in her work.

Samuel Bamford (1788-1872), a silk weaver of Middleton, close to Manchester, became involved in parliamentary reform agitation after the Napoleonic Wars and took part in the meetings and petitions that culminated in the massacre of Peterloo (1819). Committed to non-violence, he felt alienated from the Chartist demands for the franchise and electoral reform of the 1830s and 1840s, which to him threatened destruction and class hatred. For Bamford the earlier reform movement failed because it was a matter of passion, not thought: 'We looked for fruit ere the bloom was come forth; we expected will when there was no mind to produce it, to sustain it.' His creed of non-violence he saw as justified by the steady amelioration between 1819 and 1839 and he stood for the same idea of class reconciliation that sounds in *North and South;* his vision may be of a Cobbett-like Golden Age that never did and never would exist, but it is a high call for all that.

Bamford's radicalism was linked with religious tolerance; the chapel the reformers rented for meetings was open to all sects for their services.[115] Both in politics and religion he was likely to attract Gaskell's interest, and he had made a name by editing the Lancashire dialect works of 'Tim Bobbin', contributing dialect words to William Gaskell's *Lectures,* and writing poems.[116] He disclaimed being a poet – 'I was only a country rhymester',[117] but Gaskell includes his best poem in *Mary Barton* (a novel of local pride, displaying Lancashire's worthies), 'God help the poor, who, on this wintry morn,/Come forth from alleys dim and courts obscure' (pp. 125-7). They shared a passion for Tennyson; Gaskell begged a copy for him when she found that though Bamford knew many poems by heart he couldn't afford a Tennyson of his own. One other common delight Bamford and Gaskell had was the telling of stories. Though his autobiographical writings, *Passages in the Life of a Radical* and *Early Days,* are often drawn on for illustration of Lancashire life and of working-class reform movements, no one seems to have noticed the fictional shaping of many elements in them, that must cast doubts even on the clearly historical parts. Bamford appropriates to himself the St John's Eve ritual of gathering fern seed, a highly effective piece of blood curdling,[118] and has a fine ghost story which Gaskell must have relished. Going to a Methodist meeting outside Middleton of an evening as a lad, he saw a boy ahead he knew, running like himself and tried to overtake him:

> When I got nearer, I called out; but he still kept onward, not making answer. When close behind him I shouted 'Bill, Bill – why so fast?' but there was no notice or reply; which I thought

rather strange: and when I came abreast of him, I said in a
tone of defiance – 'Come on, then, and see wot theaw'rt short
of;' and darting past him like an arrow, I turned my head
with an air of triumph, and saw a face – not Bill's, but that
of one who had been dead many years.[119]

He sped on, to be rid of the figure now, and, bursting into the
meeting house, found Bill already there on his knees. Curiously
though, there were no ill consequences to Samuel or Bill; perhaps
praying more really in earnest than for a long time was enough.

Although Bamford's active life was virtually over when Gaskell
knew him, one of his contemporaries, Thomas Wright (1789–
1876), was in spate as a one-man voluntary prisoners'-aid society.
Having fallen amongst ill company in youth, Wright was granted a
personal revelation one day in Granby Row, Manchester: 'Suddenly
I was amazed by a great light which came out of the clouds. I stood
still, and inwardly I heard a voice say, "Thy sins, which are many,
are freely forgiven thee; go, sin no more." Oh, what joy I felt!'
Later, at the foundry where he worked, a convict, found to have
lied to get employment, was discharged; convinced of the man's
serious reformation, Wright guaranteed twenty pounds for his good
behaviour.[120] Subsequently he visited prison, found jobs for prisoners being released, and engaged the interest of many people, including Gaskell. At work all day from 5 a.m. to 6 p.m. he spent his
evening leisure and Sundays at his self-imposed work (still
managing to marry twice and have nineteen children). He appears
in *Mary Barton* (p. 181) as one fulfilling Jesus's injunction to visit
the prisons. Then in 1852, his health failing under the strain, a subscription raised the equivalent of his annual income and he devoted
himself entirely to prison work.[121]

Thomas Wright was often to be found at Plymouth Grove; he
'drank tea here last night,' reports Gaskell, 'and said "By Jingo"
with great unction, when very much animated, much to William's
amusement' (108). It was the society and culture of Plymouth
Grove, above all of its drawing-room, from which faint echoes
came at that auction sale of 1914. It looks a formal, rather
uninviting place (on its best behaviour for the photographer, no
doubt),[122] but for Gaskell's friends, like Charles Eliot Norton, it
was the heart: 'Does the drawing room look as it used to do, – the
piano & your table in the same place, – the flowers still blooming in

the little conservatory – the same landscape over the fireplace, – the same centre table with the books and work on it as of old?'[123] A room for Gaskell could have associations almost palpable: in *Mary Barton* (p. 308), she says 'the very house was haunted with memories and foreshadowings' and before moving to Plymouth Grove she urged her friend Eliza ('Tottie') Fox to visit soon – 'I want to get associations about that house' (111). Happy associations, but living associations, vibrant above all in friendship, for which Gaskell had a peculiar talent; she was beautiful not only physically (later portraits indeed show her rather heavy and worn) but in personality. The deepest feelings run through her life here and these feelings of friendship are the hardest to pin down, realizable perhaps only through reading her letters.

Someone like Geraldine Jewsbury might make the reservation 'that if one could get at the "Mary Barton" that is the kernel of Mrs Gaskell one would like her, but I never have done so yet';[124] Susanna Winkworth's impressions are those confirmed on all sides:

> She was a noble-looking woman, with a queenly presence, and
> her high, broad, serene brow, and finely-cut mobile features,
> were lighted up by a constantly-varying play of expression as
> she poured forth her wonderful talk. It was like the gleaming
> ripple and rush of a clear deep stream in sunshine . . . . All her
> great intellectual gifts . . . were so warmed and brightened by
> sympathy and feeling, that while actually with her, you were
> less conscious of her power than of her charm.[125]

Through her surviving letters (and it is important to stress how these can distort our idea of a relationship by the chance survival or destruction of a series) we can trace friendships with Elizabeth and Anne Gaskell, William's sisters, later Mrs Holland and Mrs Fox, and with Eliza Fox, known affectionately as 'Tottie' (as Gaskell was 'Lily' to her closest friends), to whom Gaskell characterized Charlotte Brontë as 'like you, Tottie, without your merriment' (130). These are relatives and personal friends, interested in family matters and the household and ordinary things, lively and intelligent, with whom Gaskell could relax, who might (as Anne and Tottie did with Meta) act charades 'in the outer lobby, under the gas' while the audience 'stood on the stair-case, in the inner hall, and the folding doors were thrown open' (147). Manchester friendships might develop into intimacy, as with the Winkworths, or remain slightly peripheral, as with Geraldine Jewsbury. It was Miss Jewsbury who had a doubt about the 'real' Mrs Gaskell and she criticized one of the earlier Gaskell homes as she 'lay on the floor ... and called our drawing room "such an ugly room in which we should always be unhappy"'. (813). A provincial George Sand, Geraldine was an alert, witty, impulsive woman, who smoked cigaritos,[126] wrote novels (*Zoë* was mildly scandalous), read manuscripts for the publisher Bentley, and had an (on her side) impassioned and occasionally hysterical friendship with Jane Welsh Carlyle. She moved out of Gaskell's circle in 1854 when she went to London, ending at the same time her entertainingly informative series of letters to Jane, with their pictures of Manchester life and follies like the local business man who commissioned 'ancestors' for a chapel he was fitting up.[127]

There were friends acquired later in life, like Charlotte Brontë (see chapter 5) and her publisher George Smith, who treated her generously as friend by sending new books and as businessman by offering the best terms for her writing. Gaskell's attitude to Smith is one of sympathy and trust, very unlike the uneasy, though drawn-out, relationship she had with Dickens: 'good enough for Mr Dickens' came to be a pejorative self-criticism. Other people she knew briefly or in sudden accesses of enthusiasm. She was overwhelmed by Florence Nightingale in 1854 and was stunned by her letters from Egypt, whether the consciously beautiful descriptions of the moon: 'Isis welcomed us to her country with the most delicate and silvery of crescents', or the meditation after entering an Alexandrian mosque dressed as a moslem woman, which 'seemed to reveal to one what it is to be a woman in these countries, where Christ has not been raised – God save them, for it is a hopeless life'.[128] But though she remained on friendly terms with the Nightingale family, the relationship never developed. Again, in early married life she was in contact with William and Mary Howitt about country customs and in the 1850s, while she was engaged on the life of Charlotte Brontë, Sir James Kay-Shuttleworth became important, but these were not friendships that lasted or went deep. With the publication of *Mary Barton* she was welcomed into London literary and social circles. Some encounters deepened into those friendships already touched on – Mary Mohl, Charles Eliot Norton and so on. Others were pleasant social contacts, easily made, laid down, renewed another year: Samuel Rogers, the Carlyles,

Thackeray, Barry Procter and the rest. Real pleasure and real kindnesses, but of the surface.

V

Out of all these varied elements, out of the reality of the ghostly Plymouth Grove I have sketched here, came the books: and even where direct influences are hard to trace or not relevant to the work it is out of them all that the writings came. Susanna Winkworth continued her description of Elizabeth Gaskell:

> No one ever came near her in the gift of telling a story. In her hands the simplest incident, - a meeting in the street, a talk with a factory-girl, a country walk, an old family history, - became picturesque and vivid and interesting. Her fun, her pathos, her graphic touches, her sympathetic insight, were inimitable. When, a few years later, all the world was admiring her novels we felt that what she had actually published was a mere fraction of what she might have written . . . . [129]

Six novels, a biography, and a large number of short stories is a reasonable *oeuvre;* our own wonder might be that Gaskell achieved so much. Under that brilliance and charm, though, Susanna had spoken of 'power' and it is important, despite illness, despite breakdown, to see that Gaskell was a remarkably tough person.

After a day being the woman and the housewife she would set to writing, or on holiday retire to her room, or stand at Mary Mohl's mantelpiece, or take advantage of family absences - whatever time she could find or make, if all duties of house and home were done, she spent in writing once she was established by her first novel, *Mary Barton.* She was never a professional writer in the way of Dickens or George Eliot, earning a living through writing; there are gaps in her writing when Plymouth Grove and Manchester engrossed her whole time. But even before *Mary Barton* there are signs of the writer. A poetical collaboration with William, 'Sketches among the Poor', was hopefully subtitled 'No. I', though no more appeared after its publication in *Blackwood's Magazine* (January 1837). In 1838 she was writing to the Howitts about Cheshire customs and childhood observances and rhymes - her first extended piece, a sketch of Clopton Hall in Warwickshire, was inserted by William Howitt in his *Visits to Remarkable Places* (1840, pp. 135-39), while her three earliest stories appeared in *Howitt's Journal* (September 1847 and January 1848), two of them under her punning pseudonym 'Cotton Mather Mills', a hint of Puritan ancestry and present environment. She was always prepared to write stories for special occasions – Travers Madge's Sunday-school magazine, for instance – but with *Mary Barton* she established herself primarily as a novelist.

There is little evidence as to Gaskell's theory in writing and not much more, apart from the works themselves, on her practice. Her most extended theoretical statement answers a request for criticism of someone else's novel and is therefore coloured by the nature of the work itself and a wish to be kind. She advised concision and felt introspection an unsafe training for the novelist: read Defoe, she said, 'and you will see the healthy way in which he sets *objects* not *feelings* before you' (541). Plot needed thought in shaping; each character must conduce to the growth and progress of events: then 'set to & imagine yourself a spectator & auditor of every scene & event! Work hard at this till it become a reality to you' (542). Obvious enough, yet it was good advice: the difficulty of plots is shown in Gaskell's only surviving working notes, the outline of *Mary Barton* and of its 'Conclusion yet to be written'.[130] Otherwise, Gaskell sent outlines to publishers (*Sylvia's Lovers* and *Wives and Daughters* in letters to George Smith) and discussed the progress of her stories with various people, not always with happy consequences; while at work on *Ruth*, visitors smashed into what she told them of it and 'I've been frightened off my nest' (205). Better for her was the advice and information of John Forster, Dickens's friend, who was able to reassure her, during the writing of *North and South*, that Dickens did not intend to include a strike in *Hard Times*, which her novel was to follow as a serial (281). Sometimes she seems to be thinking aloud in her letters, seeking a response by which to assess an idea, as when she wonders whether the crisis in *North and South* might be brought on by Thornton's mill being burnt down (310). The surviving manuscripts suggest that she wrote rapidly and fluently: that of *The Life of Charlotte Brontë* is fairly heavily corrected, the nature of the work demanding accuracy and the weaving together of details, though the pages are clean compared to the elaborate revision in process of writing that Dickens's manuscripts show; that of the final novel, *Wives and Daughters*, is a very clean piece of work, the original and not a corrected copy, with no hint of illness or difficulties. Presumably Gaskell thought even in the midst of household duties of what she was to write, getting it down when she could. Her clear style, with comparatively little imagery or rhetorical elaboration (the more effective when they come) no doubt helped rapid composition. The body of this book will suggest some of Gaskell's development as an artist. From early on she was concerned with form (*Mary Barton* was a 'Tragic Poem') and became increasingly skilful in plotting – toning down over-emphatic action – and in controlling the introduction and development of characters. Comments on her contemporaries suggest a moral basis to her art, in which the character of author and of work are closely if not insistently linked: to her it would be 'dreadful hypocrisy' if the Ruskin 'who wrote those books is a bad man' and initially she had problems between admiration for George Eliot's work and distress at her unmarried state. Art did prevail, though, and she confessed, 'Do you know I can't help liking her – *because* she wrote those books. Yes I do! I *have* tried to be moral, & dislike her & dislike her books – but it won't do'.[131]

Gaskell relied on her husband to correct her work in terms of grammar and spelling; he controlled her use of 'which' and 'that', as well as striking out irritatingly favourite phrases like 'tête à tête'. As well as having the help of a daughter (apparently Meta) in copying out letters for *The Life of Charlotte Brontë*, Gaskell also took William's advice over the biography and had his full support both before and after publication for what she had written. William also proofed much of her work, Gaskell drawing her publishers' attention to the possibility of inaccuracies when he was away (e.g. 465). Her characteristic format of paper is a foolscap sheet (apparently obtained by tearing a larger sheet in two), often blue but sometimes white, written in her large, usually legible, hand.

Two main publishers produced her work: Chapman and Hall, to whom she felt a loyalty since they took *Mary Barton* after 'Mr Moxon refused it as a gift' (256), and George Smith of Smith, Elder, to whom she went with publication of *The Life of Charlotte Brontë* (Smith was Charlotte's publisher). With Smith she established a lasting friendship, her break with Chapman no doubt being made easier by the firm's identification with Dickens, for whom a coolness had sprung up amidst the difficulties of publishing *North and South*. To get money, Gaskell was quite prepared to allow Sampson Low to reprint a collection of her short stories (*Round the Sofa*, 1859), but characterized him as a 'rascally publisher' for trying to pass it off as a new work (531). When he offered her £1,000 for a three-volume novel, she wrote to Smith saying she would rather have £800 from him (558) – pleased possibly to have the means to screw out a good price, but genuinely wanting to publish with Smith. In the event she had £1,000 for *Sylvia's Lovers*, which included the American rights (581). Gaskell earned well, though not in the top rank. Since she was not dependent on her work, she preferred the certainty of an outright payment rather than a royalty (William preferred the latter), though after the first two novels she tended to accept payment for a specified number of editions and profits after that – *Mary Barton* and *Ruth* were sold outright (the former for £100); for *North and South* she had £260 for serialization and about £400 for volume publication, retaining the copyright. She had an extra sum for the English edition circulated exclusively on the continent by Tauchnitz, but lost the American rights by her own carelessness, something she was more careful to secure for the future. Smith paid £800 for *The Life of Charlotte Brontë* (his original offer was £600, until Gaskell urged the expense in gathering materials) and £1,000 for *Sylvia's Lovers*, while *Wives and Daughters*, serial and volume publication, presumably promised nearly £1,600, needed for the price of The Lawn and not covered by Smith's mortgage of £1,000.[132] The sums might be compared with the original £800 offered to George Eliot in 1858 for a four-year copyright of *Adam Bede*;[133] even that early in her career, though, she was a star, and more usual was the £400 a novel Margaret Oliphant (supporting three children) got in the 1850s.[134] Gaskell did well, could have done better if she had chosen to drive her bargains. One further source of profit was translation: in the 1850s Hachette of Paris had a twelve-month option on her work, paying one-and-a-half francs a page for any work taken (433), and Mary Mohl's nieces translated *Sylvia's Lovers* into German (740). Made famous by *Mary Barton*, Gaskell was widely translated during her lifetime.

Elizabeth Gaskell's reputation survived well enough for two collected editions to appear early in the twentieth century; *Cranford* was continually reprinted (its popularity establishing a false view of Gaskell's 'sweetness') and *The Life of Charlotte Brontë* has remained continuously available. Since the early 1960s Gaskell's reputation has increased considerably, and the 1965 centenary and publication of her letters (1966) both prompted reappraisals. Much of her work is now readily available and she has been rightly assessed as amongst the most interesting of the Victorian novelists of second-rank – attempts to place her with Dickens and George Eliot are only likely to provoke an excessive counter-reaction.

2

Mary Barton (1848) and North and South (1855): Industry and Individual

'How knowest thou,' may the distressed Novel-wright exclaim,
' . . . that this my Long-ear of a fictitious Biography shall not
find one . . . into whose still longer ears it may be the means,
under Providence, of instilling somewhat?'

Thomas Carlyle, 'Biography' (1832)

I

After her marriage in 1832, Gaskell was to live for the rest of her life, except for holidays and visits, in Manchester, a city already made great by the Industrial Revolution, yet expanding immensely throughout her lifetime. That city and the reflection of its growth. in the social novel is the concern of this chapter. When William Gaskell attempted to divert his wife's grief at the death of their son by suggesting she write a story, Gaskell began a historical tale, set in eighteenth-century Yorkshire, but, as she herself said, the everyday insisted: 'I bethought me how deep might be the romance in the lives of some of those who elbowed me daily in the busy streets.'[1] In the novel she produced, Mary Barton (1848), she writes both of the workmen 'who looked as if doomed to struggle through their lives in strange alternations between work and want' (p. lxxiii) and of the tragic individual, John Barton. She wrote from what she knew and had seen, and could feel the individual gripped in a historical process that threatened England with the upheavals of the 1840s that culminated in 1848 with Europe's year of revolutions If it were 'an error that the woes, which come with ever returning tide-like flood to overwhelm the workmen in our manufacturing towns, pass unregarded by all but the sufferers' (p. lxxiv), still the error was so bitter that anything that made people aware of the truth was for good. Both to tell of Manchester and to show the tragedy of working men were primary purposes in Gaskell's first novel.

Cotton was king in Manchester and the focus of the city's splendours and miseries. The city of the 1840s was the product of a rapid growth that continued throughout the century. The main action of *Mary Barton* is set about 1838 or 1840: there was a commercial crisis in 1841 and the mood of the Hungry Forties and the demands of Chartism colour, as they provided the impulse for, the writing. *North and South* (1855) is more or less contemporary in setting and the difference between the two novels is partly in Gaskell's developing skill (she wrote *Ruth* and *Cranford* between the two industrial novels and advanced rapidly artistically), partly in changing personal attitudes, and partly in the changes that took place in Manchester between the 1840s and 1850s. Revolution at least seemed to be averted and issues could be discussed more dispassionately because there seemed time in which to find solutions.

In roughly forty years (1794-1831) Manchester grew from a parish of about 40,000 inhabitants to one of over a quarter of a million. Betwen 1800 and 1844, cotton production in the kingdom increased from 3 million lb. to 600 million lb., three-fifths of the business concentrated in Lancashire.[2] Even given the speed of development in the twentieth century, we have seen nothing so stunning and so completely unprovided for in its consequences. In the face of such changes and wealth there was understandably a sense of the romance and excitement of the cotton industry. The heroic figure was Sir Richard Arkwright (1732-92), whose practical realization of the powered spinning frame between 1767 and 1769 set things in motion. Thomas Carlyle declared (note the sense of imperative) that 'it was this man that had to give England the power of cotton',[3] and Edward Baines in his *History of the Cotton Manufacture* (1835) spoke of Sir Richard as one

> who, though not entitled to all the merit which has been
> claimed for him, possessed very high inventive talent, as well
> as an unrivalled sagacity in estimating at their true value the
> mechanical contrivances of others . . . and [in] constructing the
> factory system – itself a vast and admirable machine, which
> has been the source of great wealth, both to individuals and to
> the nation (p. 147).

A new empire, founded on commerce instead of force, was being established, with a sense of man's power in the control of natural forces, so that science becomes an aesthetic as well as economic source – Baines refers to Dr Black's 'important and beautiful discovery of latent heat'. [4] This was progress:

> Men . . . have merely to attend on this wonderful series of mechanism, to supply it with work, to oil its joints and to check its slight and frequent irregularities; – each workman performing, or rather superintending, as much work as could have been done by *two or three hundred men* sixty years ago. At the approach of darkness the building is illuminated by jets of flame, whose brilliance mimics the light of day, – the produce of an invisible vapour, generated on the spot. [5]

Thus Arkwright's mill glows for us in Thomas Wright of Derby's nocturnal painting, and the dominion of human science over the powers of nature hinted at a prospect of eternal peace, because cotton linked the spindles of Manchester with the plough and hoe of the Mississippi. There is prospective irony in Baines's comment that the 'American government cannot wage war against English manufacturers without waging it equally against the southern states of its own confederation' (p. 317); when war did come, it was North against South and cotton came close to drawing England in on the side of the South.

The changes were observed easily in a man's lifetime, so that an 1839 Manchester guide book could observe that many older inhabitants remember 'when the site of the present substantial warehouses in New Market-Buildings was a pool of water. . . . '[6] Speed of change meant advance; generally, men were better off, against agriculture's soul-destroying poverty. John Clare's parents had 'often enough to do to keep cart upon wheels, as the saying is';[7] factory wages were so good that few girls would even consider going into domestic service (a difficulty for the Hales in *North and South*); and in 1845 Lyon Playfair quoted an estimate that each family in Lancashire consumed 450 pounds of butcher's meat a year (solid red meat, that is, exclusive of bacon, pork, fish, and poultry).[8] Margaret Hale includes lack of butcher's meat, to which Higgins is used, as one argument against his proposed southern migration. Now that men might do work done by two or three hundred men sixty years before, their wages were proportionally higher, but whatever the general advantages, the individual case was often worse, particularly as urban development began to be strangled under its own pressure. The influx into towns meant worsening living conditions, while the work environment, in mills that needed to be kept damp and hot, was wretched and not improved by the attitudes of many of the masters. A foreign observer, Fanny Lewald ('an intrusive, stupid, ugly, fat Berlin Jewess, coursing about on the strength of sending windy gossip to the newspapers', Carlyle called her in a diversion from self-laceration),[9] writing in 1850 with a mixture of shrewdness and banality, shows Manchester as unplanned, wealthy and squalid:

> It is, if you exclude the majestic Market Street, the Square, and a square at the end of the town, on which, behind a clear water-fountain, a new and magnificent hospital has been constructed, really not at all beautiful. Without the character of venerable age or brand new elegance and comfort, the uniform rows of smoke-blackened houses stretch on and on in long straight lines along the streets. There is nothing but warehouses . . . . Isolated new buildings, such as the magnificent Exchange, the Town Hall, etc. are lost in the insignificant but useful masses of houses . . . . The confectioners, luxury shops and everything else are crammed into dark narrow spaces. They do not tempt you to linger there . . . .
>
> The town of Manchester is a place for working in, where people earn enough money so that they don't have to live in it; the town has, therefore, despite its great industrial traffic, a certain air of a small town which is out of date.[10]

The wealth is there, and other observers drew attention to the contrasts of a great (and dirty) city. Disraeli sets the industrial splendour of the centre of 'Mowbray' against the infinite swarming population of the suburbs, in *Sybil* (1848: Bk. II, ch. ix). Early in *Mary Barton* there is the contrast between the Davenports' miserable cellar and lighted, well-filled shops.[11]

The novelists, whatever their disparate purposes (*Sybil* presents a lively and entertaining, if untenable, historical interpretation), show awareness of industrial conditions and the unease about basic social justice that charges the work of most of the best writers in nineteenth-century England. Critics like Carlyle in *Past and Present* (1843) and Matthew Arnold in *The Function of Criticism at the*

Present Time (1864), however separated in time or attitudes, emphasized the ability of literature, including criticism, to function so that
writer and thinker are workers for good in society. What these
writers are aware of is the centrality of the individual in society
(whether in Carlyle's account of child-murder for the funeral-club
money or Arnold's mordant 'Wragg is in custody'), something
insisted upon by official reports as well. In 1845 Playfair had
declared that a 'human being is not a mere producer of wealth; his
death or existence, his happiness or misery, are much too high
objects upon which to set a pecuniary value' (p. 105). The idea that
we would be happier without the Industrial Revolution must be
resisted, and through the 1820s individual gains were greater than
losses, though this is not to ignore losses that were there, particularly
breakdown of the family, since a wife in employment had little
time or energy for baking or brewing or ordinary housecleaning.[12]
By the 1850s the balance was again decidedly in favour of the city
dweller in terms of conditions and wages: the debate is over the
1830s and 1840s – was there gain or a positive step backwards? – and
this is the principal period of the social novel (extending into the
early 1850s), of Gaskell, Dickens, Disraeli, Kingsley and minor
writers, roused by their own experience and by an awareness, never
lacking in the Victorians, that things were seriously wrong.

In 1844 the French journalist Leon Faucher (and his anonymous
translator) recognized the importance of progress as a way to a
higher sphere of social and moral development (the mood of
Tennyson in 'Locksley Hall', preferring 'fifty years of Europe to a
cycle of Cathay') and Faucher emphasized that the rise of the
industrial arts 'indicate[s] ... the real Destiny of Society. ... The
cause of Industry is the cause of humanity'. Yet Faucher also
admitted that 'Ages of transition are always painful stages in human
progress. ... They are seasons of activity it is true, but a morbid
restlessness rather than a harmonious action is their dominant
characteristic.'[13] *Mary Barton* expresses something of that 'painful
stage in human progress', while *North and South*'s qualified optimism
suggests a more stable society. Though Gaskell never takes us into a
mill (Bessy Higgins describes the spinning processes to Margaret
Hale), she shows worker's conditions, the frugality of the Barton
household and the squalor of the Davenports' filthy cellar. Even
Alice Wilson's cellar, though whitewashed, is damp, a condition of
many such dwellings, originally occupied by hand-loom weavers

who needed humidity to preserve the stretched thread. Reading accounts of Manchester, one might feel that Gaskell, if anything, shows things in their painful progress as better than they were.

The community of rich and poor alike, a theme covert or overt of the social novels, was in reality stressed only too terribly by the filth of the streets, by the rapid spread of disease bred in the poor's insanitary housing. The poor man might be the principal sufferer, 'but no man is safe who breathes the same air'.[14] Edwin Chadwick's *Poor Law Commission Report* (1842) noted of parts of Manchester:

> whole streets in these quarters are unpaved and without drains
> or main-sewers, are worn into deep ruts and holes, in which
> water constantly stagnates, and are so covered with refuse and
> excrementitious matter as to be almost impassable from depth
> of mud and intolerable from stench (p. 38).

Privies and ashpits (which received all kinds of refuse besides ashes) often adjoined or were below living-rooms, so noxious matter soaked through walls or fumes came through the floor. The Manchester and Salford Sanitary Association, a good example of action by individuals concerned at the lack of civic activity, in a report of 1854 found (one example of many) that there were two privies (or petties) for nine-ty-four people, four holes to a privy.[15] Living conditions were often disgusting: one police inspector found 'on a wretched bed', 'three persons sick, and on the point of death', and though there were instances of good cellars (and some 'preferred to more convenient and cheaper residences on account of their independent entrances'), in many houses physical and sexual overcrowding lead to beastliness of conditions:

> D.F. is a widower with one sleeping apartment, in which sleep
> his adult son and daughter; the latter has a bastard child,
> which she affiliates on the father, he upon the son, and the
> neighbours upon both.[16]

If this should seem exceptional, proximity was common enough:

> The occupants of the beds were, for the most part, in a state
> of nudity, and were huddled together in the same bed, men,
> women, and children without any reference to age or sex. . . .
> In one house . . . the floor of the upstairs room was literally
> covered with human beings, and it was almost impossible to
> take the dimensions of the room without treading on them.[17]

Although there may be something ludicrous in the earnestness with which measurements were obtained under difficulties, the Sanitary Association, with its investigating committees and Reports both printed and manuscript, was concerned with establishing the nature of conditions, with the philosophical aspect of the situation, with immediate alleviation and with long-term reform. William Gaskell was a committee member from 1853 and gave a lecture on 'The Transgression of the Laws of Health, etc.' in the 1854-5 session.

Given home conditions and long factory hours, often 5.30 a.m. to 7 p.m., which broke down family life, there was naturally a desire for escape. The Sanitary Association did what it could, printing, for instance, in 1861 cards with simple advice on looking after children, the cards 'made somewhat ornamental, and ... prepared so that they can be hung up in cottages and appealed to whenever their assistance is required'.[18] Things had improved by 1861, but the lure of streets and beerhouses and gin palaces was strong. When Carson's mill in *Mary Barton* burns down, the gin palace next to it is described with care (p. 54);[19] while in 1841 Manchester was estimated to have 285 brothels, apart from the common prostitutes walking the streets, though accosting was less rude than in most places, the girls being of a better class because Manchester was, 'in regard to promiscuous intercourse, the rendezvous of the wealthier classes'. A Mr Logan said what he perhaps did not quite mean in asserting that there 'is not a single first-rate house for assignations in Rochdale, because the *gentlemen* always go to Manchester'.[20] The working life of a prostitute was reckoned by Faucher at six years (p. 42), a grim shadow over Mary Barton's Aunt Esther.

Such accounts of Manchester necessarily stress the disgusting side of life, since bad conditions rather than satisfactory needed attention. Their extent should be borne in mind when reading *Mary Barton* – they are hinted at in the ash-heap stepping stones on which you do *not* tread if you care for cleanliness (p. 65). Gaskell does not dwell on these matters – she is not primarily a sanitary reformer; she makes her point succinctly through the Davenports' cellar and concentrates on the tragedy of John Barton. What she does, as do the reports of the Health of Towns Commission and of the voluntary Manchester Sanitary Association, is to challenge Frederick Engel's assertion that:

a person may live in Manchester for years, and go in and out
daily without coming into contact with a working-people's
quarter or even with workers. . . . I have never seen so
systematic a shutting out of the working-class from the
thoroughfare, so tender a concealment of everything which
might affront the eye and the nerves of the bourgeoisie, as in
Manchester.[21]

Apart from the doubtful nature of the process (Engel's 'shutting out'
claims a deliberate action by the middle classes) it is clear that many
people knew and sought out what might affront eye and nerves.
Gaskell's preface to *Mary Barton* and Margaret Hale's early experiences in Milton (=Manchester) in *North and South* suggest that the
industrial nature of the city could not be avoided, an impression
enforced by Fanny Lewald, who noted the workers in the largest
streets and in the public park.[22] The plight of Manchester and that of
individual workers were often desperate; yet neither was ignored.
The British Industrial Revolution has been the basis of all subsequent
industrial transformation, yet its uniqueness must be stressed both as
model and as circumstance. If others have taken advantage of
techniques and experience, so also have they been able to anticipate
problems Britain could not guess at in advance and had painfully to
live through.[23]

The problem was heightened by the double necessity of immediate
alleviation as well as the search for long-term solutions. Education
was advocated as a solution to working-class distress, yet Dickens
pointed to the lack of home influence, or worse, the home's per-
nicious influences, which worked against all efforts of education. Like
the Manchester Sanitary Association, Dickens had advanced from the
earlier belief in education as the great panacea to a conviction that
'neither education nor religion could do anything really useful in
social improvement until the way had been paved for their ministra-
tions by cleanliness and decency'.[24] In writing *Mary Barton*, Gaskell
shows conditions in incidental and illuminating detail, but often as
an assumed background to her primary purpose. Her eye and nerves
are alive to urban conditions even when she does not bring them into
direct play in the novel.

In a situation aggravated by worsening conditions and increasing
population (men married at an average age of twenty-three), the
principal threat was conditions not poverty; butcher's meat was

consumed on a scale unknown to agricultural workers, but disease, suffering and ignorance flourished. Ignorance is indicated by a set of tables drawn up in 1844 by the prison chaplain at Preston and published by Lyon Playfair the following year. One may suspect a certain lack of co-operation or playing up amongst the prisoners in those answers totally inapposite; still, of 416 prisoners at the Sessions, 50 per cent were unable to name the months of the year and 40 per cent to name the reigning sovereign. Mr Clay, the clergyman concerned, reckoned that knowledge of words like 'righteousness' would afford evidence of attendance at a place of worship; of those ignorant of meanings, the greater number admitted as much: 'some, however, guessed at their meaning; and with regard to "righteousness," said that it meant "badness," "bad company," "a bad mind," "doing wrong," "swearing," "fighting and being drunk," "that they should not be so rich," etc. etc. etc.'[25] At a time of crisis, as the 1840s undoubtedly was, poverty, ignorance and violence were the dangers, and a writer of 1844 stressed the three great aims of forward-looking people as Free Trade, sanitary regulations, and comprehensive secular education.[26] The first would guarantee the workman a proper reward for industry and prevent the recurrence of periodical slumps (1841 was a year of commercial crisis and the 1840s a recession period), the second, healthy living conditions, and the third, free of the religious dissension which impeded establishment of a state system and emphasized sectarian differences in the schools, would fit people better for their role in society and an understanding of their own situation.

It is in education and relaxation that the better side of Manchester is seen. Unitarian support for education and working men's knowledge and skill have already been touched on (pp. 18-19, 28 above), and there was a tradition of choral and vocal music emphasized by Margaret's career in *Mary Barton* and enforced by reference to the singer Deborah Travis (p. 39). Books became increasingly available, the most famous library being at Chetham's Hospital, established in 1665 as a free library, with 21,000 volumes. The Free Library was established under the Public Libraries Act of 1850 and so belongs to the period of *North and South* rather than *Mary Barton* - by November 1856 it had 32,573 volumes. Other libraries existed, though most charged some kind of subscription, the Mechanics' Institution, with 14,000 volumes, most obviously providing for the working man.[27] Leisure time was small and the English Sunday restrictive; those workmen who wanted on their one free day to look at pictures or natural curiosities found galleries and museums shut – a state of affairs adversely remarked by visitors: Faucher noted that Protestantism tends to inertia and worse on Sundays, which the more rigorously observed 'the more frequented are the public-houses and gin-shops', Manchester having 'no public promenades, no avenues, no public gardens'.[28] For exercise, people with the energy walked out into the fields on holidays, as the Bartons do to Green Heys: the modern sprawl of Manchester or London is comparatively recent. About 1847 or 1848 Geraldine Jewsbury gives a long description of the newly opened Peel Park, formerly a family residence, the house a museum, library and reading-room, 'the dirty-faced, painful-looking mechanics' reading 'with a grave attention which showed that to them, at least, books were very reverend realities', while in the park 'the men with their wives, or the women with their children alone, were scattered up and down, looking quite at home. It made me see that the "people's parks" are "no make-believes", since they use them and enjoy them'.[29]

The work people also enjoyed more zestful amusements; the liveliness of Manchester men was notable then as now.[30] Singing and · dancing was to be found at the Trafford Arms, Victoria Bridge:

> It is curious to mark the zest with which a Lancashire clog
> hornpipe, a screaming comic song, or a sentimental ditty, is
> hailed by an audience crowded from floor to ceiling. Each
> visitor pays two-pence on entrance, for which he is supplied
> with a glass of capital ale or porter. . . . Above the
> concert-room is a good dancing saloon, well lighted and
> capable of holding about 300 persons.[31]

Such rumbustiousness, though dated after the worst periods of distress, is a useful corrective to the depressing squalor, for people could enjoy life and mostly did not judge their own condition by the ideological or religious class-theories of Engels or the Sanitary Association or Gaskell or ourselves.

Gaskell makes a plea in *Mary Barton, North and South*, and in some of the short stories for reconciliation of the classes. Division, often expressed in violence, was common enough, though the most notorious outrage, the Peterloo Massacre of 1819, began as a peaceful meeting in support of political reform.[32] This violence was linked both to economic distress and to political radicalism, which in turn tended to be related, so that with increasing economic buoyancy after the 1840s radicalism and violence declined. Chartism was a force in Manchester, as John Barton's account of the petitioner's humiliation in London suggests. There were riots in 1842, with cannon planted at New Cross, and people were ready to believe there were demagogues set on stirring up revolution,[33] but the language and ritual of such working-class movements is curious in modelling itself upon Christianity, which, though undoubtedly capable of revolutionary and enthusiastic development, yet provides modes of thought tied by the very nature of the associations of form and language to the establishment they sought to change or to destroy.[34] In this sense, at least, English radicalism could be remarkably conservative and there is no doubt that revolutionary radicalism involved a very small number indeed.

If the Chartists and Owenites attracted people by democratic hymns and secular sermons and increased their adherents 'by rural excursions, and by providing cheap and innocent recreation for the working class',[35] we may be also fairly certain that many people found them an acceptable alternative to church attendance while remaining as passive as they would under a Christian minister. Even in the period of higher radicalism a newspaper like *The Poor Man's Advocate* suggests the ambivalence of using familiar forms and language for a new doctrine. The paper ran briefly in 1832-3 and belongs to the period when a society advancing along the road to industrialization was trying to

> persuade a labour force, hitherto accustomed to the freedom
> and flexibility of a mainly agricultural, craft, or domestic way
> of life, to fall easily and unprotestingly into the discipline and
> rigidity of large-scale industrial organization.[36]

Despite an epigraph from Shelley, the *Advocate* falls naturally into the language of Christianity: its general motto, 'Open thy mouth, judge righteously, and plead the cause of the poor and needy', from the Book of Proverbs, asserts that society is as in need of reform as of overthrow. It could also draw upon the story of Dives and Lazarus, the division of their fate having class overtones recognized also by John Barton and by Bessy Higgins. More importantly in this context, the *Advocate* links the interests of the middle class with those of the working class in the changes that must come, as did Gaskell from her middle-class, overtly Christian, position. 'Change of system or outrage is inevitable', declared the *Advocate*; 'it becomes a matter of interest . . . in which the middle class of society are deeply concerned, to procure at once justice to the operative, and security to themselves.'[37] Though the tone is threatening, the assertion that the middle class's 'welfare is bound up with that of the working class', since the 'one cannot be permanently injured without entailing mischief upon the other', is essentially Gaskell's point. Gaskell 'quotes' back the Christian language and ties the gospel to a social reconciliation, so that the terms of the dispute are in common between her and radicals, even if their aims are not the same. In using this language Gaskell seeks change to prevent worse disorders.

The *Advocate* gives evidence enough of faults in the system if only believed in part, and of a new relationship being established between master and men. It attacks bad masters, night work, dodges to impose fines and to get round factory legislation. Particularly galling was the unwarranted intervention of masters over customs of the men, vestiges of the older system being displaced. The imposition of fines for the old practice of 'footing' called forth a lament that suggests the conservative nature of these proletarian activists:

> A 'footing' simply means a treat given by a new hand to his
> 'shop-masters,' as a token of his desire to cultivate their
> friendship and good-will. . . . It had its origin in times when
> workmen were neither so submissive, nor masters so assuming
> as they are now become. . . . But those times are gone. We
> have exchanged 'footings,' and other occasions of innocent
> enjoyment and recreation, for one continual round of gloomy,
> unceasing, and ill-requited toil.[38]

Interestingly, this involves the breakdown of a theory of paternalism in the master/man relationship, no new theory yet having taken its place. For Carlyle the 'cash-nexus' was all that bound man to man; Gaskell feared this to be true and strove against it. There were conflicting claims, either that the master should not interfere beyond his contract (a theory asserted by masters and men alike: Thornton *and* Higgins in *North and South* doubt the propriety of association), or that the master was responsible to his men and ought to be concerned for their welfare even at the expense of his immediate profits. It is in this context of change and debate particularly that we should see Gaskell's industrial novels and it is a sign of her increasing strength that the question is presented as more complex, and left unanswered though explored in *North and South* where it had been lost amid technical problems of handling material in *Mary Barton*.

It is necessary to hold on to the fact that the Industrial Revolution is a great achievement. Yet many had woe to bear, and industrial fiction largely shows the dark side, each author taking up not only conditions but the issue of capital and labour. The novelists tend to stress a division (Disraeli's 'Two Nations' in *Sybil*, the rich and the poor, who in Dickens and Gaskell become masters and men) which ought to be bridged over, since labour and capital are not opposed but interdependent. One vexed question here was the position of the unions, emphasized by the close association of industrial organizations with Chartism in the 1830s and 1840s. Gaskell, in both *Mary Barton* and *North and South*, presents one of the most favourable pictures in Victorian fiction of the Unions,[39] writers generally showing contempt or hatred. Even Dickens, who favours the working man in *Hard Times* against masters like Bounderby, contrasts the honourable independence of Stephen Blackpool who refuses to join the union, with the rhetorical blether and self-seeking of Slackbridge, the paid delegate.

The voice (though how loud in terms of audience is difficult to say) of workmen's combination against the factory system is heard in journals such as *The Poor Man's Advocate*, which took up the question of masters' rights:

> We are quite well aware that it will be argued against us, that
> we have nothing to do with the internal regulations of a
> master's manufactory; that all his arrangements are matters
> merely between himself and his work-people – 'a mere matter
> of private business;' and that for others to meddle with them,
> is, to say the least of it, impertinent (p. iii a).

On this, Lord Brougham stood against further legislation, since he argued that any employee might make his own bargain with an employer and could go elsewhere if the situation wasn't liked; the retort of the *Advocate* and of the novelists, was that employees had no such powers and no where else to go, for there were combinations of masters. Dickens, Gaskell and others were less certain about the mode of action, where the *Advocate* saw the need for combinations of the workmen in unions. It warned that violence and destruction could only be 'averted by the kindness and sympathy shown by the middle towards the working classes' and issued the threat that since 'those only who possess something, can sustain loss', the middle class of society must be deeply concerned 'to procure at once justice to the operative, and security to themselves' (p. 3 b). These rumblings are heard in Gaskell's preface to *Mary Barton*, though she seeks conciliation rather than violence. The violence was real enough, if sporadic, as often individual initiative as union action, though any manifestation tended to militate against labour organizations. The 1831 murder of young Thomas Ashton, a consequence of a dispute with the union, forms the fictional climax of Elizabeth Stone's novel, *William Langshawe, The Cotton Lord* (1842), and is drawn on for Henry Carson's murder in *Mary Barton*. Fiction and fact reflect each other.

The unions, forbidden by the Combination Acts (1799-1800) until their repeal in 1824, were closely associated, in the popular mind at least, with political and subversive secret societies and early modelled themselves deliberately on associations like the Masons, using ritual and secrecy to make them strong and impressive to their members. Too often the representation of the unions, in attacks and in novels, saw them only as coercive mummers. The fiercely hostile pamphlet of 1834, *Character, Object, and Effects of Trades' Unions; with some Remarks on the Law concerning Them*, provided ritual colour for trade union initiation in both Elizabeth Stone's *William Langshawe, The Cotton Lord* (1842) and Disraeli's *Sybil* (1845). The pamphlet's author had gathered material from many sources, including manufacturers 'who have seen or suffered the effects of Combinations', their names being suppressed for safety to property and even lives. The cotton-spinners, though only one-tenth of all cotton operatives, had the best-organized, most extensive union, since their work was essential to the continuance of all the rest (pp. 2, 12). Successive strikes failed, the 1829 turn-out producing violence, and masters were shot at:

> these villainous attempts were unsuccessful, except in the
> instance of Mr. T. Ashton, one of the most respected of the
> manufacturers, whose yet unpunished murder attests the excess
> to which the workmen are capable of proceeding, when
> impelled by the spirit of combination (p. 20).

It says much for Gaskell's imaginative power that she, unlike Elizabeth Stone, could see young Carson's murder in Mary Barton as perpetrated not by someone 'impelled by the spirit of combination' but rather by a tragic figure whose sufferings and personal feelings had been insulted. The pamphlet is most expansive on the rituals of initiation and the forms of meeting: the wool-combers have 'a skeleton, above which is a drawn sword and a battle-axe, and in front stands a table, upon which lies a Bible' (p. 67); prayers and hymns are uttered and oaths administered: 'every necessary device is employed to strike terror into those who go through these inaugural rites' and a 'London journeyman, who entered a Union during the past year, was so overcome by the ceremonies he went through on his admission that he was literally deprived of reason, and died in the agonies of raving madness' (p. 66). Elizabeth Stone conveniently disposes of one of her characters in this last fashion. Jem Forshaw, a cotton operative, enraged when his Nancy shows favour to the mill-owner and believing that master, Balshawe, wants to expedite their marriage only as a cover for disposing of spoiled goods, agrees to take the vows of the union. Blindfolded, with the Psalm 94 chanted, he takes the oath, but overcome by the sight of skull and skeleton (borrowed by Stone from the wool-combers) he falls down in a fit, to be taken in a few days and 'carried in a coach to the asylum for such miserables – an incurable lunatic' (ii, 166-74). The ludicrous anti-climax (all seemed set for Balshawe's murder at the hands of Jem) only serves to emphasize Stone's hatred of the unions; while Disraeli's remarkably similar account of initiation (*Sybil*, bk iv, ch. iv) though infinitely more skilful, also has no real follow-up. Dickens has an initiation into the 'Prentice Knights of *Barnaby Rudge*' (ch. 8), but once he comes seriously to industrial problems in *Hard Times*, whatever his attitude to unions, he dispenses with all such claptrap, while Gaskell nowhere hints at it.[40] Not only is Gaskell sympathetic towards the unions (though not uncritical of them), she is also aware that industrial problems are not a matter of skulls and oaths but of flesh and blood, and in coming to fiction she deals both with a state of the people 'in which the lips are compressed for curses, and the hands clenched and ready to smite' and with the tragedy of John Barton, for she had 'so long felt that the bewildered life of an ignorant thoughtful man of strong power of sympathy, dwelling in a town so full of striking contrasts as this is, was a tragic poem' (70).

II

Mary Barton and *North and South* are often spoken of in the context of social fiction, and if seen as such (they after all draw their materials, impulse and strength from the Manchester that Gaskell knew) in the series of novels about conditions of the cotton industry, they give a sense of continuity, as well as of Gaskell's superiority both in approach to the problems and in fictional skill. She was remarkably early in the field: *Mary Barton* preceded *Hard Times* by six years, and though Charles Kingsley's *Yeast* began serial publication in 1848 it only appeared complete in 1851. Three novels before *Mary Barton* that deal specifically with the cotton-manufacturing areas, all interestingly by women, are: Frances Trollope's *Michael Armstrong the Factory Boy* (1839-40), Charlotte Elizabeth's *Helen Fleetwood* (1841), and Elizabeth Stone's *William Langshawe, The Cotton Lord* (1842). The historical information was available through observation, reports, even journalism; its most notable interpretation was in nineteenth-century fiction.

The preface to Frances Trollope's *Michael Armstrong* stresses the novel's concern with the evils of the factory system and in particular 'the hideous mass of injustice and suffering to which thousands of infant labourers are subjected, who toil in our monster spinning mills' (p. iii).[41] Trollope found it easier to sympathize with children than with adult labourers who might resort to combinations or violence to gain their ends. She brought the story to an abrupt close with Michael's establishment in adult life, recent industrial unrest producing doubt when

> those in whose behalf she hoped to move the sympathy of
> their country are found busy in scenes of outrage and lawless
> violence, and uniting themselves with individuals whose
> doctrines are subversive of every speepecies of social order (p. iv).

Though not specific, her reference to 'men who have stained their righteous cause with deeds of violence and blood' probably aims at the Glasgow cotton-spinners' strike of 1837, which provoked Carlyle to speak of 'Glasgow Thuggery' in his essay *Chartism* (1839). Gaskell was to claim that she had cases from Glasgow in mind when she wrote of Carson's murder in *Mary Barton* (196).[42] The cause for which Trollope wrote and which she feared she might injure if she persisted in holding up the Glasgow men of blood as objects of public sympathy was the Ten Hours' Movement, begun in 1831 and first passed, heavily modified, as law in 1844.[43] Its aim was a maximum working day of ten hours (six days a week, that is); and the innocent child victim was easier to support than men driven to articulate demands on their own behalf. Basically Tory in outlook at this time, Trollope saw the Ten Hour Bill as the panacea for all industrial injustice. Through the Rev. Mr George Bell she states the far-reaching consequences of such legislation. Bell, speaking to the conscience-stricken Miss Brotherton, who has realized her money comes from labourers' misery, insists that the factory child is more deserving than the negro slave (a hit at philanthropists whose wealth came from the factory system), for both have a master and no choice. After describing a mother forcing her child to the factory, so that she will not be fired, Bell voices Trollope's Toryism when he urges the political danger from such a system:

> Never ... did the avarice of man conceive a system so hourly
> destructive of every touch of human feeling, as that by which
> the low-priced agony of labouring infants is made to eke out
> and supply all that is wanting to enable the giant engines of
> our factories to out-spin all the world! (p. 202).

The responsibility is the masters', since Bell voices rightly (however uneasy we might feel in the context of this particular novel) that it is not from science 'that we have anything to dread, it is only from a fearfully culpable neglect of the moral power that should rule and regulate its uses, that it can be other than one of God's best gifts' (p. 205). We feel uneasy not at the sentiment but because, despite all the horrors Trollope shows so effectively, Bell seems genuinely to feel that a Ten Hour Bill will surely bring all to right.

Michael Armstrong opens in Ashleigh, which like many such places in Lancashire, is scarcely more than a village. Satire upon the manners of the newly rich, found also in Elizabeth Stone, is strong, precipitating the main action. The desire of the chief mill-owner, Sir Matthew Dowling, to stand well in his flirtation with Lady Clarissa induces him to take Michael, a mill-worker, into his own home, a ludicrous piece of plotting by Trollope, which threatens the story's credibility. Sir Matthew's amorousness is not so strong that he would willingly entertain Michael, and it is crude realism that accepts his overseer's argument that, since there is industrial unrest over a girl's death through overwork, taking up Michael plus a carefully contrived act of generosity to his mother might placate the men. The theme is scarcely pursued, no further reference being made to organized labour, trade unions, or any kind of strike. Trollope is innocent of the concerns of Elizabeth Stone or Gaskell with organized labour or industrial action except in the reaction of her novel's preface.

Trollope is more effective in describing the factory, to which Sir Matthew takes Michael in his new clothes to make clear 'the extraordinary kindness I have shown you' (p. 82). She presents it as a prison, the bell rung for admission, 'a ceremony necessary to obtain admittance both for masters and labourers; no means of entrance or exit being ever left unsecured for a single instant' (p. 79). This restraint, the worse to a population used to easier systems of agricultural organization, if apparently extreme, is backed by evidence in *The Poor Man's Advocate* of a factory where the rule was no exit without written permission.[44] Michael and his brother Edward are 'piecers', responsible for 'piecing' or repairing the cotton threads running to the spindles when they break. Edward, despite all dangers ('the over-lookers, straps in hand, [are] on the alert'), is overpowered by brotherly love and clasps Michael fondly in his arms. Every labourer in sight

> forgot all standing orders in their astonishment, and stood
> with gaping mouths and eyes fixed upon the astounding
> spectacle. Sir Matthew, too, forgot for an instant, that every
> movement made within that crowded chamber, not having for
> its object the transmutation of human life into gold, was a
> positive loss to him ... (p. 82).

He gloats on his scheme and wonders 'who would dare to mention night work and hard usage now.'[45]

In his growing hatred of Michael, however, Sir Matthew determines to be rid of him, though without sacrificing good opinion. He persuades Mrs Armstrong to sign indentures, pretending they bind Michael apprentice to a stocking-weaver, thus placing him entirely and legally in his master's power until the age of twenty-one. The mill, an ordinary cotton mill it turns out, is in the Deep Valley, near the Derbyshire Peak, where Sharpton exploits cheap labour from the parish child-pauper population, about whom no questions are asked. Some of Trollope's most effective scenes are here, in the children greedily vying for food with pigs at the trough and in the fever that strikes them down.

Meanwhile, Miss Mary Brotherton, a young lady whose wealth comes from cotton, has begun to consider the basis of her fortune. She is essentially good, yet she

> grew up in total ignorance of the moans and the misery that

lurked beneath the unsightly edifices, which she just knew
were called the factories but which were much too ugly in her
picturesque eye for her ever to look at them, when she could
help it (p. 93).

Prompted by Michael's appearance in Sir Matthew's house she begins
to wonder who these labouring people are. In Ashleigh she meets
two girls, one injured by a billy-roller wielded by the overlooker, the
other lamed by falling asleep against the machinery. Trollope then
handles very finely a death-bed scene, where the squalor of the
house, the varied feelings of dying mother and her children, the
drunken worn indifference of the father, and the Christian concern
of Miss Brotherton are all held, without any one reaction swamping
the rest, leading to Mary's cry on her return home: 'I too am living
by the profit of the factory house. Is the division just? – Oh, God! Is
it holy?' (p. 137).

After her meeting with Mr Bell the clergyman and the meagre
consolation he can offer, Mary seeks to rescue Michael, visiting
various factories, including one which provides a Sunday-school. But
the Evangelical mill-owners (Trollope's Anglicanism branded all
such as hypocrites) expect the children to be there at 7 a.m., having
worked them until five minutes to midnight the night before (so not
profaning the Sabbath) – not surprisingly the children learn nothing
and sleep as best they can. Through plot complications, Mary
believes Michael dead and she goes abroad with Edward and with
Fanny Fletcher, a friend of Michael's from Deep Valley. Michael,
escaped from the prison-mill, finds new life in Cumberland (*he*
believes his brother to be dead) where the revivifying power of
nature is enforced by quotation from Wordsworth. Discovering
Edward is not dead, his search to find him brings him to Sir
Matthew's grotesque end, who dies haunted by a vision of Michael
and five hundred maimed factory children. Michael, happily reunited with his brother and Fanny, prepares to live happily ever
after, Trollope apparently content to have made her points about the
factory system and so not worried about the Armstrongs having
made, as it were, a 'separate peace' with the system – rather as
Gaskell found emigration a solution to the problems of *Mary Barton*,
where *North and South* was to have a bolder and less final ending.

Despite all its faults (the silliness of Michael's first being taken up;
the Ten Hour Bill as panacea), the novel's often forceful appeal is
essentially to the readers's feelings, stressed by emphasis upon child

labour, while the larger issues of capital and labour, of adult workers, or the real implications of the system are largely ignored.

Against Frances Trollope's Tory and High Anglican stance, *Helen Fleetwood* by Charlotte Elizabeth (Mrs Tonna) is Evangelical in tone and concerned in particular with child labour. It is not badly constructed, but its style is flowery and its piety (a fatalistic quietism, rather than Gaskell's Christian action) dominant. Its greatest interest is when concretely dealing with life in a cotton town. Widow Green, lured by an account of town as 'one of the first places in England for furnishing good, healthful, profitable employment for industrious people ... down to the small children, whose little nimble fingers get so expert at the easy tasks given to them' (p. 27),[46] finds on arrival in M. that conditions are worse than she ever could have thought. In a system that 'occasions so pressing a demand for a supply of new labourers, that it gives rise to a traffic not very dissimilar from the slave trade' (p. 41), her grandchildren are valuable to masters, who eagerly demonstrate ways of circumventing factory regulations about the age of children in manufactories (p. 64).[47] Little Mary Green's vivid account of the machinery on her first day at work recalls the more objective account of Baines (above, p. 49):

> but only think, boys, what it must be to see ever so many great big things, frames upon carriages on each side of the room, walking up to one another, and then walking back again, with a huge wheel at the end of each, and a big man turning it with all his might, and a lot of children of all sizes keeping before the frame, going backwards and forwards, piecening and scavenging .... Move, move, everything moves. The wheels and the frames are always going, and the little reels twirl round as fast as ever they can; and the pulleys, and chains, and great iron works over-head, are all moving; and the cotton moves so fast that it is hard to piece it quick enough; and there is a great dust, and such a noise of whirr, whirr, whirr ... (p. 110).[48]

Gaskell describes scarcely any machinery, as though she wishes to concentrate on the human drama rather than compete with the wonders of steam. It is these machines that have broken Mary Green's cousin, Sarah, as they were to have destroyed Rachel's sister in *Hard Times*.[49] Sarah, besides being consumptive, has had one arm taken off and her generally lowered condition 'came from convulsions and fits' (p. 75) as well from 'the overlooker that used to strap me and kick me, when I used to get too tired to work' (p. 108).

In the approach to death, Sarah is brought to spiritual understanding and joy by Helen, an interesting parallel with Bessy Higgins in *North and South*, another victim of industrial disease, though Margaret Hale brings spiritual consolation that stresses love rather than grace. Blame for abuses is placed squarely on the Calvinistic corruption of the human heart. Early on Helen 'had spoken truly her prevailing thought when reminding the widow of the Cross that every Christian needs must bear .... She now realized the daily taking up of that Cross, and her only solicitude was to be found following Christ under its burden' (p. 101). With such belief, the danger is that the system stands while grace is sought in acceptance of its burdens and reformation deferred to heaven. But Charlotte Elizabeth does denounce the system and those who make it:

> On the system, the vile, the cruel, the body and
> soul-murdering system of factory labour, we cannot charge the
> innate depravity of the human heart; but we do denounce it as
> being in itself a foul fruit of that depravity under its hateful
> form of covetousness, and of being in turn the prolific root of
> every ill that can unhumanize man ... (p. 167).

Her answers lie in appeal to the individual; conversion is to be personal rather than social, which avoids facing the complexity and size of the problem. Helen is made to stress the individual's peril, who with access to God's truth in the Bible yet lets 'those souls perish, while their poor bodies are worn out by hard and cruel labour to swell his unholy gains!' (p. 156). Even if the creed is unpalatable, the human need is recognized and this individual conversion echoes dramatically (if ultimately unconvincingly) in Carson's serious turning over of his Bible at the end of *Mary Barton*.

For Charlotte Elizabeth the ideal model lies in the country and in the past. Just such a unit Widow Green had managed to maintain before her lease expired and she moved to the town. The novel expresses a hatred of the Industrial Revolution, for its social and political anarchy and divisiveness, a division not known when there was a proper understanding of class:

> There are districts in the land still retaining much of the
> primitive character of English rusticity – places where the

blight has not come; where the demoralizing swarm of railway excavators has never alighted, nor the firebrand of political rancour scattered its darkening smoke, nor the hell-born reptile of socialism trailed his venomous slime (p. 238).

In such places (as in the towns themselves before the slime trails) the labourer knows his master (pp. 239-40). The attitude is understandable and not without its appeal; Dickens and Gaskell felt its force. But Charlotte Elizabeth's wish to place her model in the past and in the country is clearly inadequate in the face of what actually was happening. It is a model offered too in the unsatisfactory reconciliation of John Barton and Carson, but in *North and South*, whatever relationship Thornton may establish with his men and with Higgins in particular, both sides insist upon the right of the men to exclude Thornton from their activities. What Charlotte Elizabeth saw was true in part, that two 'classes, hitherto bound together by mutual interests and mutual respect, are daily becoming more opposed the one to the other' (p. 395), but her hope of Evangelicalism or rusticity was not to be realized. The novel itself shows a certain grim realism in denying a happy ending, except in the most chastened way: Helen dies, James dies, Widow Green goes into the workhouse, Mary is apprenticed, and only Richard and Willy find reasonably happy employment in farming. The system has been exposed and the family destroyed.

The third novel, by Mrs Elizabeth Stone ('Authoress of "The Art of Needlework"'), has both a fortuitous and a real connection with Gaskell. When *Mary Barton* appeared anonymously in 1848, Gaskell took a certain pleasure in helping speculation about the novel's authorship:

> Marianne Darbishire told me it was ascertained to be the production of a Mrs Wheeler, a clergyman's wife, who once upon a time was a Miss Stone, and wrote a book called 'The Cotton-Lord'. Marianne gave me many proofs which I don't think worth repeating, but I think were quite convincing (62).

The attribution seems ludicrous now to anyone reading the two novels with close attention, since *William Langshaw, The Cotton Lord* (1842), though set in Manchester, with superficial likenesses in its setting and occasional plot detail and more likenesses in delight at Lancashire folk and ways, is in tone and method opposed to Gaskell's work. It is often racy in style, some of its sketches of Manchester and of holidays like Race Week have merit as detachable essays, but it veers erratically between the satirical and the laudatory in its dealings with the masters and between farcical and scornful with the men. The plot, with its love intrigues and revelations, is silver-fork school[50] or degenerate Walter Scott.

Elizabeth Stone, though, unlike Charlotte Elizabeth, does have a liking for Manchester (her father, John Wheeler, was proprietor of the *Manchester Chronicle* and editor of *Manchester Poetry*), and amidst her satire, reality keeps breaking in, often manifested in local pride of progress:

> Wi' the rock and the spindle our grannies began,
> Neist at their wee wheelies they spat and they span,
> O little they thought o' the beautiful plan
> That now is spread wide for the spinnin' o't.[51]

The novel opens with a sketch of the popular image of a manufacturing district: its smoking chimneys, vulgar proprietors and still more vulgar wives, 'dense populations, filthy streets, drunken men, reckless women, immoral girls, and squalid children' (i, 1), and then challenges it. In an invocation of rural Lancashire, using rhymes and traditions such as the witches of Pendle Forest, Stone suggests the Gaskell of the opening of *The Life of Charlotte Brontë*. As the manufactories spring up by running streams and 'a low, a numerous, and, in many instances, a degraded population is speedily congregated' (i, 8), she puts in a good word for their moral character against that of agricultural districts, stressing the intelligence and natural musical talent of the natives of Lancashire, with their chorus-singers and hand-bell ringers (i, 10). Yet Stone's vision has a constant wobble: after the good word, the workers are either rough malcontents or else fools like Jem Forshaw, whose collapse at a union initiation has been mentioned already.

Stone's sympathies lie with the proprietors, new men though they are, who had come into prominence so rapidly that it is 'an admitted axiom that the Manchester people "have no grandfathers"' (i, 174), ostentatious and vulgar though they are like old Balshawe, a first generation cotton-lord, whose gorging brings on an apoplectic fit at a banquet, leaving him an imbecile (ii, 106, 114-16). William Langshawe himself, however, though a self-made man, perhaps too concerned with business, is a prime example of the Manchester

69

principle of self-help, as the anecdote of him in church, as admiring as satirical, shows:

> ... our pews joined, and I have seen him ... not one time,
> nor twenty, but a hundred times, when on his knees, steal a
> small pencil from his waist-coat pocket, and while his voice
> ejaculated as loudly as any in the church, 'Lord have mercy
> upon us, miserable sinners!' the blank leaf of his prayer-book
> was rapidly filling with a myriad of complicated figures ...
> (i, 72).

Langshawe is shrewd and determined his daughter shall not marry any idle gentleman or fashionable spendthrift. His pride and display of wealth is like that of John Thornton's mother in *North and South*: to that extent, both Stone and Gaskell display a recognizable type of Mancunian. Stone is ready to accept the system as one of necessity, where man must give place to machine, for

> Let a master be ever so kindly disposed; the great magician,
> Steam, is absolute and inflexible in his exactions; and while he
> is 'on' the appointed labourers must not slacken in their
> exertions (i, 161).

The master apparently is exonerated, as though he had no responsibility or control over steam, and Stone takes a pragmatic attitude over working hours. What of children working ten hours a day? Mr Ainsley, a defender of the system, in context the author's spokesman, agrees that looked at theoretically

> every man with a humane heart would wish that children
> should be free and unfettered, and pass their early years in
> gaiety and liberty. But this is impossible. The children of the
> poor *must* work; and that being the case, the true
> philanthropist will bend his energies rather towards the
> amelioration of existing evils, than to the invention of a
> Utopian and unattainable system of freedom and happiness ...
> (i, 191-2).

Yet the mill-owners are immensely wealthy – Langshawe's daughter, Edith, is said to have £100,000 – so why cannot the parents be paid more and the children worked less? Stone is silent, though the usual answer was the risk the owners took in investing their capital (a risk no worker faced), entitling them to all the profit when it came. The novel does not try to deny the often miserable living conditions of the workmen, though extreme conditions are blamed on their own lack of education or concern. The masters generally have a sense of responsibility. Edith has been brought up by her father to have 'a just idea of wealth by seeing the toil to others by which it was obtained' (i, 62), and the personal relationship of master and man is stressed when Edith persuades her father to discharge one man's last quarter's rent. Langshawe does so, and discharges the next quarter's as well. The patriarchal attitude displayed is clearly felt to be the best. Gaskell sees the changing relationship between masters and men as more complex and more tentative in the growing and jealously guarded independence of the men.

If Stone can see good masters and bad, can mock the grossness of behaviour as well as admire the sterling qualities of cotton-folk, she has nothing but hatred and contempt for the unions, though none of Charlotte Elizabeth's Christian horror at socialism as a creed. She draws on experience and on the 1834 pamphlet, *Character, Object, and Effects of Trades' Unions.* The cotton-spinners, Stone says, 'have absolutely passed laws, levied contributions, and published their proceedings at their annual or half-yearly meetings' (ii, 159). Whatever their claim to be protecting themselves against tyranny, 'it were absurd to suppose that this power is never exerted *except* for the protection of the operative from an oppressive or illiberal master' (ii, 160). The behaviour of Unions clearly could be arbitrary – it is one of the points at issue between Margaret Hale and Nicholas Higgins – and it could be violent. There is no need to doubt Stone's factual note appended to a picture of turn-outs ending in riot, tumult, and 'insubordination of the most extreme kind'; her mother hopeless of her father's safe return, the house shuttered and barricaded against the mob (ii,164fn.). To Stone the insult lies in its being 'insubordination'; she could not accept, as Gaskell did, the challenge to paternal hierarchy. Such is the persistence of these mill-workers, says Stone, that even 'while the orators of the political clubs' and the radical press 'were declaiming on slavery and the long-protracted toil of the factory operative', they could find time for midnight meetings and cash for union organizations that included paid officials (ii, 163).

The industrial action of the novel climaxes in a strike, when taking advantage of agricultural distress the political demagogues of the manufactories 'got up a cry of distress, which did not exist *then*, though it was speedily induced by their machinations' (ii, 281). The agitation culminates in the outrage of Henry Wolstenholme's murder, based on the killing of Thomas Ashton of Hyde, the real connection of the novel with Gaskell, who herself used the incident in *Mary Barton*. The differences in treatment suggest the different concerns of the two novelists. Where Stone separates the threads of masters' immorality and union violence, Gaskell links them (though not causally) by having Carson as both would-be seducer of Mary Barton and victim of her father's violence, a psychological and social complexity that suggests the untidiness of life and yet also helps artistic concentration. And where Stone's Wolstenholme is an entirely innocent victim, Gaskell, though in no way condoning the murder, is able to show with understanding the provocation for men whose demands have not been met, whose families are starving, and who are treated with contempt in Carson's mocking doodle of a cartoon. Wolstenholme belongs to a family 'dignified and adorned by an open-hearted hospitality, and by a widely-extended and unwearying benevolence which redeems the character of Lancashire "cotton-folks" generally from much that might otherwise degrade it' (i, 53-4). During the Christmas celebrations, Henry goes out to make sure all is well at the factory. Soon

> a bustle was heard outside the door, which was instantaneously
> opened. A crowd of people appeared, and as they partly
> divided to enter the hall, Mrs Wolstenholme, who had
> nervously pushed foremost, saw her eldest son, Henry borne in
> by the men – a corpse (ii, 305).

Stone appends a long note about the truth of the incident, but makes no fictional use of it, beyond the chance to beat the unions, who are further deflated by the strike ending with no advance in wages. The murder is a climax, in that it comes almost at the end of the novel, and yet it does not really seem to be a culmination: it has all the awkwardness of a real event hoisted into a fictional context.

Mary Barton (1848) was Gaskell's first full-length work. She had collaborated with her husband in 'Sketches among the Poor – No. 1' (1837),[52] a verse portrait of a woman who returns to childhood as death approaches:

> Fancy wild
> Had placed her in her father's house a child;
> It was her mother sang her to rest . . .

She was, Gaskell later said, the germ of Alice in the novel (82). The sketch, 'Clopton Hall', for Howitt was Gaskell's earliest independent work and Howitt conducted the original negotiations for Chapman and Hall to publish *Mary Barton* (55), the novel having been completed by November 1847.[53] Mary Barton represents a rejection of romance – or rather of the false belief that romance lies in the distant or strange. Gaskell first refers to the novel as 'a Manchester Love Story' (56), although the subtitle shifted significantly when published from love to 'A Tale of Manchester Life'. Despite Gaskell's claim after publication that 'John Barton' was the original title (70), the original names suggest that Mary's love was, along with Manchester life, always central to her design.[54] Alone amongst her works a detailed preliminary working sketch exists; and Gaskell also noted down the conclusion, presumably to be certain that everyone was accounted for.[55] The outline divides the novel into the common three-volume form (it actually appeared in two); apart from names and minor details, it corresponds substantially to the finished work. In the 'Conclusion yet to be written', which goes from Mary's collapse after the trial, the only important differences are in Esther's death, originally in a lodging house, not the Barton home (a significant return to her youthful innocence) and in the settlement in Canada (originally America), now briefly shown, instead of the plan's 'and so, sailing along the path of the setting sun, they fade from my sight, and darkness mantles over their future, & shrouds it from my vision'.[56] The publishers asked her after completion to add a section to bring up the length and she inserted what substantially are chapters 36 and 37, including the conversation between Carson, Job Legh, and Jem Wilson, seemingly so vital to the novel's meaning. We may take it (there is no direct evidence) that *Mary Barton* did divert Gaskell from the painfulness of her son's loss. Certainly, it gave her a sense of purpose, as she recognized that she might be doing something for her fellows, writing to Chapman in April 1848 that 'I think the present state of public events may not be unfavourable to a tale, founded in some measure on the present relations between Masters and work people' (55).

The publication of *Mary Barton* might seem timely indeed in 1848, a decade of political and industrial unrest culminating at home in the great Chartist rally and fear of anarchy, and abroad in revolution that expelled Louis Philippe in France, convulsed Germany and the Austrian Empire, and was to spread the following year to Italy.

Gaskell was at pains to deny its opportunism, 'no catch-penny run up since the events on the Continent' (58), stressing that the story was finished 'above a year ago', yet her account of its genesis brings out her sense of its real immediacy: 'I bethought me how deep might be the romance in the lives of some of those who elbowed me daily in the busy streets of the town in which resided' (p. lxxiii). Its relevance was not to the events of a year but to the effects of a generation; its sympathies were needed when the English middle classes had been given a severe fright, and liberal feeling for the working classes was at low ebb.

The story opens about 1835/37 and the main action can be dated about 1840, perhaps coloured also by the serious depression of 1841. The opening, with its expedition out to Green Heys Fields, half an hour from town, shows the Barton and Wilson families at a period of stability and full work, establishes the ease of access to the country when holidays are allowed, and suggests the recent growth of industrialization. A different pulse from the life of towns is stressed: the farming activities of the seasons, the old-fashioned herbs and flowers 'planted long ago, when the garden was the only druggist's shop within reach' (p. 2). It is a world largely unrecognized by the Bartons and the Wilsons, assimilated into unchanging rhythms of the industrial world. And yet Wilson still sleeks 'his hair with old country habit' (p. 77). The swift temporal flux of urban society is conveyed in such vestigial gestures and finds varied expression in old Alice Wilson, who with rich memories of Cumberland childhood has never thought herself a 'townie', and in Carson the mill-owner, who began as a hand with nothing save his own labour. This society absorbs, allows rapid growth, yet can fail to accommodate and often to understand. These people are independent in prosperity, the factory men and girls remarkable not for looks but for 'an acuteness and intelligence of countenance, which has often been noticed in a manufacturing population' (p. 3). Gaskell's Manchester man is no part of the *lumpenproletariat.* He seizes eagerly on the chance full employment gives to deck out his home, though commercial crisis will be reflected there too as knick-knacks and furniture are stripped away. In the Bartons' home, on the return from Green Heys, Gaskell acts very much as conductor:

it was evident Mrs Barton was proud of her crockery and
glass, for she left her cupboard door open, with a glance round

of satisfaction and pleasure . . . The place seemed almost
crammed with furniture (sure sign of good times among the
mills). (p. 13).

It is to this room, now stripped by poverty and a fitting image of the
sinking life of the householder, that Mary returns in John Barton's
few final days, where 'dull, grey ashes, negligently left, long days ago,
coldly choked up the bars of the grate and John has 'taken the
accustomed seat from mere force of habit, which ruled his autom-
aton body' (p. 410). The characters' fluctuations can be traced in
their world of material possessions.

From Green Heys Fields and back into Manchester, Gaskell is first
concerned to establish a physical reality, unknown to her readers,
which she later utilizes without authorial explanation as when Alice
Wilson's cleanly kept cellar with its ingenious contrivances sets a
contrast for the emphatic squalor of the Davenports' subterranean
dwelling. Gaskell realizes, increasingly in her work, the close attun-
ing of physical objects to human beings, so that through association
possessions take on emotional charge. The cheerfulness of the Barton
home, the fire, the tea with ham and eggs, the splendour of the
'bright green japanned tea-tray' (p. 13) are all part of a satisfying yet
fragile life, which is gradually to be destroyed, beginning that very
night with the violent and unexpected death of Mrs Barton in
childbirth, as John Barton himself is worn away by social circumstance and by a wild internal distress. Gaskell guides readers she feels
to be venturing on unfamiliar ground (as she glosses dialect words
and phrases: William Gaskell's *Two Lectures on Lancashire Dialect*
were added as an appendix to the fifth edition of 1854). If attention
to detail, however telling – the 'triangular pieces of glass to save
carving knives and forks from dirtying table-cloths' (p. 13) – can
seem over-insistent, it is also used to suggest the complex layering of
memory and suffering through objects which contain the past in
their physical present. John Barton alone in the dark after the bustle
of his wife's death

> thought of their courtship; of his first seeing her, an
> awkward, beautiful rustic, far too shiftless for the delicate
> factory work to which she was apprenticed; of his first gift to
> her, a bead necklace, which had long ago been put by, in one
> of the deep drawers of the dresser, to be kept for Mary. He
> wondered if it was there yet, and with a strange curiosity

75

he got up to feel for it . . . His groping hand fell on the piled-up tea-things, which at his desire she had left unwashed till morning – they were all so tired (pp. 20-1).

Curiosity oddly predominates in a way perfectly natural at moments of stress. An object of the past, charged in its association with his suddenly dead wife, is recalled and even as John seeks to retrieve that past through the beads other objects press in upon him to bring him jarringly back to the present misery. Through japanned trays and dirty plates Gaskell works for a sympathy that begins in understanding the fabric of these lives.

The novel's opening stability is mirrored in John's personal stability. The roomful of furniture, 'sure sign of good times', hints at a point of fine balance and in the same way John is displayed, poised, with the character-potential to precipitate his tragedy: 'His features were strongly marked, though not irregular, and their expression was extreme earnestness; resolute either for good or evil, a sort of latent stern enthusiasm' (p. 4). With his wife dead, the wave-crest breaks and rolls through the narrative, bitter memories of his son's death, his activity in a trade union, and the growing industrial depression carrying Barton on to evil. Having conceived John Barton as a tragic figure, Gaskell never quite resolved the problem between the free will of the tragic hero and the moral determinism of the society the novel creates. Two forms – tragic poem and 'condition of England' novel – are in conflict. At the end Gaskell speaks of 'the tragedy of a poor man's life' (p. 432) and in letters of 'the bewildered life of an ignorant thoughtful man of strong power of sympathy' which is 'a tragic poem' (70). But does Barton choose or is his action determined? And how does the answer to that question affect our response to him? Part of the dilemma is in the murder. Barton, certain what he does is evil, is so racked by conscience that he rapidly dies of remorse, and yet no blame is attached to Mary for concealing her father's guilt, though much of the latter part of the novel is taken up with desperate efforts to prove an alibi for Jem Wilson, wrongly accused of Barton's crime. Gaskell fails to clarify the precise relationship between Barton and his society, between his suffering and his crime. It is as though she were trying to isolate the crime from the community in which it is committed and relate it only to Barton's own inner drama. Clearly, though, the tragedy is of a potentially good man ground down by the disparity between social (including

76

moral and religious) theory and social practice, twisted by opposition to injustice, and destroyed by his own moral awareness that he cannot himself sanction the act he commits against the oppressors. The murder of young Carson achieves nothing for the union, yet within the human fabric of the novel it reconciles two men at John's deathbed: himself and Carson senior, who has come to recognize, as John never entirely forgot, that 'we have all of us one human heart'. Combinations, whether of men or of masters, were divisive, and Gaskell strives to show in individuals what Carlyle characterized in *Past and Present* (1843):

> We call it Society, and go about professing openly the totalest
> separation .... Our life is not a mutual helpfulness; but rather,
> cloaked under due laws-of-war, named 'fair competition' and
> so forth, it is a mutual hostility. We have profoundly
> forgotten everywhere that *Cash-payment* is not the sole relation
> of human beings; we think, nothing doubting, that *it* absolves
> and liquidates all engagements of man (Bk. iii, ch. 2).

Gaskell does not want to go back in terms of mechanical progress, but to forge anew a human relationship. At times, this produces unease. It seems so clear who is suffering that John Barton's citing of the parable of Dives and Lazarus has a force untouched by Gaskell's hasty palliation.[57] But her view of society is organic, as was Carlyle's and as was Wordsworth's, notably in 'The Old Cumberland Beggar', and still Christian in that she would have all men brothers through love of God and of their own image in him, as Carson and Barton join: 'Rich and poor, masters and men, were then brothers in the deep suffering of the heart' (p. 425).

Neither *Mary Barton* nor *North and South* were justified by the course of social development, yet human concern and ability to present the situation as it is are powers that live in Gaskell's novels. She works dramatically, for instance, to achieve Carson's conversion, by the repetition in the episode of girl and errand-boy of Barton's words, the girl's kiss of forgiveness leading Carson to read his Bible. If the conversion does not convince, it is because Carson's desire for revenge has been established too well, yet the street scene shows Gaskell aware of the demands of the novel form – that what she has to say must be enacted, embodied in character and scene, not merely stated. This awareness also underlies the sense, even if only half admitted, that a Christian view cannot be a simple one; that the

Bible, however true a pattern of conduct, is full of hard sayings.
What answer is there to Barton's version of the quarrel between men
and masters?

> We're their slaves as long as we can work; we pile up their
> fortunes with the sweat of our brows; and yet we are to live
> as separate as if we were in two worlds; ay, as separate as
> Dives and Lazarus, with a great gulf betwixt us; but I know
> who was best off then (p. 8).[58]

It is part of Barton's tragedy, what makes him a tragic hero, that he
is intelligent, an idealist, unselfish, with an ability to analyse, a man
made desperate by finding he cannot reconcile theory and practice:
'At last I gave it up in despair, trying to make folks' actions square
wi' th' Bible' (p. 431). He can accept suffering for himself, but finds
it intolerable for others, whether they are his son Tom, his fellow
workers, or even the assaulted knobsticks. His humiliation in
London when a delegate is the more deeply felt because it is a failure
to help his fellows. Even as he goes to murder, Barton comes on the
lost boy whose cry opens again springs in his heart which he has
sought to close. We are not to lose sympathy with him at this crisis.
His tragedy is partly that he cannot see clearly, that he falls into
desperate action against his own conscience, yet it is also that he
shows that larger capacity of spirit which we demand in tragic
figures.[59] To have him seized by the law would not allow the final
reconciliation with Carson, part of the overall design, and would
detract also from the dramatic presentation of his character –
Gaskell's conception of the character means that Barton moves freer
than the social situation in which he is placed would normally allow.

Whatever Gaskell's later feelings about the centrality of John
Barton, she did accept the title *Mary Barton* and Mary's is the
dominant consciousness, through which much of the action is
mediated. Her vanity at being wooed by a wealthy handsome man
and her gradual understanding that she really loves Jem Wilson hold
together much of the novel: it is Carson who pursues her, it is at the
Carson mill that she sees Jem rescue his father from the fire (a fire,
not unwelcome to Carson, which increases the misery of the men),
and it is her father's murder of Harry that precipitates Mary's
declaration in open court of love for Jem. Though Gaskell never
abandons observation and detail (even late in the story, the touch is
not lost of the woman who, it being Monday washday, 'stood,

stripping the soap-suds off her arms' (p. 330)), a long stretch of the latter part of the book involves articulating character and situation where plot has taken over. Once the murder is committed, Jem accused, and Mary convinced of his innocence, action predominates; the extraordinary takes over from the ordinary tenor of life, and with the establishment of a timetable (Mary's hope to save Jem begins on Saturday: the trial is on Tuesday) events are dominated by time.

Despite this, Mary is the emotional point of growth in the novel. Gaskell meant her to be imperfect and it is this imperfection that allows her to develop through the child, open to the carelessness of youth, and the growing woman, threatened by the same fate as the pathetic 'Butterfly', Aunt Esther, a realistically conceived prostitute. In conflict with Carson and in the struggle to save Jem's life Mary reaches an emotional maturity. Gaskell's ability is the mark of her mature powers; she can already capture the flux and reflux of emotion.[60]

Gaskell's developing, often already assured, skill is seen in the tracing of Mary's passional life, counterpointed against her outward involvement with young Harry Carson and her apparent indifference to Jem. If she is shown too much with Carson, the reader's sympathies may turn away from Mary or else anticipate her union with Harry; if she is not shown with Jem – and Mary's feelings and actions largely separate her from him – then the flourishing of love may fail at the end. Gaskell tackles one difficulty by never showing Carson alone with Mary until she has resolved that, not loving him, she must cut free. The first reference to Carson, besides, is as 'a lover, not beloved, but favoured by fancy' (p. 46). So far as Mary seriously thinks of being married to Carson (and marriage is the only possibility for her), it is to set up her father in comfort, the kind of thoughtless generosity that saves Carson also in our opinions and makes him a pathetic rather than deserved victim – Harry gives Wilson five shillings even while his real thought is on 'a look and a smile from lovely Mary Barton' (p. 78). Both he and Mary are mistaken or inadequate in their responses, but not lost to essentially human feeling. When Mary realizes it is Jem she loves (in the very moment she seems to reject him for ever), she discovers also that our actions enmesh with other people's so that we cannot easily cut free from the past. Firm decision does not wipe the slate clean of circumstance or situation. Mary may set about a new life, but

Gaskell suggests the complexity of a process so much more difficult in reality than in a change-of-heart melodrama. Mary begins well as 'in her earnest sad desire to do right [she] now took much pains to secure a comfortable though scanty breakfast for her father; and when he dawdled into the room, in an evidently irritable temper, she bore all with the gentleness of penitence' (p. 151), but she has to meet Sally Leadbitter, Carson's go-between, at Mrs Simmonds's establishment, and young Carson is expert at casual meetings in the street. The only real encounter between Mary and Carson is carefully placed at this point. Harry declares he loves her so much he is *now* prepared to marry her. He judges by worldly standards (as does the foolish Sally) and believes Mary bargaining with all she has of value to secure marriage. She may have compromised in speaking to him, after her earlier resolution, but in Carson's present readiness to pay the highest price, Mary, who has never fancied anything other than marriage, only finds her decision confirmed.

By a fine stroke, the angry encounter between Jem and Carson, where Jem tries to dissuade Carson from paying attentions to Mary, and which ends with Jem's threat, part of the evidence against him at the trial, has been provoked by Esther's frantic attempt to save Mary from her own fate. Speaking when the real danger is past, she unwittingly helps to incriminate Jem – and also ultimately brings Jem and Mary together. Out of her corrupted life (again, like Barton's, one ruined by warping of a good emotion, love for her officer and her daughter) comes the final happiness of the young couple whose union determines the final comic tone of the action.

Gaskell brings the story to a happy conclusion for most of those involved. Objections might be made to the transfer of Jem and Mary to Canada, away from the Manchester which seemed so central when the novel began, but it can be historically justified and is well-grounded in the revulsion of Jem's workmates, who believe his acquittal to be more technical than real. In her first full-length work Gaskell shows a control of detail, character, and plot: a sense that feeling is a close-woven chain connecting past and present. If she is at times too eager to intervene and occasionally becomes breathily rhetorical (a weakness generally indicated by an outbreak of exclamation marks), these are faults her later works show her to have recognized and controlled. Her style is colloquial, at its best that of the informal storyteller; she says she tried to *see* the scenes and then tell them 'as nearly as I could, as if I were speaking to a friend over the fire on a winter's night and describing real occurrences' (82). What persists from reading *Mary Barton* is the revelation of a desperate situation observed with a fine eye for detail, the tragic figure of John Barton, and the emotional delicacy of Mary's present-ation, plus the humour of characters like Job Legh (particularly the mixture of pathos and comedy, as in Job's account of bringing his grand-daughter Margaret from London). All these qualities are firmly established, to be extended in the rest of her career.

Reaction to *Mary Barton* left no doubt that it had made its mark. The title became Gaskell's soubriquet, as Geraldine Jewsbury was referred to by friends as Zoë, after *her* first novel (64) and Thackeray had tactlessly presumed to call Charlotte Brontë 'Jane Eyre' on their first meeting. It was variously noticed in a number of periodicals. William Rathbone Greg, a fellow Unitarian, perceptive even when adverse, 'reviewed and abused' it and 'we are none the less friends' (275).[61] More immediate for Gaskell was the response in Man-chester, where some 'say the masters are very sore', though one 'thinks it so true he is going to buy it for his men' (67). Perhaps the most gratifying tribute was a letter from Carlyle, even if the old curmudgeon felt called on to qualify his praise by a preference for doing 'silently good actions' to writing good books.[62]

Mary Barton was constantly reprinted (it reached a fifth edition in 1854), was published on the Continent in English by Tauchnitz, and widely translated;[63] it achieved the unique distinction amongst Gaskell's works of being dramatized. Dion Boucicault's *The Long Strike* (1866) is a feeble production that concentrates upon the strike, the murder, and the trial. The needed witness is contacted (the one notable scene in the play) through the wonder of electric telegraph. Jane (i.e. Mary Barton) declares her love at the trial (whither she is accompanied by her father, sunk in madness and never finally accounted for). The wretched action ends with a stage picture, as the jury brings in 'not guilty'.

A useful transition between *Mary Barton* and *North and South* is Geraldine Jewsbury's *Marian Withers* (1851), serialized in the *Manchester Examiner and Times* and issued in three volumes. Like Gaskell's two novels, it is concerned with ideas and emphasizes as truth what its author tells. 'We have seen and conversed with most of the persons named in this tale,' writes Jewsbury in the Intro-duction, implying that reality is a 'world of inedited romance' and that she could '*invent* nothing half so good' (i, 1-3).[64] This claim for truth is important, made as it also is by Trollope, Charlotte Elizabeth and Stone, and prompting the most challenging of *Mary Barton's* reviews by Greg. Greg is the more important for his high estimate of Gaskell's ability and Gaskell's continued friendship. There are degrees and kinds of truth. Gaskell felt (not entirely fairly to herself) 'that I, in my state of feelings at that time [of writing *Mary Barton*], was not fitted to introduce the glimpses of light and happiness which might have relieved the gloom' (75) and was worried, not that what she wrote was 'a free expression of ideas' (after all, 'thought is free'), but that it might be felt she 'represented a part as the whole' and so 'people at a distance ... be misled and prejudiced against the masters, and that class be estranged from class' (73).[65] *North and South* can be seen partially as a redressing of the balance, by a more favourable representation of the masters' point of view, and it has been suggested that *Marian Withers* itself was a corrective or kind of answer to *Mary Barton*.[66]

Geraldine Jewsbury seems to have had an enthusiasm for taking people around Manchester manufactories. In the midst of an oppressive June, 'like a casing of hot lead', she 'nearly wore [a friend] out with taking him over cotton mills'.[67] The setting of her novel, though, is a village near Accrington, in 1825, so that the action is set earlier than that of any novel considered in this chapter. As with Sir Matthew Dowling's factory in *Michael Armstrong*, the countryside is all around, so that an idyllic quality is added to the scene at Mr Wilcox's mill, situated at the foot of a 'broad meadow-like hill':

> Groups of work-people were scattered about; some were sitting down, soberly drinking tea with their wives out of tin cans, and eating huge slices of thick bread and butter; boys of all ages ... were racing or playing at football. Groups of girls [were] screaming and laughing, playing practical jokes on each other, or exchanging sharp, saucy words with the young fellows who were teasing them .... Other groups ... in their cotton bedgowns and black petticoats, with their glossy hair arranged in a classical-looking knot [were] walking two or three together, with their arms round each other's waists, telling their secrets like young ladies of a higher grade (ii, 33-4).

John Withers, Marian's father, is a largely self-made man, rescued in childhood by a Miss Fenwick who, like Trollope's Mary Brotherton, discovered the living conditions of part of Manchester's population (as early as 1794); a 'whole "Satan's invisible world" was displayed to her, and she could not again become indifferent' (i, 15). But where Mary Brotherton's affluence takes the Armstrongs out of the industrial world, Miss Fenwick's concern places John as apprentice to cotton-spinners. He gains what education he can, turns, despite hardships, his mechanical skill to improvement of machinery, and rises to be a mill-owner himself.

Withers's rise is a pattern in common with William Langshawe's and Carson's. In her article, 'The Civilisation of the Lower Orders', Jewsbury described the success of such men, who

> have either risen from the ranks themselves or their fathers
> before them did so. It is quite common to find the near
> connections and relations of wealthy merchants and millowners
> quite poor and ill off, while the more fortunate members live
> in houses like palaces ... without having in the least degree
> lost the uncultivated habits of the *People*.[68]

If this suggests she might join with Stone in satire upon manners, Jewsbury yet recognized the sterling qualities of many of these men, worthy founders of the new Empire of cotton. Withers never rises to one Jewsbury mentions in a letter, who 'great, rough, and sooty-looking man as he is, has done the work of two generations towards civilising [Manchester], is always buying pictures himself, and making other people buy them too';[69] but Withers is honest, concerned for his men and his reputation, and Cunningham, the main voice of theory in the novel, defends masters like Withers and Wilcox and Sykes when Marian objects that 'they are coarse and vulgar, and destitute of all education or refinement' (ii, 27). So they may be, but, says Cunningham,

> they are full of savage and vigorous life, like that with which
> the barbarians rejuvenated the old world, when Roman
> civilisation had run to seed. These men have the old barbaric
> strength of undisciplined life; they need educating, they need
> civilising; but they will change the face of the world ...
> (ii, 29).

The terms here almost suggest a response to Gaskell's fear that she may have represented 'a part as the whole' (75), a concern for a larger view rather than a desperate representation of isolated aspects.

There is a contrast drawn, though, between men like Withers and Wilcox on the one hand and Higginbottom, whose only concern is the cash-nexus: 'He took no thought or interest in his work-people after they left his mill; he paid them their wages on Saturday night, and they might be ill or well, drunken or sober, as they pleased' (ii, 36). The issue was to be debated in *North and South*, and Jewsbury implies that masters do have a responsibility to their workmen. Wilcox is practically concerned for the well-being of his employees, providing a room where the women 'might hang their bonnets and shawls'; there was water, towels and soap, and looking-glasses suspended against the walls (ii, 49). He also has a scheme for fitting up a place where the men can wash off grease and dirt: 'My missus says it is sin to put such fine notions into poor folks' heads. But I say, that when a man is dirty, he will do actions he would be ashamed to do if he were clean' (i, 246). A later extension includes laundry facilities. This looks forward to the workers' canteen Thornton helps establish in *North and South*, though the men's independent operation of it, so that it is theirs rather than an act of patronage by the master marks an essential shift in the master - worker relationship which mirrors a whole change of theory about social interconnection. One important thing that Jewsbury is able to do that Trollope and Charlotte Elizabeth had not found possible is to show a range of masters, good, bad, and indifferent, since she does not have a thesis of opposition of interests between specific classes or groups.

The novel's primary concern is the emotional growth of Marian and her eventual marriage to Cunningham, who embodies Jewsbury's own social theory. Her father goes through a commercial crisis (a familiar plot turn), weathers it with a loan from his friend Wilcox, and is happy to have Cunningham as partner and in time as son-in-law. Though different in tone and points of detail from the relationship of Margaret and Thornton in *North and South* (Marian's involvement with the shallow Albert and her finding true love in the mature Cunningham, is closer in pattern if not in emotion to Emma and Knightley), the union of Marian and Cunningham suggests the way a novel concerned with the 'Condition of England' question could link its social concern with individual feeling. Jewsbury's interest in passion (the chapel scene in *Zoë* (1845) was considered 'warm') leads to a stress not only on her heroine's education as pupil of Cunningham but also her awakening to a world for which her upbringing and education (formally, a good one) have not prepared her. She is aroused by the performance of music from Mozart's *Don Giovanni:*

> She sat in a trance, feeling as if a stream of life was being
> poured into her; the intense enjoyment almost amounted to
> pàin, her whole being seemed fused and permeated by celestial
> fire ... (i, 131-2)

Margaret Hale's education and intellect (her good sense, one suspects) scarcely allow of such sensuous ecstasy, yet the idea of love for a man who has strength, love even though intellect may insist he is in the wrong, is something not in Mary Barton's fancy for young Carson or love for Jem Wilson. Jewsbury may not be a specific influence, but she does show how Gaskell could open up from presentation of ideas and intimately connect them with her characters' emotional life.

Cunningham is a shadowy figure compared with Thornton, largely because he is a mouthpiece for Jewsbury's social ideas and takes little part in the action. Like Gaskell and Dickens, Jewsbury essentially held a doctrine of union between classes, though not Christian union, as the one salvation of society. In a novel review, Jewsbury noted that only in 'association will be found to be the cure of the miseries produced by competition; that "association" is the watchword of the new order of things which is beginning. The age of individualism is passing away'.[70] What Cunningham provides is a statement of this idea by someone who has an overview of the cotton industry and sees its potential greatness, unlike men of Withers's or Wilcox's stamp, who are too involved in process to be able to comprehend system. In this he anticipates Thornton's larger view of industrial strength and vitality. Cunningham conveys the sense of the greatness of Manchester and the industrial north, of the new empire of peace which will supplant an empire of war, and he later speaks of the need to organize, civilize and educate the industrial masses as 'the great work of the present century, and one not to be achieved in a day' (ii, 113).

Marian Withers is no more than an interesting minor novel, but whether or not it prompted Gaskell to consider the masters' side more closely it shows, like *North and South*, an awareness of the workers' point of view and of the masters', and of a viewpoint above both. Gaskell moves from *Mary Barton*, a novel primarily of ideas (that is, pressing arguments, as her epigraph suggests) designed as 'a spur to inactive thought and languid conscience' (119)), to *North and South*, a novel with an industrial setting offering a dynamic interaction of its characters. An interest in the aesthetic dimension was already clear in John Barton's tragedy, but it is fully realized in *North and South*.

Charles Dickens published the first episode of *North and South* on 2 September 1854 in his weekly periodical *Household Words*. It continued until 27 January 1855 and was then issued in two volumes, a second revised edition appearing within the year. By this time Gaskell was a well-established writer. Her second novel, *Ruth*, was published in 1853 and she had already contributed to *Household Words*. When Dickens was soliciting potential contributions before its first appearance (30 March 1850), he wrote:

> I do not know what your literary vows of temperance or abstinence may be, but as I do honestly know that there is no living English writer whose aid I would desire to enlist in preference to the authoress of Mary Barton (a book that most profoundly affected and impressed me), I venture to ask you whether you can give me any hope that you will write a short tale, or any number of tales, for the projected pages.[71]

Gaskell's response was the three-part story *Lizzie Leigh*, which leads in the first issue of *Household Words*, after Dickens's 'A Preliminary Word'. Nearly a dozen other stories appeared during the next decade, as well as articles on matters as diverse as French salons and Cumberland sheep-shearers. Most famous are the eight papers which finally formed *Cranford*. Dickens greatly admired *Mary Barton* and *Ruth* ('My dear friends', he called them),[72] while in skill and in general agreement of ideas, Dickens recognized a contributor of value to his magazine. When he received part of *North and South* in manuscript (about the first quarter), though it bore a close relationship in theme and argument to his own *Hard Times* then being serialized (1 April to 12 August 1854), he welcomed it and later spoke of an 'admirable story, [which] is full of character and power, has a strong suspended interest in it (the end of which, I don't in the least foresee)'.[73] Gaskell herself was well aware, in planning and writing, that she was dealing with themes Dickens himself was using – she was delighted to find he did not mean to have a strike – and Dickens stressed the affinity of their concern:

The monstrous claims at domination made by a certain class
of manufacturers, and the extent to which the way is made
easy for working men to slide down into discontent under
such hands, are within my scheme; but I am not going to
strike. So don't be afraid of me. But I wish you would look at
the story yourself, and judge where and how near I seem to be
approaching what you have in your mind.[74]

Whatever the separate form their tales took both were concerned
with class reconciliation, a point stressed by Gaskell's choice of
epigraph for the serial:

> Ah, yet, though all the world forsake,
>   Though fortune clip my wings,
> I will not cramp my heart, nor take
>   Half-views of men and things.
> Let Whigs and Tories stir their blood;
>   There must be stormy weather;
> But for some true result of good
>   All parties work together.[75]

The closeness of theme – industrial conditions as a matrix for
personal relations – brings out striking differences between the form
of the two works: Dicken's, a moral fable presented in a mixture of
realistic and emblematic characters and situations, essentially satirical
and caricaturing; Gaskell's, a human comedy traced through consistent and developing characters set in conditions understood from
long personal experience. To compare Dickens's Bounderby with
Thornton is not simply to move from an unfeeling hypocrite to an
independently honest figure, it is to move from the grotesque to the
naturalistic. Dickens's successes (the sinister hilarity of Mrs Sparsit,
Harthouse's attempted seduction of Louisa) are things missing from
North and South. Perhaps its tone is too subdued; but Gaskell is able
in the way she raises questions to leave us finally with the feeling that
they have been explored and are left unanswered only because she is
aware of the complexity of the situation she has created. This is a
technical advance from *Mary Barton* where the impression is often of
Gaskell's own unease about the problems set up and her need to
reassure with a 'I know it is not so' or 'as it seemed to him'.

Writing the novel was a painful experience. At one point early
in composition, Gaskell admitted she had not written one line for
three weeks because of headaches and dizziness, and that 'it is dull'

(290, 294). Later she seemed easier. By 26 July 1854 Dickens had approximately half the manuscript in hand and proposed beginning publication at once;[76] yet she wryly observed, 'I dare say I shall like my story, when I am a little further from it; at present I can only feel depressed about it, I meant it to have been so much better' (323). Part of her depression no doubt came with the difficulties of serialization, of which this was her first experience with a full-scale work.[77] Annette Hopkins's account too readily takes the view that *North and South*, 'with all this attention devoted to characters and problems, was by its very nature entirely unsuited to the form of serialisation regularly followed in *Household Words*';[78] too readily, that is, because character and problems are no necessary difficulty. Gaskell, however, could not (or would not) see her novel as a serial. There was no need for her to provide a cliff-hanger to end each episode (Dickens himself certainly does not), but the episodes should have some kind of shape and individual dynamic. Dickens was at fault, by being overconfident of his own ability to shape up what she sent him and there are two letters of Dickens's which suggest divisions (covering the first half of the novel) and roughly corresponding to the serial issue.[79]

Later, having asked for compression in proof of the second episode (chapters 3 and 4, including Hale's conversation with Margaret about his doubts, which Dickens had mentioned in talking of the manuscript and 'where we agreed that there should be a great condensation'),[80] Dickens found to his dismay that Gaskell returned the proofs unaltered. By this time he was beginning to doubt the wisdom of publication at all, for a preliminary setting up in type to estimate length had been seriously wrong. Though he handled Gaskell diplomatically, her apparent lack of response, plus declining sales during publication, cannot have helped Dickens's temper. He had tried to draw her attention to the need to think about the nature of weekly serialization and its problems, and a natural irritation (probably making itself felt in his letters) was the result. Gaskell meanwhile had other, more pressing problems; she wanted room (Dickens remarked himself when writing *Hard Times* for weekly as against his more usual monthly serialization that 'the difficulty of the space is CRUSHING'), and matters were worse as she drew near the end. Dickens had proposed (perhaps too loosely) 'about 20 weekly portions':[81]

in this way of publishing it, I had to write pretty hard
without waiting for the happy leisure hours. And then
20 numbers was, I found my allowance; instead of the
too scanty 22, which I had fancied were included in 'five
months'; and at last the story is huddled & hurried up,
especially in the rapidity with which the sudden death
of Mr Bell, succeeds to the sudden death of Mr Hale.
But what could I do? Every page was grudged me, just
at last, when I did certainly infringe all the bounds &
limits they set me as to quantity (328–9).

For the volume publication she was able to add extra material;[82]
Margaret's changing attitude to the south could be stressed by the
visit to Helstone and necessary interval allowed before the death of
Mr Bell, though there is still the sense that the novel is somewhat
huddled at the end.

However, in January 1855, when *North and South* was concluded,
Dickens wrote to Gaskell:

Let me congratulate you on the conclusion of your story; not
because it is the end of a task to which you had conceived a
dislike (for I imagine you to have got the better of that
delusion by this time), but because it is the vigorous and
powerful accomplishment of an anxious labour. It seems to me
that you have felt the ground thoroughly firmly under your
feet, and have strided on with a force and purpose that MUST
now give you pleasure.[83]

He hoped for further work from her; despite adverse remarks to
Wilkie Collins,[84] Dickens was prepared to offer Gaskell more than
the £250 he paid for *North and South* for another novel and doubled
the sum when she refused. She continued to contribute, including
two substantial stories, 'My Lady Ludlow' and 'A Dark Night's
Work'. Dickens knew her value and Gaskell *his:* prompt payment
for anything he took – and though their relations implied a measure
of reserve the essential fellowship of mind and wish had been there.

In *Hard Times* Dickens stresses the plight of the individual, in a
moral fable which if often angularly schematic, often confused, and
finally unsatisfactory in offering the fun and games of Sleary's circus
as a panacea for society's ills, is yet one where the pressure of
institutions and the danger of the cash-nexus are clearly stated.[85]

Louisa and her near disaster are among *Hard Times'*s most memorable achievements, and it is on similar ground that Gaskell triumphs: the exploration of an awakened consciousness, receptive to environment, which in Margaret Hale seeks to respond to and expand with her new experiences. Margaret's temptations and problems are not those of Louisa Gradgrind, but both writers show their skill in presenting a young girl who must deal virtually unassisted with the unknown.

There is no final solution in *North and South;* not even the escape to Canada of *Mary Barton.* Margaret indeed specifically rejects the household of her aunt Shaw where she might without fuss live free from the problems of Milton Northern (the town is virtually identical with Manchester). Gaskell does not try to suggest that there can be any such solution, even in marriage: the sense of a continuing situation helps to tie the novel to the world it depicts. Here, Margaret's ability to save Thornton at the end from financial disaster perhaps seems too happily fortuitous. None the less, I would see this ending as more truly connected with the concerns of the novel than does, say, Raymond Williams in *Culture and Society 1780-1950.* Despite Williams's claim (pp. 91-2), Thornton is not affected by the superior gentleness and humanity of the south (he is affected by Margaret, never, despite the title, the embodied representative of the values of the south), nor is Margaret's money the first practical opportunity to make his humanitarian experiment – he has already started with the workers' kitchen. While Margaret's money allows him to return to business, I do not think we are to see Thornton as a bankrupt patronized by her. The legacy indeed is convenient; yet it helps Thornton, not to start, but to continue.

The situation is viewed through the consciousness – more fully a single point-of-view than Mary Barton was allowed to be – of Margaret herself; the title indeed originally was *Margaret Hale.*[86] That title, though not exciting, does better suggest the interest of the novel. Instead of the more schematic arrangement that the juxtaposition of *North and South* suggests, 'Margaret Hale' insists on a central human drama – the mental and emotional conflict of a single person, whose fate is bound up with her experience.

The novel's opening is on neutral ground, the London of Edith's home – a luxurious and, for Margaret, inadequate place, though it is in the power of Gaskell's handling that Edith, sensual and happy in marriage, is never condemned. Margaret's horizons are not simply the narrow ones of Helstone; the world she has seen, caught in its shallowness with Aunt Shaw's trivial if comic grumbles and Edith's childish passion, is a comfortable if unsatisfactory one. London is never to be a place for Margaret to live in. Helstone in time may no longer be possible and Milton may be oppressive, but Margaret is already clear about London. Gaskell points this up by the love and eventual prosposal of Mr Lennox. Lennox is a reasonable man, suited to be Margaret's friend, though not her husband, and who recognizes the good that is in her. Yet she has a vein of seriousness, as her remarks on the conversation heard at London dinner-parties show, to which he has no response. Henry Lennox is the man Margaret could have married, a contrast to Thornton. His proposal suggests Margaret's attractiveness, and her rejection of him emphasizes that dissatisfaction with London that makes her the more ready to be responsive to the north.

Later, Lennox is to continue a friend (there is no melodramatic desire for revenge after a slight) and Margaret is to find in Thornton someone who demands of her that he be more than a friend, full as he is of that 'savage and vigorous life' that Jewsbury spoke of in *Marian Withers*. This London section and Lennox's proposal are not a false start, though given serialization Dickens might well fret as the story's direction is not rapidly established.[87] The opening is an accumulation of all that Margaret will have to give up, along with Helstone. The dream of the south (though we see how qualified it is when her realism (p. 9) opposes Lennox's romantic fiction of Helstone as a place where roses bloom all the year) is destroyed by her own insistence on the realities of the place and an individual recognition that though dreams may, life does not stand still - all this, called from her by her *experience* of the north. She is to champion the north against Bessy Higgins's delusive vision (pp. 156-7), she warns Nicholas against his desire to move to the south, and when she returns to Helstone, she finds the dream finally passed in the jarrings of the new incumbent's family and the ignorant brutality of the cat-roasting anecdote. The opening scenes of the novel establish that Margaret does not need the forms and ceremonies of the idle well-to-do even while suggesting that she will have to adapt herself when she meets the north. Still, her reactions to situations make it clear that she is capable of responding to people as people and not simply as concepts.

The south is evoked too sharply for its impression to be lost as we move north.

> And when the brilliant fourteen fine days of October came on, her cares were all blown away as lightly as thistledown, and she thought of nothing but the glories of the forest. The fern-harvest was over; and now that the rain was gone, many a deep glade was accessible, into which Margaret had only peeped in July and August weather (p. 21).

The initial impression of Milton, in contrast, is gloomy and forbidding, promising no new delights with change of season: 'For several miles before they reached Milton, they saw a deep lead-coloured cloud hanging over the horizon . . . all the darker from contrast with the pale grey-blue of the wintry sky . . .' (pp. 66-7). In *Mary Barton*, however unfamiliar such scenes to the reader, they were largely the norm (Green Heys Fields were the unfamiliar); here, it is a whole alien world that the reader has to come to terms with, at least imaginatively, through the process of Margaret's experience. The first sights are of scenery *en masse*, then particular physical conditions of streets with the 'great loaded lurries' which 'bore cotton, either in the raw shape in bags, or the woven shape in bales of calico' (p. 67), grim enough, but, Margaret is to learn, inhabited by human beings – the Higginses, the Bouchers, the Thorntons – who respond and evoke response. Earlier, even Mrs Hale has moments when the habitual deadening of her response is vivified – in telling Margaret of Frederick's disgrace at sea or when, after Margaret reveals Hale's decision to leave Helstone, her first coldness changes when she sees her husband with 'a timid, fearful look in his eyes' and 'that look of despondent uncertainty, of mental and bodily languor touched his wife's heart. She went to him, and threw herself on his breast, crying out – "Oh! Richard, Richard, you should have told me sooner!"' (p. 52.)

This touches the deeper responses, springs dried during the custom of marriage still capable of reopening (however temporarily) as love makes new demands. Such emotional links may be no more than hinted at or may lie in physical objects which are fused with human meaning: the rose that Thornton has taken on his visit to Helstone (p. 520), which echoes back to the roses in the jug of water on Margaret's return to the village (p. 462) and the roses that Lennox jokingly saw blooming all the year round (p. 9). From pastoral idyll (Lennox) to pleasing reality (the water-jug) to a love token, the object is the same but the human response gives it varying significance.

For whether in north or south, Gaskell insists on human reactions before schematic responses, on the spirit and not the letter, and these responses lie not in one geographical area rather than another, though with the breakdown of feudal responsibility they are more urgently needed perhaps in the north. The novel does not so much establish the polarity of north and south as insist that we must deal with problems in hand, which are as real in one area as another. Margaret herself, back in London with Aunt Shaw, finds plenty of social work to do. After all, part of the novel's purpose is to reconcile, not separate, whether at a social or geographical level.

Gaskell, learning that Dickens was not utilizing his Preston visit to have a strike in *Hard Times,* seized her chance and depicted one both in its quietness of stubborn passive resistance and in the dramatic activity of the attack on the mill, where Margaret demands Thornton do his duty by the imported Irish labourers and seems publicly to declare her love for him by her defence. The issues of the strike and its breaking before the unity of the masters is much more carefully worked out than in *Mary Barton* and not allowed virtually to disappear as it did after the murder of young Carson. The novel insists upon debate and finds no facile solution such as that suggested by Carson senior's conversion and reconciliation at Barton's death-bed, which seemed to declare that a new life was to lead to a new heaven and new earth. A reading of *Mary Barton* shows that Gaskell's view was not so naïvely apocalyptic as this, but it is the tenor of that scene. *North and South* is open-ended in this respect. Thornton is a good master, Higgins is a good worker, and so they can co-operate. We are aware though that there are bad of both.

The debate, provoked by Margaret's involvement with industrial life and personal contact with those who live in Milton, begins with her encounter with Nicholas Higgins and Bessy; an impulsive generous action leads to an acquaintance which, Margaret finds, demands adjustment of her past. She is no longer the vicar's daughter visiting the parish poor; such roles have broken in this society. She has no clear social position and Higgins has no conception that she might have. From the personal life of the Higginses, she is drawn to the union and labour difficulties, which in turn, through Thornton, draw her back to the personal crisis of love, beginning with respect

93

and then shame at knowing Thornton has covered up the lie for her, and so the growing awareness that it can and ought to be something more than respect she feels for him.

Gaskell particularly draws together the concerns of the debate in Boucher, whose part is comparatively slight and yet who provokes a crisis for Higgins. Boucher is weak, someone unable to bear hardships for the good of his fellow workmen, who stirs up the riot at the mill, expressly against the orders of the union. He is a poor workman, unlike Higgins, who effectually accepts Thornton's values though not Thornton's wage-level. Though Gaskell accepts the unions and presents their views at large, she questions their ends through Mr Hale, who says their ideal 'would be beautiful, glorious – it would be Christianity itself – if it were but for an end which affected the good of all, instead of that merely of one class as opposed to another' (p. 276), even if Higgins speaks effectively, with the force of personal experience. Gaskell moves carefully to the dramatic situation that is the climax of Boucher's story. Tormented by his family's need, now fiercely anti-union, sent to Coventry, Boucher is a wretched specimen, 'wi' his mealy-mouthed face, that turns me sick to look at' (p. 349), and Higgins justifies the union's conduct. Margaret declares that Higgins and the union have made Boucher what he is – and he is brought in, a suicide, grotesquely dyed by the stream's industrial filth, with Higgins's incredulous cry, 'It's not John Boucher? He had na spunk enough' (p. 350). We see what Boucher has been made; courage has only been misdirected to his death.

The handling of this scene, as with so many others, shows Gaskell's technical development from *Mary Barton*. It is carefully contrived, an answer to the debate between Margaret and Higgins; almost too pat, one might feel, but it succeeds, unlike some other dramatic moments in the novel (the coincidental presence of Frederick, Leonards and Thornton at the railway station, for instance), since Boucher's plight has itself provoked the debate, and the very conditions being discussed have forced Boucher's fate upon him. Yet if the union loses at this moment (and it is no permanent defeat), Gaskell is too dramatically concerned with the truth of her story for a sudden conversion on Higgins's part. He does not curse the union. Rather, he works for Boucher's family and gains Thornton's individual respect. The situation is too complex for any easy solution. Like Stephen Blackpool in *Hard Times*, who mutters that 'Aw's a muddle', Higgins finds that 'th' world is in a confusion that passes me or any other man to understand' (p. 365). But Gaskell shows the unions as now an accepted reality of industrial life, and in Nicholas's practical solution there is none of the desperate futility of Stephen Blackpool or the frustrated anger of episodes like Barton's London humiliation.

Gaskell is perhaps more optimistic than Dickens, for she not only presents the unions more or less sympathetically, but she has also Thornton with his proud defence of the north and industrialism against a cycle of Cathay. There are no melancholy-mad elephants in Thornton's mills: 'I won't deny that I am proud of belonging to a town . . . the necessities of which give birth to such grandeur of conception' (p. 93). It is the note again of the glory of King Cotton. Margaret and Thornton confront one another; perhaps their debate is not quite satisfactorily worked into the texture of the novel, but it does find a resolution in the developing relationship of Margaret and Thornton. If they begin as standing in some sort for north and south, they end by merging to form an entity, though any allegorical blending is pretty remote in the actuality of their love.

The industrial and personal issues of the novel are held together in Thornton and Margaret. Mary Barton's love story was a strand, but theirs is of the fabric. Gaskell advances character and social interests by a developing train of reactions, each meeting extending itself into meditation and analysed development. Although Margaret's is established as the point of view through which events are followed, she still has to be schooled in the facts of Milton life, just as Thornton has to be schooled by her in the demands of the heart. These demands meet most clearly in the attack on the mill (p. 212). Each finds in the other the seriousness Margaret felt so painfully lacking in Henry Lennox. Thornton shows his love as she lies semi-conscious on the sofa, struck by a pebble: 'Oh, my Margaret – my Margaret! no one can tell what you are to me!' (p. 214). Thornton loves her because of her demands upon him, while his response shows her that he has need of protection. Their relations after this are a gradual process of finding one another, a process beset by difficulties, yet none the less certain. The casual mention of a gentleman's visit to Helstone, when Margaret revisits her home, falls into place when Thornton shows Margaret that rose gathered from the old home. Margaret, always set strong for life, now learns that she can fulfil herself in one particular life and the pair accept the truth about each other, despite what the world, personified by Aunt Shaw and Mrs Thornton, may have to say about the matter.

North and South is Gaskell's final sustained treatment of industrial themes, indeed of social problems. After this she increasingly concentrated upon her strength: the pattern and development of personal emotion, which the progress from *Mary Barton* to *North and South* shows her exploring and developing.

3

Cranford (1853)

If stationary men would pay some attention to the districts in which they reside, and would publish their thoughts respecting the objects that surround them, from such materials might be drawn the most complete county-histories, which are still wanting in several parts of this kingdom . . .

Gilbert White, 'Advertisement',
The Natural History of Selborne (1789)

The germ of Gaskell's best-known book (at one time, for most people, her only book) was a story-article, 'The Last Generation in England'. Published in the American *Sartain's Union Magazine* (July 1849) and not reprinted until Elizabeth Watson's edition of *Cranford* (1972), it has affinities in its close observation and delight in social detail with her early 'Clopton Hall', with a letter of August 1838 to Mary Howitt describing Knutsford customs of her youth (28-30) – sand pictures for weddings and rejoicings, well-dressings, 'riding stang' for scolding women (a form of Skimmerton ride) – and with the later sketches 'Company Manners' and 'French Life'.[1] She begins 'The Last Generation' by referring to an *Edinburgh Review* article, 'in which it is said that Southey had proposed to himself to write a "history of English domestic life" '.[2] Gaskell, regretting the loss of Southey's own book, stated her wish to record details observed by herself or handed down by others, 'for even in small towns, scarcely removed from villages, the phases of society are rapidly changing', change hinted at in *Cranford* by the railways and by Drumble, the manufacturing town.[3] In 'The Last Generation' Gaskell vouches for the truth of what she describes and claimed in a letter to Ruskin (February 1865) that she had seen the cow with its grey flannel waistcoat and drawers and knew the cat that swallowed the lace, adding an extra Cranford anecdote about a new carpet and a new housemaid (747-8). In the article and in the expanded fictive form of *Cranford*, the sense that she is writing a 'history of English domestic life' helps make the work distinctive.

'The Last Generation' suggests a social spread considerably narrowed in *Cranford*, where society's upper reaches are the daughters of large landed proprietors of very old family. Violence, of a kind only imagined during the Cranford panic (ch. x) or set outside in the story of the pedlar's pack (p. 111), flashes out in 'The Last Generation' amongst

> a set of young men, ready for mischief and brutality, and
> every now and then dropping off the pit's brink into crime
> . . . . They would stop ladies returning from the card-parties,
> which were the staple gaiety of the place, and who were only
> attended by a maidservant bearing a lantern, and whip them;
> literally whip them as you whip a little child . . . (pp. 162-3).

This violence, a useful reminder of Gaskell's own toughness,[4] is curbed in *Cranford* by omission, and apparently no place was found for the individuality of the lady who would drive out 'with a carriage full of dogs; each dressed in the male or female fashion of the day, as the case might be; each dog provided with a pair of house-shoes, for which his carriage boots were changed on his return' (p. 163).[5] Eccentricity in *Cranford* it is to be no longer an end but the means to an analysis of manners and feeling.

I have claimed that *Cranford* is distinctive in kind, and a brief comparison with an obvious forebear, *Our Village* by Mary Russell Mitford (1787-1855),[6] based on Swallowfield, near Reading, may help to bring out that particularity. After a preliminary description of the village, Mitford traces through a year from January to November, the focus being the narrator's observation on her walks or small expeditions, alone or with a friend or with Lizzy, a child of the neighbourhood; her only constant companion is May the greyhound. The narrator's character (almost identical with Mitford's) and the chronology are the only structural elements. The society is small (nothing like the township of Cranford); the social observation is not of manners; and social distinctions are very little regarded – in the end, it is true, social distinctions do not rule Cranford, but their very presence is necessary to feel the strength of goodness in breaking them: an important characteristic of Miss Matty or even Miss Jenkyns who display, by an eventual disregard of taboos, the heroism which Mrs Jamieson, for instance, is never able to find. The occasional anecdote of Mitford's reminds us of *Cranford*: the whimsical man who, thinking the lime trees darkened his rooms

> had all the leaves stripped from every tree. There they stood,
> poor miserable skeletons, as bare as Christmas under the
> glowing midsummer sun. Nature revenged herself, in her own
> sweet and gracious manner; fresh leaves sprang out, and at
> nearly Christmas the foliage was as brilliant as when the
> outrage was committed (p.14).

And certain of the characters, glimpsed briefly, have pathos and humour. There is John Evans, the gardener, who, becoming insane on his wife's death, was 'sent to St. Luke's, and dismissed as cured; but his power was gone and his strength; he could no longer manage a garden, nor submit to the restraint, nor encounter the fatigue of regular employment' (p. 20); and again, Miss Sally Mearing, who scorned the new ways of agriculture, and lives out her days at one end of a bluff bachelor's farmhouse 'untempted by matrimony, and unassailed (as far as I hear) by love or by scandal' (p. 85). The most extended sketch of character, of Hannah Bint the young dairymaid, who supports father and siblings by her efforts, is still essentially anecdotal, not carried beyond the moment. The landscape's progress is more fully charted and the importance of natural observation over figures suggests that Mitford's affinities are more with Gilbert White in *The Natural History of Selborne* than with Gaskell. She does not have White's scientific curiosity (testing a theory, for example, why cuckoos do not hatch their own eggs – Letter xxx), but she can observe a kingfisher by a frozen stream with the precision that gives pleasure (pp. 36-7).

One of the great powers of *Cranford* is Gaskell's handling and control of emotion, but Mitford never extends and hardly reveals her persona's feelings, beyond delight and wonder in the glory of God's creation. Her own life had been a difficult one and she no doubt felt it proper to conceal it. Even when she touches on points of entry into the past, Mitford tends to make them vaguely general: she rambles to the house where she lived for eighteen happy years, but though 'three years ago, it nearly broke my heart to leave' (p. 54), she never tells us the reason for leaving; and when she lies upon the bank of violets it is to call up an idealized past and experience: 'What a renewal of heart and mind! To inhabit such a scene of peace and sweetness is again to be fearless, gay, and gentle as a child. Then it is that thought becomes poetry, and feeling religion' (pp. 67-8).

Our Village harks back to the periodical essay; its Regency prose reveals affinities with Lamb and Leigh Hunt; and is given coherence by its common landscape, narrator, and the progression of the seasons, rather as the characters of the *Spectator* link the separate papers. It is good and Gaskell probably read it. In contrast, *Cranford*, despite its sporadic production, is essentially fictive and might be called a novel; character and action combine to produce climax. Interestingly, it was one of the books George Eliot read while writing her first fiction, *Scenes of Clerical Life* (1858), and to Gaskell later she wrote of an affinity that suggests she saw the links of craft between them as novelists.[7] Mitford's place is with the earlier essayists, Addison, Goldsmith, Leigh Hunt, perhaps with Gilbert White, though his scientific rigour, an intellectual toughness absent in Mitford, makes him distinctively a professional. Gaskell's is with George Eliot, since both are concerned with fictions, with telling stories, and it can only mislead, perhaps lower our idea of her, if we compare, as Anne Thackeray Ritchie does, *Cranford* with the *Essays of Elia*, though she is right in seeing that the book is imbued with the 'force of sentiment'.[8] Mitford turns aside from people to landscape, whereas in her Keatsian feeling that 'Scenery is fine – but human nature is finer', Gaskell has an avidity for people. Mitford gives little sense of the connective feelings of past and present, and she lacks a controlling tone. She says that

> There are moments in life when, without any visible or
> immediate cause, the spirits sink and fail. . . . They who have
> known these feelings . . . will understand . . . why even
> needle-work, the most effectual sedative, that grand soother and
> composer of woman's distress, fails to comfort me today
> (p. 125).

We may wonder whether this is not simply a painful truth that Mitford like most of us has experienced, rather than the complexities a Gaskell narrator can hint at, of changing attitudes, of learning, and of growth. When rumours fly in Cranford, Mary Smith says 'it seemed to me then that there was every reason to believe' (p. 109); and the word 'then' controls our sense of her ability to look forward and back within the structure of the work, rather than nakedly out from the world beyond the book.

Martin Dodsworth, in a perceptive essay,[9] insisted that 'the fundamentally serious concerns of her book have been neglected for a belle-lettristic study of incidental detail', and while I query his suggestion that we should treat the novel as symbolic of a conflict within the mind of the author, I do want to argue for a serious concern with the pattern of behaviour and feeling, for the pathos which (along with evident comedy) lies in the book. Without invoking too direct a comparison *Cranford* and Twain's *Huckleberry Finn* both offer an accepted surface of society's beliefs, challenged by the reader and eventually defied within the story. When Huck declares, 'All right, then, I'll *go* to hell' (ch. 31), he ironically still accepts society's laws, yet finds he cannot live by them; Miss Jenkyns, Miss Matty and the other ladies all find at some time or other that though they had rather not openly break society's rules, human nature will keep breaking in. *Cranford* often has a sense of deep loss consequent on this doubleness that is akin to the tragic idea.

Cranford's sense of unity only came through hindsight. The initial story, 'Our Society at Cranford', was published in *Household Words*, 13 December 1851.[10] Many years later Gaskell wrote that the 'beginning of "Cranford" was *one* paper in "Household Words"; and I never meant to write more, so killed Capt. Brown very much against my will' (748);[11] this may strictly be true, but the second paper, 'A Love Affair at Cranford', was published so soon afterwards (3 January 1852) that it is clear they were conceived at much the same time. The first is, however, complete in itself and establishes a pattern for most of the parts that followed as well as the larger structure; the plot lies in suffering, quiet heroism, death, and a projection forward into happiness, though this is necessarily qualified by what went before. Captain Brown's rescue of the child even at the expense of his own life (the more poignant because he was not making a gesture of sacrifice) and his daughter's death are relieved by their own value and by the happy ending in marriage for Miss Jessie. Yet if this serves as a model for the structure of individual units and for the novel's whole, an important development between the first episode and the rest of the narrative is a shift of relationship between the Jenkyns sisters.

In 'Our Society' Deborah, in attitude and manners, sets a pattern of rectitude happily broken through in her response to Miss Brown's situation. After Deborah's death, she stands as the revered exemplum to whom Miss Matty tries to conform, yet whose standards are constantly challenged, both by what we learn of her (Deborah's part in preventing Miss Matty's marriage, for instance, or her bank investment) and by Matty's need to find ways of acting for herself. There is a shift in Gaskell's attitude to Deborah after 'Our Society', unfair perhaps, but finely exploited in Miss Matty's gradual breaking from her sister's leading strings. The pattern established, Gaskell in time saw her way to make episode dependent upon episode and so to form an interdependent narrative. The meeting between Miss Matty and her old suitor Mr Holbrook is followed by his death and Miss Matty's ability to defy the shade of her sister in allowing Martha a follower, so that a sense of life and possible happiness leads us on to a suggested future larger than Miss Matty's could be, yet in which Miss Matty shares by helping create it. The loss of Peter, the great mystery of the third story, 'Memory at Cranford' (13 March 1852), is resolved in the final episode with the Aga Jenkyns's return. Gaskell could look back as the stories continued to be produced and integrate new material by retrospective reference and development.[12] Miss Matty's frustrated marriage is remembered again by the reader (part of the power is our sense of sharing secrets with certain characters) when she defends the wedded state against Miss Pole's aspersions (pp. 127-8) and Peter wonders that she is not married ('I could have sworn you were on the high road to matrimony when I left England') (p. 187)), while Mrs Fitz-Adam unwittingly recalls the part Miss Jenkyns played in frustrating the match when she remembers Matty's kindness of long ago in the midst of sorrow:

> she was looking down at some primroses she had gathered,
> and pulling them all to pieces, and I do believe she was crying.
> But after she had passed, she turned round and ran after me
> to ask – oh, so kindly – about my poor mother (p. 167).

We perceive more than Mrs Fitz-Adam can; in a minor key it is like the comedy of 'Curious if True', where we have to supply the connection between what we are told and what we are to understand. The retrospective development of Martha is also a sustaining thread, though one easier to develop: Martha's story is never complete since so much of her life is before her; Gaskell has to make later detail about Miss Matty and Mr Holbrook fit into an already completed pattern, though the rejection of Deborah is a forward development. Martha is allowed a follower, but the kiss heard by Matty at the end of the third story is more subtle than the renewal at the close of the second; not only does it assert life, it also brings home to Matty, as already felt in reading the letters, what she has missed. Its comedy is qualified, made complex by the pathos of the listener, whose apparent failure to understand is counteracted by the reader supplying understanding from experience of the whole knot.

The third and fourth stories, 'Memory at Cranford' and 'Visiting at Cranford', appeared on 13 March and 3 April 1852; a gap followed before 'The Great Cranford Panic', a double part (8 and 15 January 1853), and the final three episodes – 'Stopped Payment', 'Friends in Need' and 'A Happy Return' – came together on 2 April, 7 and 21 May 1853, the complete story being published in mid-1853. It is the double-length 'The Great Cranford Panic' which first clearly shows, in unresolved action, that Gaskell intended to extend the work and treat it as a whole. Mary Smith hears Mrs Brunoni's account of her journey through India and of the meeting with Aga Jenkyns, and determines to 'make further enquiry' (p. 133). There is also a hint of Lady Glenmire's marriage (only understood in the next episode) when she breaks in with doubts of Mr Hoggins's having been robbed and grows red at the implication of what she is saying (p. 127). Because of this construction, *Cranford* is unlike most sustained fictions, where extension of narrative determines the structure; rather, it is extension of character as Miss Matty develops from subordinate younger sister to central interest. Each episode is moved along by a plot primarily concentrated in that section, but a sense of character and manners (tied in with character) is dominant. One of Gaskell's achievements is the grasp she has on her creations, the ability to carry them through the whole work, to show while charting them that however strict the rules of manners, they are not absolute since the women of Cranford render 'real tender good offices to each other whenever they are in distress' (p. 1). Human nature, feeling, often clashes with custom and gains in the confrontation, the ladies usually being at their best when they 'hypocritically' renege on what they declare are sacred principles – a marked difference from Jane Austen, with whom Gaskell is sometimes carelessly compared, where identification of inner and outer is essential for probity of character. Gaskell's skill lies so often in her ability to surprise us because she proceeds in this work often not by analysis of feeling and crises of conscience long meditated but by a seemingly sudden description of actions that make us aware at *that* moment of a train of past consideration that defeats the coldness of ceremony. One such moment, unexpected yet entirely believable, was Miss Jenkyns's response to the news of Captain Brown's death.

Deborah seems to live on in Miss Matty's determination to be called Matilda and to enforce Miss Jenkyn's rules with a religious strictness (p. 30). Alterations come, though: Martha is allowed Jem as follower, while the devotion to Deborah's memory, almost remorse as at personal failure, is severely questioned when the 'rebel' who had dared to whisper against the living sister is shown to have had a lover who was not 'enough of a gentleman for the rector and Miss Jenkyns' (p. 35) and whose quiet devoted life is none the less that of a cripple, just as Thomas Holbrook's eccentricity is the outward roughness of a man, his love rejected, who yet has not soured – has crusted, rather:

> with something of the 'pride which apes humility,' he had
> refused to push himself on, as so many of his class had done,
> into the ranks of the squires. He would not allow himself to
> be called Thomas Holbrook, *Esq*; he even sent back letters
> with this address, telling the postmistress at Cranford that his
> name was *Mr.* Thomas Holbrook, yeoman (p. 34).

He is not a misanthrope, though, and both the main terms ('refinement', 'humanity') are important when we are told he despised every refinement 'which had not its root deep down in humanity' (p. 34). If age has overtaken him (Mary Smith's brief romantic vision of him and Miss Matty reunited in love is dashed to the ground), his strangeness is that of Don Quixote rather than of Timon. His domestic state, with the welcoming kitchen – which might so easily have been turned into a dining-parlour – and regret for the passing of old customs in eating, is arrested, so we may take it, at that very point when Miss Matty felt obliged to give him up. A bluff man, he might have become another Squire Hamley in *Wives and Daughters* if he had had the wife and domestic tenderness that social rank would not allow him. His very pride in his rank is a defiance of 'the rector and Miss Jenkyns', who thought him too low for them, though they neither were to be his wife.

The brief encounter after so many years is enough to call up in Miss Matty all the tremulous emotion of thirty years before, which vainly (she thinks successfully) she tries to hide. The very effort at concealment of what she feels after Holbrook's death brings on 'the tremulous motion of head and hands which I have seen ever since in Miss Matty' (p. 48), such is the force of love.

With the second story, Gaskell had needed to reintroduce Mary Smith into Cranford society, a narrator important for the sense of the larger life of Drumble, the pattern of the advancing world, behind which Cranford falls further and further. Even Mary develops, marginally, in her contacts between the two worlds, and she mediates for the reader between his opinions, which she now holds, and Cranford's opinions, which she has shed but does not despise. Mary's observation chronicles the 'history of English domestic life'. Mary had feared her connection with Cranford would cease after Miss Jenkyns's death:

> at least, that it would have to be kept up by correspondence,
> which bears much the same relation to personal intercourse
> that the books of dried plants I sometimes see ('Hortus Siccus,'
> I think they call the thing) do to the living and fresh flowers
> in the lanes and meadows (p. 27).

So Mary may believe, yet Gaskell is able in 'Old Letters' to show a past age brought to light through its correspondence. Old letters may be like dried plants to those that have no key; still, read with memory and feeling they expand out like Japanese flowers into new life. Miss Matty brings out the family letters soon after Holbrook's death, as though reminded of her own mortality and the need for preparation. In her acceptance of her father's, of Deborah's, judgment on Holbrook we may see little more than the burden of the past, of convention. The reading of the letters animates that intermingling, like wheat and tares, of the love and custom which are Miss Matty's life. The ritual springs typically for Gaskell out of physical circumstances: the economy on candles, the detail of contrivance necessary 'to keep our two candles of the same length, ready to be lighted, and to look as if we burnt two always' (p. 50). The customs of Cranford are not quaint eccentricities divorced from human nature, but habits linked by past experience to present need. Gaskell uses these quirks to tell the story:

> One night, I remember that this candle economy particularly
> annoyed me ... especially as Miss Matty had fallen asleep, and
> I did not like to stir the fire and run the risk of awakening

her; so I could not even sit on the rug, and scorch myself with
sewing by firelight, according to my usual custom. I fancied
Miss Matty must be dreaming of her early life; for she spoke
one or two words in her uneasy sleep bearing reference to
persons who were dead long before. When Martha brought in
the lighted candle and tea, Miss Matty started into
wakefulness, with a strange, bewildered look around, as if we
were not the people she expected to see about her. There was
a little sad expression that shadowed her face as she recognized
me; but immediately afterwards she tried to give me her usual
smile. All through tea-time, her talk ran upon the days of her
childhood and youth. Perhaps this reminded her of the
desirableness of looking over all the old family letters, and
destroying such as ought not to be allowed to fall into the
hands of strangers; for she had often spoken of the necessity of
this task, but had always shrunk from it, with a timid dread
of something painful (pp. 50-1).

The first impression of the letters is sensuous, the smell of Tonquin
beans that Mary 'had always noticed ... about any of the things
which had belonged' to Miss Matty's mother (p. 51). The letters,
yellow now with age, have in them 'a vivid and intense sense of the
present time', so that Miss Matty's father, the Rector, whom Mary
has only known 'from a picture in the dining-parlour, stiff and
stately, in a huge full-bottomed wig, with gown, cassock, and bands,
and his hand upon a copy of the only sermon he ever published'
(p. 52), becomes a lover, wooing his wife with 'short homely
sentences, right fresh from the heart', while his bride-to-be is full of
clothes, particularly the white 'Paduasoy', which in time is material
for a christening robe as marriage directs her from self to a new
object of affection in the child. Gaskell never mocks, though she
delights in the delicate human comedy; when, for instance, the
Rector discovered that dress did mean something to his bride 'and
then he sent her a letter, which had evidently accompanied a whole
box full of finery. ... This was the first letter, ticketed in a frail,
delicate hand, "From my dearest John" ' (p. 53). It is human because
it is two people coming together in a union where there is an
intellectual incompatibility, even an emotional one, and yet which
can develop as a working, loving relationship, from the ideal ardour
of the Rector, who dominates the early part of the correspondence,

to the domestic practicality of his wife, who had workaday qualities that stand the wear of years:

> But this was nothing to a fit of writing classical poetry which
> soon seized him, in which his Molly figured as 'Maria'. The
> letter containing the *carmen* was endorsed by her, 'Hebrew
> verses sent me by my honoured husband. I thowt to have had
> a letter about killing the pig, but must wait . . .' (p. 55).

Other letters follow – including Miss Jenkyns's own compositions – and Peter begins to emerge. After the strange joke on Deborah, all those years ago, it is Mary who first reads one of the letters returned unopened to his mother, 'and I, a stranger, not born at the time when this occurrence took place, was the one to open it' (p. 68). So past and present mell together: Mrs Jenkyns speaks to Mary Smith and Gaskell achieves what Southey wished to write, a history of English domestic manners, conveying the strangeness, the otherness of early times and the way such manners were articulated in the frame of human behaviour, in Miss Matty's parents and her lover and the world of candle economy.

The seriousness of *Cranford* lies above all in the episode of Miss Matty's greatest heroism, her insistence that as a shareholder she is responsible for the Town and Country Bank's integrity. She is put to the test partly through that model sister Miss Jenkyns, the invest-ment made at Deborah's insistence against Mary's father's advice. The heroism (the quiet heroism of the sufferer, unperceived as something even required of her; only the observer fully understands the nature of the action) is made more poignant by the pleasure it frustrates, one significantly related back again to Deborah:

> We began to talk of Miss Matty's new silk gown. I discovered
> that it would be really the first time in her life that she had
> had to choose anything of consequence for herself: for Miss
> Jenkyns had always been the more decided character, whatever
> her taste had been . . . (p. 145).

The choice proves to be one of more consequence than Mary imagined. Miss Matty's qualities are pity and integrity, the heart against the head: 'My dear, I never feel as if my mind was what people call very strong. . . . I was very thankful, that I saw my duty this morning, with the poor man standing by me' (p. 151). So Miss Matty rises to the challenge and sells tea, while Martha precipitates

Jem into marriage to help (well that Matty allowed her a follower) and the ladies of Cranford show their kind offices in response to real need (significantly Mrs Jamieson, the most positively dislikeable, is away in Cheltenham). Peter's return, then, after this dismissal of Deborah, is a kind of reward, but not a melodramatic release from misery by a *deus ex machina*. Not only has the possibility of his arrival been rumoured far off, his return does not artificially rescue Miss Matty from the consequences of her action; she has already rescued herself (indeed, she enjoys selling tea) and Peter's return is an emotional rather than material completion – though his sister's financial circumstances certainly improve immensely.

Cranford seems to have passed into folk consciousness. On my first reading, many years ago, I was intrigued to find in the tale of the pedlar's pack (p. 111) a variant of a horror story well known from my grandmother's telling: her version was of a coffin and suspicion was roused by the servant insisting 'I see a grey eye'. Whether they have a common source, I don't know, but the power of both suggests how Gaskell could call on the art of the folk narrator.[13] The book has been reprinted many times and it was Gaskell's own favourite amongst her works (747).

A curious pendant to Cranford is the short satire, 'The Cage at Cranford', published in *All the Year Round*,[14] 28 November 1863, and set in 1856, by which time Miss Matty on a strict chronology would be in her early seventies. The focus shifts though to Miss Pole and to the 'cage' that Mary Smith has sent from France, in reality the support for the excessive crinoline dresses of the late 1850s and 1860s, but taken literally by Cranford to be a bird cage. Satire on fashion is the main point, and presumably Cranford was a convenient, established milieu (certainly backward in fashions) for the ridicule, where only Fanny the maid, a charity child, recognizes what the object is and she is snubbed for her offered information. The vast crinolines were much mocked (as *Punch* cartoons show), yet despite being the 'ugliest fashion that ever caricatured the human form divine' and symptomatic, as Mme Mohl's biographer saw them, of the general corruption of French society under the Second Empire,[15] and despite Jane Welsh Carlyle's glum reaction to the photograph of a friend, that the 'crinoline quite changes her character and makes her a stranger for me. I want the one that is, as I have always seen her, a sensible girl with no crinoline',[16] no mockery was to remove it and Gaskell's assault remains a good-humoured and ineffective joke.

4

Ruth (1853): 'An Unfit Subject for Fiction'

Thus my poor Ruth was wretched and undone,
Nor had a husband for her only son,
Nor had he father.

George Crabbe, 'Ruth', Tales of the Hall

Ruth was Gaskell's second full-length work. Since *Mary Barton* she had written a number of short stories, mainly for *Household Words*; even *Cranford*, which began to appear in December 1851, only saw volume publication in mid-1853. Planned like her first novel to appear in three volumes, *Ruth* is a large advance in construction. Not only was there no need to add extra material at a late stage (p. 73 above), but the plot is tightly knit up, so that Ruth's story is always at the centre and the other plot developments (the Bradshaw children, for instance) play their part by forwarding it and by commenting – optimistically in the case of Jemima's finding of happiness, ironically through Richard's forgery and its challenge to his father. The story falls roughly into three parts, corresponding to volume division: the first up to Ruth's arrival at Eccleston with the Bensons, the second ending with the rejection of Bellingham's marriage offer. The three-volume novel was the established form for any hoping to be bought in large numbers by the circulating libraries.[1] It was a mark of *Ruth*'s success that one London librarian withdrew the novel as 'unfit for family reading' (223).

The success was moral rather than financial, since like *Mary Barton*, *Ruth* is a novel with a purpose, Gaskell in the first half of her career being as concerned with the didactic as the aesthetic function of the novel. How closely moral and aesthetic feeling were linked for her is suggested by her reaction on a visit to Bishop Lee of

Manchester (p. 26 above) to 'an exquisitely painted picture of a dead baby', the child having been burnt and lingered in greatest agony: 'I would not send my child to be educated by the man who could hang up such a picture as that for an object of contemplation' (112-13). However exquisite the treatment, the subject could not justify the result; moral judgment is brought to bear – though it is one of the paradoxes of the situation that *Ruth* was often judged as an unfit subject, however 'exquisitely painted'. Gaskell's justification was that she meant to take her reader beyond contemplation to action both practical and ethical.[2]

Ruth is a 'fallen woman' and Gaskell's letters before and after publication make it clear that she knew she was tackling a subject likely to bring adverse, even painful criticism upon herself, yet felt that she was called to do something ('the means, under Providence, of instilling somewhat') both about women who by offending against sexual mores were cast off by 'respectable' society and about the double standard that sharply differentiated the accepted moral behaviour of men from women. Anthony Trollope in 1870, defending his portrayal of Carry Brattle in *The Vicar of Bullhampton*, wrote of such women that

> a poor creature may fall, – as we call it – and yet be worth redeeming. Fathers and mothers will forgive anything in a son, debauchery, gambling, lying – even the worst dishonesty and fraud – but the 'fallen' daughter is too often regarded as an outcast for whom no hope can be entertained.[3]

When Anna Jameson praised *Ruth* she felt Gaskell's aim had been to lift up 'your voice against "that demoralising laxity of principle," which I regard as the ulcer lying round the roots of Society'.[4] For her the 'laxity of principle' was not in attitudes to the woman or an indifference towards such offences, but laxity rather about the man's part in such women's fall and the gross disparity between what was, at least officially, expected of men and what of women.[5] In *Ruth* the operation of a double standard is clear and clearly condemned; the ambiguity lies in Ruth's 'fall'.

Gaskell had discussed the subject of the novel with friends, including Charlotte Brontë early in 1852, expected a hostile reaction if the novel were published and wondered whether she ever would publish, for 'I hate publishing because of the talk people make' (209). Any doubts were resolved by John Forster sending the manuscript to her publishers, Chapman, and even when she wrote the letter just quoted, two volumes were in print, a stimulus to completing the novel: 'I set to on the trumpet sound thereof, and was writing away vigorously' (205), her heart full of it, and despite the interruption of friends she finished by mid-December 1852. Anticipating the worst she wrote to people forbidding them to send her opinions of it: ' "An unfit subject for fiction" is *the* thing to say about it ... but I determined notwithstanding to speak my mind out about it' (220). Despite a favourable notice in the *North British Review* which made her 'swear with delight', the majority of periodicals and newspapers criticized it adversely (on grounds variously of subject and treatment); it was forbidden in many households – including her own as 'not a book for young people, unless read with someone older' (221) – and she heard of two men who had burnt volume one, while a third 'has forbidden his wife to read it' (223). Men reacted fiercely against it, as moral guardians; Josephine Butler at Oxford listened in hostile silence as a 'young man solemnly declared that he would not allow his mother to read such a book'.[6]

Opinion, though, was not all one way, the purpose expressed in those early discussions was achieved in the favourable response of many individuals. Gaskell was congratulated by Anna Jameson, Monckton Milnes, Charlotte Brontë, Mrs Stanley, wife of the Bishop of Norwich. As early as April 1853 Dickens speaks of Ruth as a dear friend, George Eliot wrote well of it, with reservations, and Henry Crabb Robinson, though unable to finish the story (anticipating the sad end) found it a great improvement on *Mary Barton*.[7] No bad company to be abused in. Gaskell might see herself as St Sebastian, shot through with arrows, yet by March she could begin to assess the effect more objectively and while surprised 'how very many people – good kind people – and *women* infinitely more than men, really & earnestly disapprove of what I have said', she could congratulate herself on putting 'the small edge of the wedge in, if only I have made people talk & discuss the subject a little more than they did' (226). The novel, once established, was frequently reprinted (twice in the 1850s and an eighth edition in 1867).

Gaskell knew, as well as did most of her readers, of the problems 'fallen' women faced. One of her earliest contacts with Dickens was for advice about sending a girl of sixteen to Australia – she had been seduced (after working for a dressmaker) 'by a surgeon ... who was called in when the poor creature was ill', decoyed into prostitution, and had agreed to emigrate (98-9). Dickens himself had been interested in the plight of such girls by Angela Burdett Coutts, and in the 1840s and 1850s together they ran Urania Cottage, a refuge for the protection and training of prostitutes who wished to escape their way of life. Gaskell's readiness to help and to face realities is indicated by a conversation in June 1853 with a Mr Allen, who visited hospitals and amongst prostitutes: 'We talked (a propos of Ruth) a good deal about the difficulty of reclaiming this class *after they had once taken to the street life'*, and she asked for details of Lieutenant Blackmore and his refuge in London (236). Clearly Ruth is not a prostitute, indeed she is startlingly unlike, but one suggestion of the novel is that she is only saved from being so by Benson's Christian charity in taking her in and lying about her past. Financial necessity and social ostracism by both family and society at large made it difficult for any woman, once 'fallen', to be accepted again.

Blackmore deserves a little attention, for he, like many of his contemporaries, was concerned with saving these girls if they would accept help. After naval service – he was severely injured in an explosion while saluting the king of the Belgians – Blackmore experienced a personal conversion and from about 1847 he had 'been actively engaged in endeavouring to rescue from temporal and eternal ruin some of those unhappy girls who are found thronging the streets of London by night', distributing also tracts 'to the male sex, their co-partners in sin'.[8] Blackmore called his nightly expeditions, ludicrously to our ears, 'cruisings' and is sanctimonious in his evangelical piety (Gaskell had heard worse of him (236)), but he recognized, as did Dickens, the claims of human dignity and self-respect if these efforts were to succeed. The appeals were given in envelopes like letters and the two refuges, in St John's Wood and Marylebone Road, were run in the spirit of family homes:

> Here, thought I, lies the secret of success. Mere patronage or benevolence will never call forth such an expression as this:- "I feels at home!" If we wish to benefit our fellow creatures, we must get hold of their hearts, and cause them to feel we have a *brother's* sympathy, and are prepared to act a *brother's* part.[9]

The extreme isolation of such women is stressed by Blackmore (p. 72), while the double standard also is an object of his scorn:

Oh, ladies of England! arouse from your apathy! Which of the
two is more to be dreaded or scorned:- He who the following
day is to be seen in the drawing-room – welcomed by the
virtuous and unsuspecting; or she who has been ruined by him,
and, if known, is scowled upon in the distance – or if
unknown, is pining away in solitude, an outcast from society
(p. 101)?

Social awareness, concern, and action are apparent, whether in
Dickens, Coutts, Blackmore, Allen, or Gaskell, yet Gaskell antici-
pated and found trouble when she wrote a novel about such a
woman. The most likely reason is that what was true in fact and
not necessarily accepted as inevitable or right, or was dealt with in
factual accounts and reports, was still not proper in fiction ('unfit
subject') because novels were so widely read. Not that unmarried
mothers and illegitimate children are uncommon in earlier fiction.
Fielding's Tom Jones is a foundling, Oliver Twist is illegitimate
(the 'surgeon leant over the body, and raised the left hand. "The
old story," he said, shaking his head: "no wedding-ring, I see . . ." ')
– Trollope sent a list of such works to Thackeray in 1860,
including George Eliot's Hetty Sorel, 'with almost the whole story
of how the child was gotten'.[10]

Unlike earlier writers, Gaskell insists upon placing Ruth at the
centre of the novel, makes us aware throughout of her unmarried
state and of her author's approval, and shows her redeemed through
suffering. The subject is before us all the time, so if distasteful it
cannot be avoided. Ruth is not of the same nature as Blackmore's
streetwalkers or even the seduced girl Gaskell had written to Dickens
about, she demands not pity but admiration, and her very status as
heroine (not only the central figure but with heroic qualities)
would be objectionable. Trollope in *The Vicar of Bullhampton* felt he
could not defy conventions to make Carry Brattle his heroine, partly
because he wanted to avoid 'heroic' implications, partly because the
novel, though conceived around her, 'with the object of exciting not
only pity but sympathy',[11] could not have the 'fallen woman' as its
dominant character. Gaskell herself had shown Esther (Butterfly) in
Mary Barton, with great sympathy despite a painful sense that she
never could return to a respectable life, and in her short story 'Lizzie
Leigh' (published in the essentially popular *Household Words*), Lizzie
falls, but the interest concentrates upon her family and their search

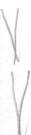

113

for the wanderer. Though neither Esther nor Lizzie are central, the sympathetic handling of Esther's motive for going on the streets is important, since it shows Gaskell's capacity for independence. In social terms many women were tempted by the money, especially sempstresses, who worked long hours for little reward, or having once been seduced found no one would employ them. The popular fictional image was of someone wilfully inflamed, whose nature led to her condition (so alleviating the need for compassion or action). Esther's fall, for Gaskell, is not a psychological perversity but a social responsibility. Esther sells herself for love of her daughter and so saves her soul alive: up to the child's illness, though unmarried and virtually deserted, she had been faithful to one man. Only desperation leads her to seek money that way and though the situation may be sentimental it demands our sympathy and suggests pressures upon the individual where other novelists remained circumscribed by convention.

Gaskell is the first novelist in nineteenth-century England to take a fallen woman as her central character, and even if we look at an earlier American example, Hawthorne's *The Scarlet Letter* (1850), we find at the beginning that the 'crime' is already committed and acknowledged by Hesther. She is punished and isolated, so that much of the attention focuses on Dimmesdale's tortured state. Hawthorne's romance was generally enthusiastically received, though Henry Chorley, who clearly admired it, in his *Athenaeum* review spoke of it as 'a most powerful but painful story', warned that he was 'by no means satisfied that passions and tragedies like these are the legitimate subjects for fiction', and deliberately avoided the conventional practice of giving extracts.[12] Henry James remembered as a child 'the sensation the book produced, and the little shudder with which people alluded to it, as if a peculiar horror was mixed with its attractions',[13] though in characterizing the handling and main interest he scarcely concerns himself with the morality (p. 112). Gaskell never forgets love, whether in Ruth's interview on the sands with Bellingham or her nursing of him in fever at the end, though she too is concerned with the moral situation and shows Ruth's 'redemption' partly through her child as Hesther's is through Pearl. Ruth in her tragic dignity, spirituality and self-abnegation, is closer to Hesther than to Blackmore's hauls on his cruises or even Aunt Esther: direct imitation is unlikely, though Gaskell probably knew *The Scarlet Letter* well already, as later she came to know Hawthorne himself. Still, in associating Ruth with countryside and small-town life, Gaskell has her closer to the New England Hesther than Blackmore's needle-woman who, failing to make an honourable livelihood and taking to prostitution, 'must go on with it, or starve' (p. 163). If Gaskell's declared intentions in writing seem bound up with such urban victims (her conversation with Mr Allen suggests others took her point), Ruth is yet curiously heroic and pastoral as a character. The atmosphere of the book removes us from the evil of cities, the social evil, and weakens any argument so far as the *class* of fallen women is concerned, though Ruth makes her own challenge.

The pastoralism of the novel lies not only in its natural settings. It is also strongly felt in the distancing of the action back in time: precisely when is not clear – Ruth's story begins 'many years ago now'. In fact, though less than fifty years ago, the sense of past sets the action back from our own experience. The opening description of the town a hundred years before, in all its provincial dignity, is an important gloss of Ruth's story, no mere preliminary scene-painting:

> The daily life into which people are born . . . forms chains
> which only one in a hundred has moral strength enough to
> despise, and to break when the right time comes – when an
> inward necessity for independent individual action arises, which
> is superior to all outward conventionalities (p. 2).

Memories of her mother and the affectionate distress of the old farmhand are, of course, links for Ruth, and her later behaviour is determined by Mr Benson rather than 'an inward necessity'. Yet in her love for Leonard, her son, and the rejection of Bellingham she shows the moral strength to break the chains of daily life, to work out a course for herself.

Ruth's difference from the other girls at Mrs Mason's is not only her newness to dress making, but also her larger sense of the world outside. In the half-hour interval for refreshment (at 2 a.m. on a winter's morning) she springs to the window to look out on snow and moonlight. She is poetically presented from the first glimpse of her, passing the stained glass window 'through which the moonlight fell on her with a glory of many colours' (p. 3), which links Ruth to vivid life as well as to the chastity of snow and moon even while it invokes echoes of Keat's Madeline, on whose breast the moonlight threw 'warm gules', or more complexly of Shelley's dome of many coloured glass: scenery is felt as an extension of Ruth's self. The atmosphere cleaves to her even in the sharp contrast between the romantic past of the aristocratic house and its squalid present of partitioning with a dozen girls stitching away. Ruth chooses the coldest part, where she can look at the old decorated panels, a response to beauty which suggests a capacity for feeling and suffering both, a sign of her larger destiny, a nature not subdued to the task in hand nor even to the security of apprenticeship. The painted flowers give more than momentary aesthetic pleasure; they keep open also lines of communication, young as Ruth is (not quite sixteen here), with a past from which death would seem to have cut her off (p. 7).

Ruth is isolated, unprotected. Just how completely so is deliberately held back by Gaskell until the third chapter, by when her character has taken our imagination and we can pause to understand her lone circumstances – her guardian is indifferent, Jenny is removed by illness, Mrs Mason, not particularly hardhearted, is yet a Mrs Worldly-Wise who finds it easier not to enquire what the girls do of a Sunday, 'perhaps because she dreaded to hear that one or two had occasionally nowhere to go to, and that it would be sometimes necessary to order a Sunday's dinner, and leave a lighted fire on that day' (p. 35). The dressmaker's wisdom in selecting Ruth to attend at the ball, since her beauty will do credit to the establishment, comes into collison with Ruth's truth, which cannot accept that she should be 'rewarded' (Mrs Mason's specious cover in choosing) for diligence. Gaskell's technical progress is seen in this skilful establishment of Ruth's moral sense, firm if undeveloped, the rock she builds on amidst all her troubles.

At the ball, Ruth attracts the attention of Bellingham, who, having dawdled through some months of life, can be roused by her appearance as 'a new, passionate, hearty feeling shot through his whole being' (p. 32). He takes pleasure, careless rather than vicious, in pursuing Ruth, circumstance throwing in his way the rescue of the village lad – no stage-managed act like that of Richardson's Lovelace in sparing Rosebud or the charity of Laclos's Vicomte de Valmont,[14] since Bellingham has not the calculation, not, one feels, the intelligence of those seducers. Bellingham none the less turns the chance to personal advantage, and thoughtlessness begins to seem callous. The pleasure of friendship leads Ruth to love Bellingham, the prospect of loss brings the force of her emotion home to her. Already Bellingham's absence, after her show of annoyance, has made her wonder 'why a strange, undefined feeling, had made her imagine she was doing wrong in walking alongside of one so kind and good' (p. 39). As Bellingham's rescue of the boy was right, but the impression wrought upon Ruth turned to bad, so Gaskell is careful to distinguish the effect of natural scenes, innocent in themselves, and moral impulses. It is a moral growth, hesitating perhaps, that she traces. Ruth, largely ignorant of what she is doing, is not unaware that something may be wrong, however much pleasure she feels in the advancing spring when shared with a man like Bellingham:

> Among the last year's brown ruins, heaped together by the
> wind in the hedgerows, she found the fresh, green, crinkled leaves
> and pale star-like flowers of the primroses. Here and there a
> golden celandine made brilliant the sides of the little brook . . .
> and once . . . Ruth burst into an exclamation of delight at the
> evening glory of mellow light which was in the sky behind the
> purple distance . . .
>
> 'How strange it is,' she thought that evening, 'that I should
> feel as if this charming afternoon's walk were, somehow, not
> exactly wrong, but yet as if it were not right . . .' (p. 40).

It is one damning criticism of Bellingham that in Wales he cannot see beauty in rain or clouds, where Ruth's sensibility is open to 'the purple darkness on the heathery mountain-side, and then the pale golden gleam that succeeded' (p. 64). We may wonder on what basis society may destroy such living vitality, yet the 'exquisitely painted' scene is not the only factor in human response: there is our moral nature and here Ruth is herself to a degree at fault. The difficulty, on the evidence, is to determine the degree. The need that Gaskell feels throughout to intervene on Ruth's behalf, as she does when Ruth ponders Bellingham's plea to join him for London – 'Still she did not speak. Remember how young, and innocent, and motherless she was!' (p. 56) – suggests how strong was the current of popular feeling against which Gaskell was striving and how uncertain she can still be that what she shows will convince the reader of her meaning (only in her later work or with a character as narrator as in *Cranford* does she solve the problems of personal intervention and authorial commentary). Unfortunately, such comments damagingly suggest that Gaskell is not convinced of the innocence herself.

Disaster overtakes Ruth as the climax of a sequence expertly controlled in feeling and language. Gaskell alerts us to the impending tragedy, for no 'coming shadow threw its gloom over this week's dream of happiness'. As they start on their Sunday walk to the farmhouse of Ruth's childhood, the young couple are caught in a tangle of events and time that makes them echo Romeo and Juliet. They saunter 'through the fragrant lanes, as if their loitering would prolong the time and check the fiery-footed steeds galloping apace towards the close of the happy day' (p. 44). No great irony, perhaps, is intended by using Juliet's wish for time's flight as a warning unheeded by these lovers in a world where 'sorrow, or death, or guilt' *do* exist. Still, attention drawn, the reader is aware of the closed safety of the old farm and garden, with its faithful guardian who would warn if possible, deepening the painful sense of Ruth doomed and unconscious, unable to make any connection between the devil like a roaring lion and 'the handsome young man who awaited her with a countenance beaming with love' (p. 50). Part of the pain comes from our being so close to Ruth and yet unable to save her; we can only participate, not intervene. All too quickly Mrs Mason comes upon Ruth, dismisses her (dismissal acerbated by Ruth's childlike belief that this sentence is absolute); Bellingham urges and Ruth 'falls' – she 'entered the carriage and drove towards London' (p. 60).

The break in narrative at this point is very marked, by the chapter ending, by the gap of time and shift to Wales, and by the blank in Ruth's history, a flaw in Gaskell's handling of her theme in the novel. Hawthorne got round the problem of Hesther and Dimmesdale in bed by beginning his story nine months and more afterwards. The problem indeed is not so much one of bed, as of Ruth's awareness, if any, of what it is she has done. Hazel Mews is surely right to ask, 'would not the shock of discovery of what was involved in cohabitation have had a greater effect upon a young girl's mind than is portrayed in the book' and she suggests a 'touch of false refinement' may be detected here.[15]

Given the tenor of the rest of the book – not only Ruth's salvation but more importantly her belief, which is her author's too, that she stands in need of salvation after sin – hasn't Gaskell, in presenting her character sympathetically, contrived to make her sinless in the event and yet to react afterwards as though she had sinned? That is, Gaskell seems to confound society's view of what has happened with God's, despite quoting 'God judgeth not as man judgeth' (p. 54).[16] Crabb Robinson hit on it when he noted that the 'assignable fault, if

any, might be an excess of repentance'.[17] Ruth seems to understand what Mrs Mason meant ('I'll have no slur on the character of my apprentices' (p.54)), yet not to understand what she has been doing until in Wales the small boy, who heard mamma call her 'a bad, naughty girl', repulses her. Gaskell herself forcefully extenuates, before the fall, Ruth's part in it:

> She was too young when her mother died to have received
> any cautions or words of advice respecting *the* subject of a
> woman's life – if, indeed, wise parents ever directly speak of
> what, in its depth and power, cannot be put into words –
> which is a brooding spirit with no definite form or shape that
> men should know it, but which is there, and present before we
> have recognised and realised its existence. Ruth was innocent
> and snow-pure (p. 43).

What, then, passed between her and Bellingham after leaving Fordham: did she think their behaviour usual or permissible until society (though out of the mouths of babes) brought it home to her? It seems so. Yet, she acknowledges guilt, seeks to be repentant, whereas if she were truly ignorant then she has committed no sin, however men judge, since, as Benson at least ought to know, sin demands knowledge, consent and will. Being undecided whether Ruth is wholly victim or wholly penitent, Gaskell blurs the particular issue she is concerned with. Is the novel a protest against society's victimization of an innocent, or a protest against society's belief that no woman, once fallen, can live a decent life? Gaskell might in everyday life be involved with both, but since, given a single character, one case precludes the other, fictionally she can only deal with one. Apart from the excess of repentance, Gaskell seems not in the end to be able to step outside the terms of her own society. She says she strove

> to make the story and the writing as quiet as I could, in order
> that 'people' (my great bugbear) might not say that they
> could not see what the writer felt to be very plain and earnest
> truth, for romantic incidents or exaggerated writing (225).

Though largely successful in this aim, at this crisis, as occasionally elsewhere – Leonard's reaction to his bastardy, the need for Ruth's death – she is 'misled', as George Eliot put it, 'by a love of sharp contrast – of "dramatic" effect',[18] here the contrast between Ruth's purity and the opinion of the world, between her innocence and Bellingham's responsibility.

It was this blurring of authorial intention that particularly drew out W. R. Greg's criticism of Gaskell's 'most beautiful and touching tale', written, he felt, to enforce Jesus's knowledge that

> in the woman who has gone astray through the weakness of
> an ill-placed or thirsting affection, there might yet lie
> untouched depths of purity, self-devotion, and capacity for the
> loftiest virtue, which it would be vain to look for in the man
> whose cold and selfish bosom no tender or generous emotion
> had ever thawed. . . .[19]

His objection was to the creation of the pure Ruth and a lapse 'as faultless as such a fault can be' followed inconsistently by Gaskell giving in 'to the world's estimate in such matters, by assuming that the sin committed was of so deep a dye that only a life of atoning and enduring penitence could wipe it out' (p. 136). It was partly to avoid having to present a woman totally blameless that led Trollope to deny Carry Brattle the heroine's status. To place all the blame on the man, though, can be as one-sided as society's requiring that the woman pays for all.

Ruth's idyll in Wales, already disturbed by the child's repulse, is destroyed by Bellingham's illness (illness, emphasizing the narrative rhythm of encounter and crisis, is crucial at those climaxes which correspond closely to the three-volume division: Bellingham's in Wales and Eccleston, and between them Leonard's after Ruth's meeting with her lover on the sands). Here Bellingham's guilt is plain, for, if incapacitated, he is still the mother's spoilt child, making no attempt to trace Ruth and so forfeiting all claim to her love and to their child. Whatever legal claim he might have to Leonard (Gaskell rightly, I think, does not pursue that possibility), he has no moral claim. His love for Ruth may have been a 'passionate, hearty feeling', but his developed character is established for us clearly by report shortly before his reappearance at Eccleston as prospective Radical candidate: 'Plenty of money – does not know what to do with it, in fact – tired of yachting, travelling; wants something new' (p. 248). Though attracted by Ruth and excited by Leonard, that his final and trump card with Ruth should be the offer of marriage, the last desperate bid for her affection, suggests how rotten he is. At the end, his offer to educate Leonard is rejected by Benson who indignantly judges him and makes Gaskell's point that 'Men may call such actions as yours youthful follies! There is another name for them with God' (p. 450). Gaskell damns Bellingham finally (as a Laodicean rather than someone positively vicious) by his ability to go away and not care. If he escapes lightly in worldly terms – *he* does not die nor even make an inconvenient marriage to the penniless daughter of a disgraced baronet – stern judgment lies in revelation of a shallow nature. His memories have none of the emotional significance of other Gaskell characters, vitally linking past and present. In his second illness he sees Ruth again as the simple child:

> her looks were riveted on his softly-unclosing eyes, which met
> hers as they opened languidly. She could not stir or speak. She
> was held fast by that gaze of his, in which a faint recognition
> dawned, and grew to strength.
>
> He murmured some words. They strained their sense to
> hear.
> 'Where are the water-lilies? Where are the lilies in her hair?'
> (pp. 441-2).

Recall imposes one moment upon another; he fails to recognize the new Ruth or the change in her (understandable enough in terms of his illness, but significant in the larger pattern) as he fails to regret his part in that former life or to perceive that what he recalls is a moment when Ruth was already aware of the world's regard and beginning her progress in moral growth, the path he has avoided. Ruth has grown completely separate from Bellingham as he would understand if he could perceive the significance of the forced meeting on the beach. Unlike Bellingham, Ruth, in the shock of recognition, goes back not to a moment of joy but to that outside the inn when Mrs Mason rejected her. Their relationship is for her one of crisis and choice, as the night scene after the beach meeting confirms.

Ruth's growth, mental and moral, is produced largely through the concern and love of the Bensons. They rescue her in Wales and by concealing what she is, they allow time so she can face the hostile world when the truth comes out. Benson insists, despite her guilt (and the word is supplied without qualification or irony by the author (p. 116)), upon another view from that expressed initially by his sister. He can speak of Ruth's errors, agree that they are part of her shame, yet see also the coming child as 'God's messenger to lead her back to him' (p. 118); Leonard is later imaged as Jesus himself in

121

a nativity scene, while Ruth (Mary and Magdalene both) lies on the moonlit calm of her sick bed – compare the moonlight of the novel's opening scene, just a year before – 'so near, so real and present did heaven and eternity, and God seem to Ruth, as she lay encircling her mysterious holy child' (p. 163). Benson holds rightly to the Christian doctrine of loving the sinner, hating the sin, and insists that a distinction must be made between the sin and the consequences (p. 120), which Faith finds difficult until the physical presence of Leonard calls out motherly instincts and assures her naturally of what Benson can feel ethically. Benson is against the lie, but the brand of illegitimacy, society visiting retribution upon the innocent, determines him on deception. Gaskell makes this stigma concrete by Thomas Wilkins's history, though spoils the effect by melodrama of language: 'the obnoxious word in the baptismal registry told him that he must go forth branded into the world, with his hand against every man's, and every man's against him'; and by melodrama of event: 'he went to sea and was drowned, rather than present the record of his shame' (pp. 121; 120). Comparable is Leonard's reaction, good when his shame is a child's one but fudged where it is to the social implications of illegitimacy, something he can know from neither precept nor experience. It is difficult to know what the stigma of illegitimacy really was in this period; with Oliver Twist, though he clearly is a figure of romance, it doesn't matter at all. Yet even in *Ruth* itself Gaskell gives us Mr Davis the doctor, who offers to take Leonard as apprentice, with prospect of succeeding to his practice, a man who, illegitimate himself (p. 437), has yet done very well. The two examples, Wilkins and Davis, are not so much contradictory as serving different functions, the first needed to persuade Benson that he must lie, the second to persuade Ruth that revealing the truth had been worthwhile.

Benson is a Dissenting minister and so his lie is the worse from one whose life should be an example, as he knows when he thinks of the influential Mr Bradshaw, who objects to charades let alone profligacy. Most readers nowadays probably feel that Benson has done very little evil, if we would want to use the term at all. The life that he leads, with his sister and the faithful Sally, is active Christianity; it would be difficult from the novel alone to guess exactly what form his Dissent takes, though we know it is not Methodism, and Unitarianism is certainly meant (the Eccleston chapel is modelled closely on that at Knutsford, with its external staircase). His creed has none of the sentimental or grovelling drivel about Jesus that is expressed by certain Calvinistic Dissenters or Evangelicals of the period.[20] Jesus indeed, save as ethical teacher, example, and loving man, is hardly invoked by Benson – he turns naturally to God rather than Jesus.

Set against the spirit of the Bensons is the pharisaism of Bradshaw, a formalist, who adheres to the letter, not a hypocrite. He has been compared to Gradgrind in Dickens's *Hard Times* (1854) or to Bounderby. A gross hypocrite like Bounderby, whose whole life is a sham, he is not, and though there is some likeness to Gradgrind's raising of his family by system, there is not Dickens's insistence upon direct cause and effect. Richard Bradshaw's failure is more in the nature of poetic justice after his father's treatment of Ruth (an irony, perhaps, that father lives by the letter and son forges the letter) – rather than a demolition of his father's system it serves as proof that all are sinners, who need mercy. Bradshaw's collapse is brought about by his attempt to act according to his code and deny the love he feels for his son, when he cannot allow himself to hate the sin yet love the sinner. He can only accept the possibility of Richard's return when he understands what he has done to himself. The destruction of his formalism began, though Gaskell does not press the point, with Bellingham's election, sponsored by Bradshaw – the grain of mustard-seed that springs, as Bradshaw reluctantly recognizes, into the tree of his own corruptibility.

The whole election episode shows Gaskell's technical skill, as she prepares for Bellingham's return. First come the hints of the election, then the removal of Ruth to Wales, furtherings of the plot, while the discussion at Bradshaw's dinner renews the moral themes of the novel. The very cause of discussion, the prospect of bribery, involves Bradshaw in an action that ought to tell him he can no longer insist that evil may not be done to bring about good. The irony strikes Benson when he himself utters the words to the political agent Hickson. At the same time Farquhar is restored to Jemima's good graces by recognizing the complexity inherent in ethical problems. And if Benson is silent when Farquhar asks him to expand, because he is 'questioning himself as to how far his practice tallied with his principle' (p. 254), that silence is part of the minister's dignity and importance, recognized by even so worldly a figure as Hickson and exercised in his refusal to give Ruth up when the truth comes out.

The truth does come out, by coincidence. Mrs Pearce, the dressmaker newly come to Eccleston, is a coincidence less acceptable than Bellingham's reappearance simply because it is the second necessary coincidence, palpably manipulated to precipitate crisis. When Ruth accepts Bradshaw's frenzied dismissal, she is ready, almost welcomes it, since she no longer need live a lie. She has grown up - and Gaskell cunningly fills out the long time gaps in the story by significant detail, further evidence that the blank after Ruth's departure for London was deliberate - grown up both in intellect and moral dignity:

> Her mind was uncultivated, her reading scant; beyond the
> mere mechanical arts of education she knew nothing; but she
> had a refined taste, and excellent sense and judgment to
> separate the true from the false (p. 176).

We have no details of the education, but she is spurred on by it being eventually for Leonard's benefit; even when Sally is about to rebuke her for not putting her whole self into everyday tasks, the old servant 'was quelled into silence by the gentle composure, the self-command over her passionate sorrow, which gave to Ruth an unconscious grandeur of demeanour' (p. 172). Perhaps if it had not been for Benson's lie, certainly if it had not been for her fall, she could never have achieved her final status of Christian heroine. So far, at least, her sin is a *felix culpa*, the 'happy fault' which, bad in itself, produces the greater good. Perhaps we 'are not to do evil that good may come', yet by God's providence good *can* come out of evil. She has potential before she loves Bellingham, which might have been realized if she had not fallen, but in Wales it seems Ruth would have been destroyed or at best gone into a penitentiary as Mrs Bellingham recommended if Benson had not been on hand. Only through suffering can human beings come to full moral growth. In this, Gaskell is much closer to the poetic allegories of Hawthorne than the grim realities of the nineteenth-century streetwalker. Ruth is like the Lady of the May in Hawthorne's short story 'The May Pole of Merrymount', who at the end goes to a grimmer, yet (Hawthorne suggests) a more real life because she is supported in love by her Lord and their love is deepened by the challenge. Ruth finds that 'Life had become significant and full of duty to her' (p. 189) and her flowery garland is in Leonard, the Bensons and, eventually, the nursing which provides her with the martyrdom and reward of Christian virtue. This last perhaps is symptomatic of the pastoralism of the story, in the sense I used earlier, since why should Ruth die, especially by typhus taken from Bellingham rather than from the fever hospital?[21] Charlotte Brontë had protested against the ending when Gaskell sent her the outline of the story early in 1852. She was clear, as Gaskell wished, that it was a novel with a purpose, which might 'restore hope and energy to many who thought they had forfeited their right to both; and open a clear course for honourable effort to some who deemed that they and all honour had parted company in this world.' She burst out, though:

> Yet – hear my protest!
> Why should she die? Why are we to shut up the book weeping?
> My heart fails me already at the thought of the pang it will have to undergo. And yet you must follow the impulse of your own inspiration. If *that* commands the slaying of the victim, no bystander has a right to put out his hand to stay the sacrificial knife: but I hold you a stern priestess in these matters.[22]

'Victim' seems a key word here; Gaskell's purpose was partly to show that the fallen woman could lead a full and useful life, yet she couldn't escape the conventional idea that Ruth, the heroic dignified expansive creature, is also a victim, who must have her tragedy. She has not yet grasped fully, as she was to in *Sylvia's Lovers*, that to live can be more tragic than to die. It may seem carping, but what the novel lacks is ordinariness – not so much in style as in conception of character and plot. In pleading a case Gaskell overstates it. Yet in boldly attempting something new, something she felt necessary to be said, and in development of techniques of construction and mood, we recognize in *Ruth* the work of someone constantly extending her range. *Ruth*'s true successor is not the next novel with a purpose, *North and South* (1855), but the most tragic of all Gaskell's works, *Sylvia's Lovers* (1863).

5

The Life of Charlotte Brontë (1857)

> – How shall we honour the young,
> The ardent, the gifted? how mourn?
> Console we cannot, her ear
> Is deaf . . .
>   . . . a little earth
> Stops it for ever to praise.
>
> Matthew Arnold, 'Haworth Churchyard'

I

Although the work is the reason we are interested in the artist, our curiosity is rarely satisfied by knowing him through the work alone. Our curiosity is natural; the personality of the artist may provide illumination or a sense of the struggle of the human spirit in the process of creation. Gaskell knew that curiosity, though her readers' interest in *her* identity she dismissed as mere idleness. In a note to her publisher, Chapman, in the December after *Mary Barton*'s appearance, she commented with asperity on attempts to probe her anonymity:

> the whole affair of publication has been one of extreme
> annoyance to me, from the impertinent and unjustifiable
> curiosity of people, who have tried to force me either into an
> absolute denial, or an acknowledgement of what they must
> have seen the writer wished to keep concealed (64).

Though she could turn Emily Winkworth's enquiry aside with a tongue-in-cheek report (62), she insisted she had a right to the privacy requested by the silence of the title-page. Fascinated though

126

she was by Charlotte Brontë, this reaction to public speculation coloured the writing of the biography, for Charlotte had tried, under the guise of Currer Bell, to preserve her privacy and yet had been the subject of personal comment. Discussing in the biography a notice of *Jane Eyre* in the *Quarterly Review*, Gaskell noticed how the harm was not in the comments on the novel, harsh and even flippant though they were, but in biographical conjectures: that Currer Bell was a woman, and that any woman who could write *Jane Eyre* 'must be one who for some sufficient reason has long forfeited the society of her sex' (p. 360).[1] That this attack was in Gaskell's mind at least from starting on the biography is shown by a quotation from another *Quarterly Review* article which counters this 'cowardly insolence' with Southey's practice in such cases:

> In reviewing anonymous works myself, when I have known
> the authors I have never mentioned them, taking it for
> granted they had sufficient reasons for avoiding the publicity
> (p. 360).

This also appears as one of a number of quotations copied by Gaskell onto a sheet, now bound up with the manuscript, presumably preparatory to writing the *Life,* evidence of a concern in the biography to vindicate Charlotte's work and life.[2] The *Quarterly's* reviewer, Elizabeth Rigby, had not only failed to respect the 'sufficient reasons' of Currer Bell; she compounded her fault by going 'into gossiping conjectures', pretending 'to decide on what the writer may be from the book' (p. 360).

Yet if such were Gaskell's experience and feeling, she shared other people's interest in the identity of the author of *Jane Eyre* – the appearance of a remarkable novel supposes the existence of a remarkable person. On its first appearance (1847) Gaskell wrote to a friend,

> Read 'Jane Eyre', it is an uncommon book. I don't know if I
> like or dislike it. I take the opposite side to the person I am
> talking with always in order to hear some convincing
> arguments to clear up my opinions (57).

In November 1849 she is asking for biographical information (90) and, teasing having its charms, when she received a copy of *Shirley* (1849) from the author, Gaskell was eager to half reveal and half conceal her new-won information: 'Currer Bell (aha! what will you give me for a secret?) She's a she – that I will tell you' (93).

127

Whatever her own tribulations in authorship and her certainty that her own life held no interest for others, the more Gaskell came to learn about Charlotte Brontë, the more certain she was that this was a remarkable life, one which assumed tragic dimensions. She never thought until after Charlotte's death of the possibility even of publishing any kind of biography, yet she eagerly collected all the information she could, from others who had met Charlotte and, with their own meeting and rapid friendship, from Charlotte herself.

Even before she met Charlotte, Gaskell had a detailed account from Harriet Martineau, who, despite opposing views, not least on religion, was able to win Charlotte's confidence and affection. Charlotte had been particularly moved by the handling of her hero, the Duke of Wellington, in Martineau's history of the Peninsular War.[3] Harriet told Gaskell of their first meeting (December 1849) at Richard Martineau's house and Gaskell eagerly passed on the account (96-97).

Charlotte's character was beginning to fascinate her. In May 1850 Gaskell expressed her desire to hear more about Charlotte, 'as I have been so much interested in what she has written', since she felt a personality in the work beyond story and the mode of narration – 'the glimpses one gets of *her*, and her modes of thought, and, all unconsciously, to herself, of the way in wh she has suffered' (116). The interrelationship of work and writer was one Gaskell found emotionally important[4] and she wondered, since Bradford was not far away (indeed, Haworth's position near the Lancashire border makes westward travel simple) whether Charlotte ever came to Manchester. Charlotte had been there in 1846, when her father was successfully operated on for cataracts that had brought total blindness and she, 'in those grey, weary, uniform streets', had begun *Jane Eyre*,[5] but it was in the Lake District that Gaskell first met her. Charlotte had been taken up, rather fiercely, by Sir James and Lady Kay-Shuttleworth – a kindness, since Sir James recognized the dangers for Charlotte in a family where tuberculosis was endemic, but exercised in a style that was superior and often without concern for Charlotte's feelings. Sir James was to be useful later in coolly taking over for Gaskell's use letters and papers in the possession of Charlotte's widower, the Rev. Arthur Bell Nicholls, and now on Tuesday 20 August 1850 Gaskell came by Sir James's invitation from Silverdale, where the family was on holiday, to Briery Close, 'about two-thirds of the way on the main road between Windermere and Ambleside'.

She arrived late: 'Dark when I got to Windermere station; a drive along the level road to Low-wood, then a regular clamber up a steep lane; then a stoppage at a pretty house'. Here in the drawing-room she met, beside her hosts, 'a little lady in black silk gown, whom I could not see at first for the dazzle in the room; she came up & shook hands with me at once'. During tea, when Charlotte hardly spoke, Gaskell took good note of her:

> She is, (as she calls herself) *undeveloped*; thin and more than ½
> a head shorter than I, soft brown hair not so dark as mine;
> eyes (very good and expressive looking straight & open at
> you) of the same colour, a reddish face; large mouth & many
> teeth gone; altogether *plain*; the forehead square, broad, and
> *rather* overhanging. She has a very sweet voice, rather hesitates
> in choosing her expressions, but when chosen they seem
> without an effort, *admirable* and *just* befitting the occasion.
> There is nothing overstrained but perfectly simple. (123-4)

Charlotte wore black, partly because usual with her, partly because she, the only remaining child, was in a kind of perpetual mourning, Branwell, Emily and Anne having all died within a little over eight months (September 1848 to May 1849). Gaskell was always to know Charlotte as a solitary figure, an impression enforced, as Winifred Gérin points out,[6] by Gaskell's one visit to Haworth, which coincided with the crisis leading up to Charlotte's engagement. The sense of laughter in Charlotte springs, for instance, from her letter about the visit she paid with Anne to the publisher George Smith as proof that there was more than one Bell and that they were ladies: 'He looked at [the letter] – then at me – again – yet again. I laughed at his queer perplexity'.[7] This humour Gaskell could not know strongly in their relationship, though Smith's own insistence that this same letter be considerably condensed for this episode in the *Life* helped darken the picture Gaskell was drawing. At Low-wood, Lady Kay-Shuttleworth provided a good deal of information, true and false jumbled together, including some of those stories that exaggerate the Rev. Patrick Brontë's oddity near to insanity, the quite false story of Mrs Brontë being disowned by her family on marrying him, and the ways he had of venting irritation (124). Undoubtedly Mr Brontë was strange, certainly he did avoid his children, ate only in his study and never asked the

129

children in unless occasionally for tea. More important, because Gaskell was much influenced by it, was an incorrect version of events at Cowan Bridge School.

Writing to a friend about this Lake District meeting, Gaskell gives the impression that Charlotte had told her these things herself; that, for instance, she ascribed her stunted person 'to the scanty supply of food she had as a growing girl, when at that school' (128), but presumably Lady Kay-Shuttleworth was her channel. Yet that smallness, the sense of the child, helpless in its physical and social disadvantages, was one of the things that drew Gaskell to her. She pitied Charlotte, came to admire and love her, and was determined that justice should be done to a woman who had suffered and triumphed. 'Her hands are like birds' claws', she wrote; 'She is said to be frightfully shy, and almost cries at the thought of going amongst strangers' (127). The sadness was underlined by threat of imminent death, though Charlotte was to survive another four-and-a-half years, during which she produced a great novel, *Villette* (1853), and had a reasonably happy marriage. In return, Charlotte felt deeply drawn towards Gaskell. There was the motherly charm, the sense of a woman whose beauty was not so much in looks as in a full life, and there was an emotional and intellectual affinity. They might disagree over individual preferences – Charlotte could not bear Tennyson – but both were deeply attached to poetry and both were highly successful novelists, facing alike the problems of writing and of being women.

The pair were to meet on only four other occasions, three times at Plymouth Grove and once at Haworth. Other visits, projected, had to be cancelled. Their relationship developed by letter, Charlotte beginning by sending a copy of *Poems by Currer, Ellis, and Acton Bell* (1846), the sisters' first jointly published venture, pressing the claims of Emily's contribution. Yet even this emotional sympathy could not be a substitute for knowledge in a future biographer. Gaskell had no early project of memoir or biography, she essentially enjoyed the friendship; yet if she had no thought of storing up materials, the desire to *know* Charlotte led her from the beginning to analyse her circumstances. 'Indeed I never heard of so hard and dreary a life', she wrote to a friend (128), and again, to Eliza Fox, 'Miss Brontë *is* a nice person ... poor thing she can hardly smile ... the wonder to me is how she can have kept heart and power alive in her life of desolation' (130). The biography's leading themes – of the harshness of life, of the heart and power possessed and made manifest – are already sounded here.

Charlotte stayed in Manchester at the end of June 1851, for two days, on her way home from London; for a week at the end of April 1853; and for four days at the beginning of May 1854. Charlotte was much taken by these glimpses of the Gaskell home. She felt unbothered and was not forced to meet people or to perform, as too often the expectation on visits to London. Shyness still gripped her, but the children charmed her, Julia, the youngest, above all. The last of these visits was when, despite her father's opposition and self-doubt, she found herself 'what people call "engaged" ',[8] and she had long discussions about her future with Gaskell and with Catherine Winkworth. The marriage itself, I think, provides, though obscurely – it was a topic handled very cautiously – another theme within the *Life*, related for Gaskell to her sense of the power this woman possessed and the way it was subordinated in a world dominated by men, where a husband, regardless of intellect or abilities, became legally master of his wife and of all she possessed. Gaskell knew occasions when William pocketed up her literary earnings, and William was no tyrant. Even she, though not strong on women's rights (379), would have hoped with Geraldine Jewsbury that women in future 'will make themselves women, as men are allowed to make themselves men.'[9] More important in matrimony than cash, though, was general compatibility; and it is significant that when Gaskell came to choose one of Charlotte's letters announcing her engagement, she printed the more guarded one to her old schoolteacher, Miss Wooler (12 April 1854), rather than that to Ellen Nussey, her closest friend. To Miss Wooler she is suitably formal, with no gush of emotionalism for a destiny which did not appear brilliant, 'but I trust I see in it some germs of real happiness' (p. 515). To Ellen, though she dwells more on love, she shows greater awareness of the roots of incompatibility:

> I trust to love my husband – I am grateful for his tender love
> to me. I believe him to be an affectionate, a conscientious, a
> high-principled man; and if, with all this, I should yield to
> regrets, that fine talents, congenial taste and thoughts are not
> added, it seems to me I should be most presumptuous and
> thankless.[10]

Yet should she not contemplate with some trepidation the prospect of union with a man who, though undoubtedly in love with her, was a bigot and without much feeling for literature?[11]

In conversation during that last visit to Manchester, Gaskell and Catherine Winkworth, uncertain perhaps but knowing they could not advise against the marriage, seem to have spent a good deal of time reassuring Charlotte. Catherine's account of the visit, a splendid piece of reporting, laments the loss: 'Alas! Alas! I am very glad for Miss Brontë's sake, but sorry for ours, for we can never reckon on seeing her much again when she is "a married woman".'[12] She concluded, shrewdly, 'But I *guess* the true love was Paul Emanuel after all, and is dead; but I don't know, and don't think that Lily knows.'[13] She was right: M. Heger of Brussels, original of Paul Emanuel in *Villette*, had been the great love, as Gaskell was to know (and conceal) by the time she came to write the *Life*. Gaskell could sense the lack of fulfilment, that any happiness must be limited by the husband's personality – Charlotte would even be happy, but would she be satisfied? It is dangerous to press our own feelings about other people too far; they are frail means of judging others. Yet Gaskell felt that Charlotte's life had only allowed the most minimal concession to happiness and another sober-coloured thread was entwined in the *Life*.

Elizabeth Gaskell's only visit to Haworth during Charlotte's life was for four days from 19 September 1853. She wrote at least two detailed accounts of this visit, both to unknown correspondents, and inserted part of one in the *Life*, where she found

> Copying this letter has brought the days of that pleasant visit very clear before me, – very sad in their clearness. We were so happy together . . . I understood her life the better for seeing the place where it had been spent – where she had loved and suffered (p. 508).

The sense of place is essential in the vividness of the biography, from the careful evocation at the beginning with its progress from Leeds by Keighley to Haworth until we face that terrible memorial stone which ends the first chapter, to the gathering of the mourners at the book's conclusion. The visit went well, despite the recent dismissal of Nicholls and Mr Brontë's edginess (he had backed up his daughter's invitation by a note cordial enough in its stiff formality).[14] But there were ghosts in the house for Gaskell – Charlotte showed her Branwell's crude portrait of the sisters (249) and Martha Brown was persuaded to show the graves and the church without the knowledge of the family (246). And though they both stayed up at night, talking, after the household had retired at nine, Gaskell found that Charlotte would come down again, after they had both said good-night, 'and begin that slow monotonous incessant walk in which I am sure I should fancy I heard the steps of the dead following me. She says she could not sleep without it' (247). Though the version of the visit in the *Life* is briefer, Gaskell must have recalled as she copies out her own words the picture she gave of the three sisters when they had just begun writing for the public, 'putting away their work at nine o'clock, and beginning their steady pacing up and down the sitting room. At this time, they talked over the stories they were engaged upon, and discussed their plots' (p. 307).[15] Then they were three and had been creating; now, in 1853, Charlotte was alone, fruitless in work and in love; and as Gaskell copied she knew there was no more work to come. There was a fragment of a tale, *Emma* (eventually published in the *Cornhill Magazine*, 1860), but nothing was written or even attempted once she was married.

The stay was a great success, 'monotonous even in sound, but not a bit in reality' (246). What she saw and heard did not alter first basic impressions. Then the last Manchester visit and virtual silence. Nicholls's insistence upon reading his wife's correspondence curbed her spontaneity, and he disapproved of people whose religious beliefs were different from his own. In October 1854 Gaskell wrote, knowing Nicholls would see the letter, setting out her religious opinions, perhaps with some hope of conciliating him (346), and she heard through a mutual friend in December that Charlotte was well and happy (336). The next news was of Charlotte's death on 31 March 1855, conveyed to her by John Greenwood, from the village, who had supplied the Brontës with the writing paper they used to his mystification in such vast quantities. Shocked by the news, Gaskell wrote,

> You may well say you have lost your best friend; strangers
> might know her by her great fame, but we loved her dearly
> for her goodness, truth, and kindness, & those lovely qualities
> she carried with her where she is gone' (336).

And in a perhaps unguarded moment, she wrote to George Smith, Charlotte's publisher,

> I had never heard of her being ill; or I would have gone to
> her at once; she would have disliked my doing so, as I am
> fully aware, but I think I could have overcome that, and
> perhaps saved her life (346).

To be a little hyperbolical, Gaskell was entering her claim on
Charlotte and in eventually writing her life she was, in a sense,
seeking to save it, from oblivion if not from the grave.

II

Charlotte Brontë was dead. Since she died famous, rather than in the
obscurity of her sisters, her passing was noticed by many and
curiosity grew apace about a life seemingly insignificant, yet which
must surely have been eventful to produce three such novels. Gaskell
could not forget her friend, as correspondence with John Greenwood
and Charlotte's publisher, George Smith, shows, yet she was startled
by a letter from Patrick Brontë, dated 16 June 1855. Brontë asked
that Gaskell should write the life of his daughter:

> Finding that a great many scribblers, as well as some clever
> and truthful writers, have published articles in newspapers and
> tracts respecting my dear daughter Charlotte since her death,
> and seeing that many things that have been stated are untrue,
> but more false; and having reason to think that some may
> venture to write her life who will be ill-qualified for the
> undertaking, I can see no better plan under the circumstances
> than to apply to some established author to write a brief
> account of her life and to make some remarks on her works.
> You seem to me to be the best qualified for doing what I
> wish should be done.[16]

The request was all the more startling to Gaskell, who had been
overawed by the old man at Haworth, where, despite his coming in
to tea – 'an honour to me I believe' – and his 'paying rather elaborate
old-fashioned compliments', she felt 'sadly afraid of him in my
inmost soul; for I caught a glare of his stern eyes over his spectacles at
Miss Brontë once or twice which made me know my man' (245).
Despite this, Gaskell was to find a rapport with this old man, stoical
in his grief, which failed to develop in the face of Nicholls's attitudes.

Brontë was right about the notices of his daughter. An excellent
one (not correct in every detail) published by Harriet Martineau in

the *Daily News* (April 1855) ended on a sustained note of eulogy, noble from a woman who had quarrelled with Charlotte over the obsession with love she found in the novels:

> Others now mourn her, in a domestic sense; and, as for the
> public, there can be no doubt that a pang will be felt in the
> midst of the stronger interests of the day ... that the 'Currer
> Bell,' who so lately stole a shadow into the field of
> contemporary literature had already become a shadow again –
> vanishing from our view, and henceforth haunting only the
> memory of the multitude whose expectation was fixed upon her.[17]

Gaskell herself was aware of errors in this account. More disturbing to the Brontë circle were accounts like that of the *Belfast Mercury* (April 1855), which claimed not only that the family came from County Down but that the name was originally Prunty (it *had* been Brunty).[18]

It was not Patrick Brontë or Nicholls, though, who was roused initially to commission Gaskell to correct misapprehensions. They seem to have read the various reports and remained silent. It was Ellen Nussey, Charlotte's schoolfriend and life-long correspondent, who flamed out over an article in *Sharpe's London Magazine* entitled 'A Few Words about "Jane Eyre" ',[19] and demanded, writing to Nicholls of the pain it gave her, whether its readers would be left 'to imbibe a tissue of malignant falsehoods' or whether an attempt would be made for justice 'to one who so highly deserved justice'? The rhetoric might have appealed to Gaskell and it was on her that Nussey's choice fell: 'I wish Mrs Gaskell, who is every way capable, would undertake a reply'.[20] Nicholls saw no such need and reported that Brontë had laughed at the article. Still, only five days later, Brontë wrote his request, Gaskell noting in her letter informing George Smith of her acceptance of the task that she would have to omit much about Charlotte's home and circumstances, 'which must have had so much to do in forming her character', since they could be 'merely indicated' in the lifetime of her father and husband (349). For if the request came as a surprise, the idea of a memoir written by herself was not a new one. In writing to John Greenwood she had asked for information about the new study made by Charlotte for her husband's use, and when it was Greenwood first knew 'Currer Bell' (343). To George Smith in early June, a fortnight before she received Brontë's letter, she wrote that she was preparing a memoir for herself and her family, disturbed by the speed with which details of names and dates were fading. She hoped to do this 'in our country-leisure this summer', for though neither Brontë nor Nicholls would like it, still,

> my children, who loved her would like to have what I could write about her; and the time may come when her wild sad life, and the beautiful character that grew out of it may be made public (347-8).

Her surprise was therefore the greater when the man she *knew* would not want the memoir made public asked her to do just that, but her response was never in doubt. 'I am very anxious to perform this grave duty laid upon me well and fully' and she asked Smith for all the information he could give her – and he was to comply through-out the collaboration that followed, for despite Gaskell's control and final responsibility *The Life of Charlotte Brontë*, like any other good biography, is a collective effort of friends, acquaintances, and even of the subject herself.

Gaskell had one model for a possible memoir in Charlotte's 'Biographical Notice of Ellis and Acton Bell' (Emily and Anne) prefixed to the Literary Remains edition (1850), a brief sketch of about two thousand words, but any possibility of producing some-thing short enough to preface the reprinting of one of Charlotte's works was abandoned as the amount of possible material became clear. The chance of it coming out with the as yet unpublished *The Professor*, Charlotte's first novel, considerably shorter than her other work, seemed not worth canvassing further (if it had been suggested, even), since Nicholls had not even allowed Gaskell to see the manuscript.[21] She felt, though, that she already had enough material 'to make a vol: about the size of Carlyle's Life of Sterling'. Carlyle's work (1851) is not so very short, running to about 90,000 words; the life of a friend essentially obscure in worldly terms, it may have contributed in its intentions to Gaskell's own commemoration:

> Like other such lives, like all lives, this is a tragedy; high hopes, noble efforts; under thickening difficulties and impediments, ever-new nobleness of valiant effort; – and the result death ... 'Why write the Life of Sterling?' I imagine I had a commission higher than the world's, the dictate of Nature herself, to do what is now done.[22]

Gaskell's task was still to do, and her work proved about twice the length of Carlyle's, for as she began to collect material, so she found more and more. In the same letter to Smith quoted above, when thanking him for loan of Charlotte's letters to him, she announces that she has 'a series of 350 to one friend, the earliest written in 1832, & continued up to a few days before her death' (372). This was the correspondence with Ellen Nussey, initiator of the *Life,* whose character, colouring as it did Charlotte's tone in letters to her, was to impress itself upon the finished work.

Collection of material began in the obvious place, at Haworth, from Brontë and Nicholls. Accompanied by Catherine Winkworth, Gaskell went there on 23 July 1855, finding it 'a most painful visit. Both Mr Brontë and Mr Nicholls cried sadly' (364), yet Nicholls, who was aware of the dangers as well as the need to have a full and authorized history 'if it were done at all', supplied her with materials, all 'he could furnish me with' (361). On this, their first meeting, she felt she liked Nicholls, and had been amused by Brontë's parting words, 'No quailing Mrs Gaskell! no drawing back!' (364, 361). If her initial feeling about Nicholls was not to be confirmed, in fairness one should say, perhaps, that Nicholls had by marrying Charlotte been brought to share her fame willy-nilly and had yielded to Brontë's insistence over the biography.[23] None the less, having agreed in principle, Nicholls proceeded to raise various obstacles and was later to be almost pathological in attempts to deal with those who threatened to make a claim upon his wife.[24]

If Nicholls presented Gaskell with many problems, not least because she was a 'dissenter', Brontë won her affection.[25] A second visit to Haworth, in July 1856, with the work reasonably advanced, showed how far Nicholls had reservations about the project. Fortunately, she went with Sir James Kay-Shuttleworth, who, if not the most tactful of men, at least was 'not prevented by fear of giving pain from asking in a peremptory manner for whatever he thinks desirable'. As a result Gaskell was able to take away for examination *The Professor,* the fragment called *Emma,* and most extraordinary of all, as she recognized, 'a packet about the size of a lady's travelling writing case, full of paper books of different sizes, from the one I enclose upwards to the full ½ sheet size, but all in this indescribably fine writing'. These were the childhood writings of the Brontë's, the 'little writings', so important for an understanding of their literary development, as Fanny E. Ratchford has brilliantly shown in *The*

137

Brontës' Web of Childhood (1941). She thought of a photograph 'to give some idea of the fineness of the writing, – for no words of mine could explain it'; in the event a lithograph was prepared and printed in volume one.[26] What impressed Gaskell about these writings was their wildness and incoherence, reminding her of some manuscripts by Blake (possibly she means his engraved books) that Richard Monckton Milnes had given her to read: each gave 'the idea of creative power carried to the verge of insanity'. She had these precious things in her possession, however briefly, and all because Sir James 'coolly took actual possession of them while Mr Nicholls was saying he could not possibly part with them' (398-9). So we owe to the officious Sir James one debt of gratitude at least, for the *Life* would be poorer without the knowledge he helped provide: the manuscripts gave new lights into Charlotte's literary career and the comparison with Blake, though not to be taken far, does suggest kinship in private worlds of the imagination.[27]

Various information came from Patrick Brontë, though Gaskell found that he dressed up facts she asked for on *Jane Eyre*'s first appearance 'in such clouds of vague writing, that it is of no use to apply to him' (424). As she wrote, she had to keep an eye open for Nicholls's sensibilities. He vexed her by refusing to have Charlotte's portrait by Richmond copied (to gain this point was another of Sir James's achievements: the portrait provided the frontispiece) and he objected to letters (copyright was invested in him) being printed at all. To Gaskell these were of the work's essence, since Charlotte's 'language, where it can be used, is so powerful & living, that it would be a shame not to express everything that can be, in her own words' (405). Gaskell meant to use the form of the 'Life and Letters', established by William Mason when he prefixed his Memoirs of Thomas Gray to the 1775 edition of the Poems, so that 'Mr. Gray will become his own biographer' (p. 5). The model, followed and established by Boswell's *Life of Johnson* (1791), allows the subject to bear witness and reveal herself through words which spring from her own personality. Again, the possessiveness of the men of Haworth asserted itself when both Brontë and Nicholls imposed a ban on anyone apart from Smith, as publisher, and William Gaskell seeing the manuscript before publication, though Gaskell felt that Ellen Nussey, as a major contributor, was entitled to do so. In slightly Jesuitical vein, Gaskell finally decided that Ellen would have to come to Manchester and have the manuscript read to her. Amidst the strain imposed by these tender personalities, the work went forward.

Gaskell rapidly began to reconstitute the Brontë circle. As soon as she determined to undertake her friend's memorial, she started to contact people who might give information and provide letters or other help. She learnt rapidly, followed up every clue, corrected her errors as she went, and impressed her family as helpers. William Gaskell overlooked the manuscript, to check spelling and make stylistic changes, while Meta and Marianne conducted correspondence when their mother was overwhelmed and copied Charlotte's letters into the manuscript, which Gaskell at leisure went over, erasing what would not do for public eyes. One of her first contacts, naturally, was with Ellen Nussey, friend from Roe Head schooldays, where in January 1831 Ellen, herself a late arrival, had first found the lonely Charlotte, 'a silent, weeping, dark little figure' in the deserted schoolroom, and Ellen's offer of comfort had led to reciprocal affection as Ellen too began to cry: a 'faint quavering smile then lighted her face ... we silently took each other's hands, and at once we felt that genuine sympathy which always consoles'.[28] Charlotte's first letter to Ellen is dated 11 May 1831 and the last was from her deathbed in February or March 1855. About four hundred letters survive, remarkable in their range and the closeness of friendship they show, remarkable therefore in the detail Charlotte was prepared to reveal. Because of this range and their vividness, Gaskell drew on them extensively. In giving pride of place to these letters, the tone of the biography was radically coloured by them. Gaskell herself noticed after reading another series, to W. S. Williams, that 'it is curious how much the spirit in which she wrote varies according to the correspondent whom she was addressing' (375). Ellen was necessary to Charlotte, as someone reliable, affectionate, undemanding, but she was also pietistic in a way that did not jump with some of Charlotte's religious feelings and she was limited intellectually. Charlotte summed up Ellen to George Smith: 'We were contrasts – still, we suited ... She is without romance ... but she is good; she is true; she is faithful, and I love her'.[29] Allowance must equally be made for the tone Charlotte used to Smith, yet in her letters to Ellen she herself emerges at times as no more than the 'conscientious, observant, calm, well-bred Yorkshire girl' she called Ellen in that same letter. Fortunately, Gaskell recognized this and had other series to draw on. Parts of Charlotte's life were silent to Ellen – she was told nothing, whatever she may have suspected, about the writing and publication either of the *Poems* or of the sisters' novels. Later in life, Ellen grew querulous, inclined to maintain that she, in effect, had co-written the *Life*.[30] A sad figure in old age, she yet got on well with Gaskell, co-operated largely with information, and wrote an account of Anne Brontë's last days, where, accompanying the sisters to Scarborough, she had indeed been good, true and faithful.

In handling these letters, Gaskell mined them for their ore. She omitted more personal as well as merely trivial details and at Ellen's request reduced her to the initial E, though Gaskell felt this was 'so like a mathematical proposition' (396). Ellen's insistence meant Gaskell crossing out the full name in the manuscript or making sure it was altered in proof, until she caught up, though she could still forget, and at one point 'my dear Nell' slipped into the text.[31] Since she could not mark the letters and since some (not all) of the copying was done by her daughters, Gaskell often found it easiest to cut a letter after it was in her manuscript. She was also prepared to touch up Ellen's own contribution. The affecting account of Anne's journey to Scarborough and death there in Spring 1849 is told in Ellen's own words, yet Gaskell boldly cut out overemphases and the more sentimental phrases – Ellen called Anne throughout 'our dear invalid', an irritating repetition that Gaskell removed, and though the total changes in the passage are slight, they all work to make Anne's death movingly simple.

From amongst others who had found letters worth preserving, Gaskell received a good number from Miss Wooler, Charlotte's teacher and then employer at Roe Head school, and then an important collection from William Smith Williams, George Smith's agent, who had first read *Jane Eyre* and recognized its merits. Williams, a middle-aged man, felt he had never achieved the success he might have had. Charlotte tried to show in their epistolary friendship why he should accept his lot; the correspondence is often lively, intellectual in tone, touching on books and politics, and suggests the wider range of Charlotte's interests. The letters to Miss Wooler are narrower, yet each series, by calling forth another side, allows us to see that much more of Charlotte. With Ellen, these two provided Gaskell with the bulk of letters she used and to each she expressed the pleasure in reading what they sent, tracing out to Ellen the character she found of someone used 'to study the path of duty well, and, having ascertained what it was right to do, to follow out her ideas strictly' (370).

People were pursued indefatigably. Gaskell found the other great schoolfriend, Mary Taylor. Mary, a lively and outspoken person, had 'said she did not see why she was to be debarred from entering into trade because she was a woman' (359) and had emigrated to New Zealand. Unfortunately, though she could contribute her recollections, she had destroyed all Charlotte's ltters, save one. That one, though, is amongst the best, the account of the visit by Charlotte and Anne in July 1848 to George Smith's Cornhill office. Compression by Gaskell and the availability, until recently, only of a badly corrupt printed text, have concealed the full humour in the original.[32] When she sent this letter to Gaskell in January 1856, Mary also provided much information of her own as well as an interpretation of Charlotte's life. A quirk of irony has preserved the envelope, its date-stamps showing the letter's progress from Wellington, while Mary's original letter has disappeared.[33] Gaskell found Mary's view close to her own; she quoted largely from Mary's letter (probably most of it is preserved to us in the *Life*) and Joan Stevens has pointed out how Mary's words are a major element in Gaskell's finale.[34] The manuscript provides some evidence of how deliberately this effect was produced. When Mary was about to emigrate, Charlotte visited her, in wretched health aggravated by her love for Heger (though Gaskell discreetly made the cause Branwell's degeneration). Mary urged her to leave home, arguing, in her own words,

> that to spend the next five years at home, in solitude and
> weak health, would ruin her; that she would never recover it.
> Such a dark shadow came over her face when I said, 'Think of
> what you'll be five years hence!' that I stopped, and said
> 'Don't cry, Charlotte!' She did not cry, but went on walking
> up and down the room, and said in a little while, 'But I
> intend to stay, Polly' (p. 275).

In the printed version, the extract ends here, but the manuscript continues, without a break, to give Mary's view of this action:

> She thought much of her duty, and had loftier and clearer
> notions of it than most people, and held fast to them with
> more success. It was done, it seems to me, with much more
> difficulty than people have of stronger nerves, and better
> fortunes. All her life was but labour and pain, and she never
> threw down the burden for the sake of present pleasure.[35]

This passage is not deleted in the manuscript, but it was transferred to the very end of the printed text, where it stands as a keystone completing the arch of personality that Gaskell has striven to raise, the locking-piece in holding true the personality of Charlotte developed in the memoir. Mary's theme of duty sustained in the midst of labour and pain, in the face of a world which had judged and failed to understand her, was Gaskell's, who had now brought her friend to judgment again, but this time before those who 'know how to look with tender humility at faults and errors; how to admire generously extraordinary genius, and how to reverence with warm, full hearts all noble virtue' (p. 526). Reading Mary's letter, Gaskell found no new insight, rather a confirmation, but she seized on it as one more witness to the justice she tried for.

III

By the end of 1855 Gaskell felt she had enough material to begin writing, though her investigations had by no means ended, and every step in writing threw up fresh problems and fresh trails to follow, where despite the time involved she found she could 'do so much more by *seeing* people than by writing' (876). In April 1856 she began to chase up the Wheelwright sisters, who had been in Brussels during Charlotte's residence, and she called on them in London before leaving for Belgium in May. She wrote to Jemima Quillinan, daughter of Wordsworth's son-in-law, about the poet's advice to Branwell,[36] and tracked down the correspondence between Charlotte and G. M. Lewes, with George Smith as intermediary, the hunt showing typically how she traced a scent:

> The letter to the Editor of the Edinburgh Review *was* written
> & sent. Mr Empson showed it to Mr W. R. Greg . . . who
> told me 'it was a *pungent* note'. Since I have been engaged in
> writing this Memoir I asked Mr Greg to ask Mrs Empson to
> look through Mr Empson's papers for this letter. She did so, &
> it was not to be found, & we all consequently conjectured that
> it had been sent to Mr Lewes (414; see 405, 412, 418).

The letter to the editor did not turn up, but Lewes sent several, including Charlotte's flash response to his review of *Shirley* (p. 397). Information was obtained from anyone who might help and each enquiry took up time. From an unknown correspondent she wanted to 'know all I can respecting the character of the population she lived amongst' and, after specific requests, asked if he knew of any publications on local customs – she already had the life of Mr Grimshaw, an eighteenth-century Haworth incumbent (369). In September 1855 she met by chance Dr Scoresby, Vicar of Bradford (later to help on Whitby background for *Sylvia's Lovers*), who had known Patrick Brontë and 'told me many curious anecdotes about the extraordinary character of the people round Haworth' (872). And in a letter challenging Ellen Nussey as model for Caroline Helstone in *Shirley*, she added, 'Any chance of borrowing Scatcherd's History of Birstall &c?' (875). Scatcherd, Newton's *Life of Grimshaw*, and Hunter's *Life of Oliver Heywood*, amongst others, were all laid under contribution for evocation of Haworth life in chapter 2, along with others' information and her own recollections. The little adventure of the villagers' indifference to the lad who cut himself open in the rubbish-cluttered stream, 'which happened to my husband and myself', was so much the property of William Gaskell that a gap was left in the manuscript for him to write it out, the space provided being more than enough in his neat script.[37]

The places Charlotte knew were assiduously visited. Haworth she already had seen and saw again, but now Gaskell went to Cowan Bridge ('Cowan's Bridge' throughout the first edition), original site of the Clergy Daughters' School, the Lowood of *Jane Eyre*, to Roe Head of happier schooldays under Miss Wooler, to Brussels to see the Hegers (only M. Heger, in the event), even to the Chapter Coffee House, where Charlotte and Anne stayed during their 1848 expedition as the only place they knew of in London. By early July 1856, Gaskell had gone to every place where Charlotte had lived. The need to complete her materials led then to her second visit to the men of Haworth, though she feared the encounter (394); in the event Sir James Kay-Shuttleworth was to smooth that path – or at any rate ride over it rough-shod.

Gaskell seems to have expected a more rapid completion of her task than proved the case. She admitted to Ellen Nussey in December 1855 that she had not yet written a line, all time to spare being spent in writing for information, though she had thought to be a quarter finished by New Year (876). None the less, she soon plunged in. By 22 February 1856 about twenty pages had been written (878), about midway in chapter 2, describing 'the peculiar forms of population and society' around Haworth. As she wrote, she sent sections to

George Smith for comments, anxious about how others would react to a work in which she was so emotionally involved. In April she was heartened by a note from him, being, she stressed, 'very anxious to do it thoroughly *well*', not minding how much she laboured at it, 'only I am vexed to find on reading it over, that my English is so bad' (387). The manuscript shows frequent corrections, both grammatical and stylistic. Repetition of words within an uncomfortably short space, a common feature of hasty writing, is dealt with as are grammatical features, particularly Gaskell's use of 'which' rather than 'that', altered presumably by William Gaskell. The word 'very', a sign of weakness in the desire to stress things, is frequently deleted. The first paragraph of chapter 2 shows a typical example of correction and resulting elevation of style. The text reads: 'I shall endeavour, therefore, before proceeding further with my work, to present some idea of the character of the people of Haworth'. Originally Gaskell wrote: 'Accordingly I shall try to present some idea' (MS f.10), and a second hand (William Gaskell's, I take it) going over the simple statement has produced the end result. This process is sporadic and produces only minor changes, few as definite even as this, many removing clumsiness or too idiomatic a phrasing. The results largely are a gain in greater smoothness and (often) tautness.

Even as she wrote, so Gaskell kept up her correspondence, and it is often possible, reading her letters, to see the point she has reached in composition by the questions she asks. Often she was forced to go back or (in one case at least) to leave a gap until she obtained fuller information. In July 1856, with neither Marianne nor Meta at home to help and with between thirty and forty notes to write, she asks Ellen whether Emily went with Charlotte to Roe Head; why Branwell didn't go to the Royal Academy school; whether Emily went out as governess – all questions indicating she was somewhere about chapter 8, though Emily's going to Roe Head mentioned in the first paragraph of the chapter is not in the manuscript (MS f.137B) because Ellen could not supply the detail. Only in January 1857, having found the reference in Charlotte's biographical memoir of Emily and Anne, could she send the information for insertion, when the work was already printing. Gaskell seized what time she could, writing twenty pages the day before, as she told Ellen in that same letter of enquiry, 'because it rained perpetually, and I was uninterrupted' (393–4, 439). In summer 1856 her writing day stretched from breakfast to five o'clock, with a short lunch break, though in mid-August she wrote only until lunch and a little later not at all, until she took up the task again at the end of the first week in September (403, 411, 408). She paid for the effort, 'head & health suffering', and towards the end of September she gave over entirely for a time, having 'had a long fainting-fit one day ('quite promiscuous' as servants say)' and consequently forbidden work by her doctor (415).

None the less, her progress was remarkable. On 19 August 1856 she reckoned she was about half-way through (an overestimate, in the event) and fancied the rest would not take long, so much would consist of letters. Two hundred and forty pages were ready, bringing her to the Brussels period of 1842, and three days later (confirmation of this stage) she was writing to Laetitia Wheelwright for details of her Belgian schooldays (404, 405). A constant problem was working in new material. The second visit to Haworth in July 1856 and consequent examination of the 'little writings' meant rewriting about forty pages; indeed chapter 5, once Tabby, the faithful servant, is dealt with, stands conspicuously by itself, though the extant manuscript shows no sign of this radical reconstruction. Minor details were easily corrected – Mrs Jenkins at Brussels becomes the wife of the British Chaplain, not of the British Consul (MS f.215). Occasionally Gaskell became aware that an anecdote would be more effective if placed elsewhere; this meant tedious search through the manuscript, recopying and deletion. The account of Tabby (Tabitha Aykroyd) had appeared from the first near the beginning of chapter 5 (pp. 110-11). A later reference to her in a letter of 1833 prompted additional information including her averring that when woolspinning was done by hand in the farmhouses, 'there were fairies to be seen every moonlit night in the hollows',[38] presumably taken from notes Gaskell had by her, for part of it was already written out. Evidently the point struck her, for she turned back and transferred from 1833 those details not already in the earlier portrait, which was thus strengthened by Tabby being presented all at once. She became a presence from early on and the account under 1833 was deleted.[39]

One unfortunate result of necessary haste was that Gaskell could not read anything like all the 'little writings' (a vast quantity by any reckoning) and so missed, for instance, the Roe Head diary fragments of 1835-37, including the strange tale ending with a prosaic return to the schoolroom, for while 'this apparition was before me the dining-room door opened and Miss W[ooler] came in with a plate of butter ... "A very stormy night, my dear," said she'.[40] Still, another hundred and twenty pages had been written before illness and necessary home duties slowed her down in autumn (411) and, despite the fainting, by 2 October she had upwards of three hundred pages, and was just ending 1845 – the end of volume one was in sight and Gaskell now claimed to be half-way through and that the whole would be ready by February (882, 413, 417-8). In December, she had reached publication of *Jane Eyre* and plied Smith and Ellen Nussey with questions, but rather than impede the narrative flow, Gaskell left a space, in chapter 16, with a note that material was 'to come in here about Jane Eyre as soon as I have heard from Mr Smith' (MS f.347), thirteen sheets eventually being inserted for the account of the novel's progress from publisher's reading to public reception.

By December, completion date seemed to be January, and since she hoped still for February publication and to be away in Italy when reviews came out, she asked whether printing could begin. Early in January Gaskell wrote that she still had two hundred pages to go and that 'they begin to print to-morrow' (426, 434). There were problems: Smith waiting for new type; no capital Es with a diaresis for 'BRONTË' in the headlines – they should have 'a ë as soon as they can', the back of a manuscript page notes (MS f.21v); proofs were tardy. Gaskell was writing and correcting manuscript and proofs throughout January, helped by her husband, their haste allowing in many of the discrepancies between manuscript and printed text, particularly in spelling and lay-out of quotations and in details like quotation marks – in common with many authors, the Gaskells seem to have corrected proofs by the test of the print making sense, without further reference to the manuscript.

Gaskell's speed as she neared the end is astonishing, even allowing for greater preponderance of Charlotte's letters. On 7 January 1857 a remark to Smith implies she still has another one hundred and twenty pages of manuscript to complete (437), yet exactly a month later she could announce to Laetitia Wheelwright that 'I have today finished my Life of Miss Brontë; and next week we set out for Rome' (443). Not only was the *Life* completed and sent to Smith by 10 February, but Gaskell confidently expected to have finished the proofs by her departure (437, 443-4). So the task seemed completed and she set out for Italy, for 'the delicious quiet & dolce far niente'

(450), a quiet and indolence rudely destroyed on her return at the end of May.

IV

A biography can expect to be examined closely by all those who feel they have some claim on the subject. Gaskell thought a rough passage likely enough for the *Life* on its first appearance and, unlike Charlotte, she was no avid reader of reviews, good and bad alike. Things might be easier if she came to them after an interval, whatever heat was produced on publication. Before she left for Italy she quoted to George Smith a comment of Mary Taylor's: 'Does Mrs Gaskell know "what a nest of hornets she is pulling about her ears?" ' (446).[41] On her return she found over a hundred letters waiting for her, some, like Charles Kingsley's, praising 'the picture of a valiant woman made perfect by sufferings',[42] others critical or abusive. Even Patrick Brontë, who had expressed delight at the completion of a work he would himself have taken up if no one else had been found, now fastened on the statement that he had obliged his daughters to live chiefly on a vegetable diet (his extraordinary behaviour with household furniture and his wife's dress, stories now generally discredited, never seemed to worry him) and even the Haworth servants objected to the information, apropos of the supposed lack of meat, that it 'was from no wish ffor saving, for there was plenty and even waste in the house, with young servants and no mistress to see after them' (p. 87). Brontë eventually provided Nancy and Sarah Garrs with a signed testimonial that they were 'not wasteful, but sufficiently careful in regard to food'[43] and the whole passage was afterwards omitted.

But these were comparatively minor matters, to be dealt with amicably in printing a third edition (the second – properly only a reprint – had appeared during Gaskell's absence). Worse was the threat of two legal actions, for which Gaskell must herself take a good deal of the blame, though one may wonder that Smith did not exercise more care or assert his right as publisher. Gaskell had relished the prospect of letting herself go on three matters. 'Do you mind the law of libel', she had written to Smith. 'I have three people I want to libel – Lady Scott (that bad woman who corrupted Branwell Brontë) Mr Newby, & Lady Eastlake' (418). Newby, publisher of Emily's and Anne's novels, had behaved very shabbily, precipitating the Cornhill visit of Charlotte and Anne by claiming that all the novels were Currer Bell's, the author of *Jane Eyre*. The case was clearest against him, yet Smith stood firm against his 'gibbeting', and all references to his name, along with many to his activities, were deleted in manuscript.[44] As Miss Rigby, Lady Eastlake had written that *Quarterly Review* article attacking not only *Jane Eyre* but also the moral character of Charlotte. In dealing with the review, we may feel Gaskell has allowed *her* feelings to lead her into unworthy insults. She dismisses the attack on *Jane Eyre* as flippant, but after calling the attack on the author 'cowardly insolence' she rises embarrassingly through a series of rhetorical questions that culminate in Charlotte as Christ in agony (p. 360). Happily Lady Eastlake seemed content to let the matter rest and no change was needed here for the third edition.

Lady Scott was not so content. During her first marriage, as Mrs Robinson, Branwell, employed in the family as tutor, had been led to think she had some tenderness for him. After her husband's death, her lack of interest was made quite clear and Gaskell felt Branwell's destruction was in part her responsibility (p. 281). Lady Scott threatened an action and she was offered a full retraction of 'every statement . . . which imputes to a widowed lady, referred to, but not named therein, any breach of her conjugal, or of her maternal, or of her social duties'.[45] In rewriting, Gaskell removes all references to the woman and to Branwell's 'agony of guilty love', so that in chapter 13 we move from Branwell's dismissal, on unspecified grounds, to the suffering 'which his conduct entailed upon his poor father and his innocent sisters' (p. 554). The account of Branwell's death was truncated, the absurd assertion that he died standing retained, the narrative passing on immediately to Emily's condition (pp. 353-4).

Lady Scott was comparatively easy to deal with. She was a single protestor and came to terms once satisfaction was offered. More formidable were the supporters of the late Rev. Carus Wilson, founder and 'overseer' of the Clergy Daughters' school, model for Mr Brocklehurst in *Jane Eyre*. Gaskell believed that conditions at the school killed Charlotte's elder sisters, Elizabeth and Maria, and had permanently stunted Charlotte's growth. Gaskell's account contained inconsistencies that her critics eagerly seized on: she talked of bad diet at Cowan Bridge, yet stressed lack of meat at Haworth; said bad conditions produced ill-health, yet Maria and Elizabeth arrived at school barely recovered from 'a complication of measles and hooping-cough'. Opposition lodged mainly on these points, together with the claim that Carus Wilson was grossly misrepresented. Though convinced that what she had written was basically the truth and though she received letters of support against the Wilsonites, Gaskell felt there was little she could do except rewrite, and in rewriting, some of the weaknesses in her own argument disappear: lack of meat is now omitted, the character of Patrick Brontë (at Nicholls's insistence) becomes less 'peculiar', and while she adds that Charlotte only once spoke of Cowan Bridge herself, enforces her general point by reporting Charlotte's insistence 'that the food itself was spoilt by the dirty carelessness of the cook' (p. 532).[46] What was originally stated as fact is either corrected, omitted, or given as what she accepted in good faith, but might be otherwise: Wilson ceases to be 'wealthy', his willingness 'to sacrifice everything but power' goes, and errors 'which he certainly committed' become errors 'which he was believed to have committed'. It was not so much a retreat as a strategic withdrawal and regrouping.

Already before publication Gaskell had trouble with people's touchiness: Smith had been chary of too much emphasis on his relationship with Charlotte, and the presentation of Thackeray had demanded certain reticences. She had had to exercise caution in expressing opinions, whether of Emily's behaviour during her last illness ('the very essence of stern selfishness') or of Charlotte's religious feelings.[47] Writing about Patrick Brontë and Branwell had been a constant problem, and Nicholls a perpetual worry. To find all her care and anxiety so ill-repaid was painful, yet her sense of responsibility to Smith made her express readiness 'to do anything you may wish towards preparing the 3rd edition for the Press' (449). To Ellen Nussey she wrote, more openly, 'as if I were in famous spirits, and I think I *am* so *angry* that I am almost merry in my bitterness'. She had cried 'more since I came home [than] I ever did in the same space of time before', wearily asserting, '*I did so try* to *tell the truth*, & I believe *now* I hit as near the truth as any one *could* do' (454). With advice from William Shaen, acting as her lawyer, and with extra information about Haworth customs, she began 'my weary & oppressive task' (461). Work went on through August, the new edition being ready at the beginning of September. Revisions were sent on sheets of paper with instructions to the printers, the sheets where necessary being cut up into strips for easier setting-up. Printing began as soon as possible and her letters have last-minute

149

instructions, like omission of apostrophes after 'Cowan' (464). In September 1857, Gaskell had finished her duty and *The Life of Charlotte Brontë* has established itself since as one of the great literary biographies. The alterations between editions have been exaggerated. Mary Taylor, always outspoken, declared that 'libellous or not, the first edition was all true', though she talked oddly of Gaskell's 'needful drawing back'. She called the new edition 'mutilated',[48] yet she is hardly an informed witness. In setting certain details straight, in moderating her tone over Wilson and Scott, in adding extra information, Gaskell was improving her work, and to regard the third edition as 'mutilated' or 'expurgated'[49] is misleading. Gaskell herself felt that her first version was essentially correct; the revised edition does not radically alter the account. In half-humorous vein she wrote that 'for the future I intend to confine myself to lies (i.e. fiction)' and more bitterly perhaps she offered Smith a preface sent to her: 'If anybody is displeased with any statement or words in the following pages I beg leave to with-draw it, and to express my deep regret for having offered so expensive an article as truth to the Public' (455). There is truth in tone, though, as well as in fact and the truth of the third edition is often more persuasive than the truth of the first.

V

Gaskell wished above all to do justice to Charlotte Brontë, to tell the truth, so that others might come to know her as she was. The idea of 'right understanding' is stressed throughout, Charlotte having been condemned, by those who neither knew nor understood, as a coarse woman, obsessed by love, where Gaskell knew her to be devoted to duty and tried by suffering. The book develops from this need for understanding. On a loose sheet now bound with the manuscript, Gaskell copied out notes from her reading of two articles on biography in the *Quarterly Review* (1856, vol. xcviii) together with an extract from a letter of Anna Jameson's. They suggest how she saw from the first the need to reveal the real life beneath the often mundane or dreary surface of everyday existence. Jameson had written of the 'truth of that wonderful infinite life – in which there seems to have been so little of external fact or circumstance, and such a boundless sphere of feeling and intellect crammed into a silent existence',[50] while the *Quarterly Review* extracts stressed how

'Character manifests itself in little things, just as a sunbeam finds its way through a chink'. Gaskell sought the chinks through which light can fall and the real life emerge.

Near the beginning Gaskell writes that for 'a right understanding of the life of my dear friend ... it appears to me more necessary in her case than in most others' for the reader to have a proper idea of the people and society from whom her first impressions came' (p. 60). Even Patrick Brontë's eccentricities are not spared, 'because I hold the knowledge of them to be necessary for a right understanding of the life of his daughter' (p. 90). Anyone coming to the *Life* for detailed information of Charlotte's work, her theories of literature, her processes of composition, or critical discussion of her achievement, will be disappointed. There are passing references, necessarily, and something is suggested by incidentals like Charlotte's adverse view of Jane Austen – 'Can there be a great artist without poetry?' (p. 338). We learn that in writing she strove for the one set of words that was 'the truthful mirror of her thoughts' (p. 307) and that she sought for Truth and Nature, perhaps a deliberate echo of the strange childhood scene when from behind the mask she named 'The Book of Nature' as the second best in the world. But Gaskell always stresses the woman. Charlotte produced her fiction partly because, deprived of 'the multitude of small talks, plans, duties, pleasures', she was able 'to go through long and deep histories of feeling and imagination, for which others ... have rarely time' (p. 210). Yet what did she endure daily, while these voyages of the imagination were undertaken? If the idea of publishing the *Poems* was a new interest in 1845, home circumstances meant that for Charlotte it was an interest 'faint, indeed, and often lost sight of in the vivid pain and constant pressure of anxiety' respecting Branwell (p. 285); while the start of *Jane Eyre* shows the author as hero. This 'brave genius' began the novel in Manchester while tending her father after an operation for cataract, crushed though she was by the repeated rejection of *The Professor*. Charlotte's life is a triumph of the spirit, a triumph only fully realized in contrast to the deadening repetition of suffering and misfortune.

The literary greatness of Charlotte Brontë is taken for granted. It needs no justification or explanation; the life of the author does. Detail, often trivial in itself, is accumulated to show how 'it is necessary that the difficulties she had to encounter in her various phases of life, should be fairly and frankly made known, before the

151

force "of what was resisted" can be at all understood' (p. 186). This woman had been humiliated by the employer whose response to her child's 'I love 'ou, Miss Brontë', was the astonished 'Love the *governess,* my dear!' (p. 187) and the suffering demanded justice. Gaskell's view colours the work. She shows the gaiety of Charlotte's early life, yet tends to throw in a dark background. At Cowan Bridge, Charlotte is described as a 'bright, clever little child', though, Gaskell continues, 'I suspect that this year of 1825 was the last time it could ever be applied to her' (p. 108). Here as elsewhere the reader's response, controlled by the author's, as onlooker who knows the end, is important. Later, Gaskell extends the range of response by quoting a visitor to Haworth touched by sight of Charlotte, 'that little creature entombed in such a place, and moving about herself like a spirit, especially when you think that the slight still frame encloses a force of strong fiery life, which nothing has been able to freeze or extinguish' (p. 431). At the end Gaskell insists 'I cannot measure or judge of such a character as hers' (p. 526), yet through stimulating our emotional reaction she surely has led the reader to judgment.

Gaskell sought for this reaction above all through detail, concrete and vivid, the chinks through which the sun 'of that wonderful infinite life' might shine. Certain things were lost to her – tact forbade her using Thackeray's account of how *Jane Eyre* 'made me cry – to the astonishment of John, who came in with the coals' (MS f. 347/2), while Smith's modesty curtailed Charlotte's account of the Cornhill confrontation and of a later visit where Charlotte named 'with grateful obligation, and as circumstances of comfort to which she was not accustomed, the having a fire & candles in her bedroom'.[51] Authentic details are established as the book opens with a journey to Haworth, the reader moving away from an urban civilization to something older, more elemental – even as the houses of Keighley straggle on along the road, the moors come to dominate, 'grand, from the ideas of solitude and loneliness which they suggest' (p. 55) until we arrive at church, parsonage, and the graveyard 'terribly full of upright tombstones', a statement of death emphasized by the commemorative tablets in the church, so untimely filled by the Brontë family dead. Instead of a biography opening with a birth, Charlotte's death is recorded on that extra tablet, needed once Anne's death, even when recorded in letters small and cramped, had filled up the tablet on the right hand of the communion table. Haworth's society is then developed, its past in men like Grimshaw, friend of

Wesley, who rebuked a visiting preacher rash enough to say that a congregation would need little exhorting which had so pious a minister (p. 70), and its present in details that Gaskell is at pains to authenticate by her own presence – 'I remember Miss Brontë once telling me', 'Miss Brontë related to my husband', 'A good neighbour of the Brontës ... told me a characteristic little incident'. The personal relationship of Gaskell to her subject is never obscured, so that she can recall later the pleasure of one of Charlotte's visits to Manchester, make the point about Charlotte's affection for those who were part of her life, and bring the reader close to her subject: 'The weather was so intensely hot, and she herself so much fatigued ... that we did little but sit in-doors, with open windows, and talk. The only thing she made a point of exerting herself to procure was a present for Tabby' (pp. 450-1).

Charlotte begins to emerge from her background, along with her family. Their stark memorial, climax of the journey to Haworth, begins to expand into living figures. Maria Branwell, Charlotte's mother, is briefly sketched, with evidence from her letters, upon which Gaskell comments, with that play of humour so much the life of the biography, that without 'having anything of her daughter's rare talents, Mrs Brontë must have been, I imagine, that unusual creature, a well-balanced and consistent woman' (p. 83). The humour is as much directed against the readers' stereotypes as against women. Gaskell no more forgot the family servant, Tabby, than did Charlotte. She it is who peoples the landscape with talk of fairies and the folk who had seen them, before the mills came (p. 110), the roughness which overlies essential good nature linking her with men like Grimshaw, while her grumbles at factories enforce the spread of Keighley and the mills at the foot of Haworth itself. Unlike the characters of the children she tended, Emily, Anne, and Branwell, which are to be developed in relation to Charlotte's, Tabitha's is established with her first appearance, to be a fixed point, unchanging, though never forgotten, until her death shortly before Charlotte's own. Of Charlotte's siblings, Emily remains something of a mystery to Gaskell. She tries to be sympathetic, stresses her own lack of knowledge, and the extraordinary figure that does emerge corresponds in many ways to Charlotte's description of her as 'stronger than a man; simpler than a child'. If she could appear 'egotistical and exacting' (p. 231) and pained Charlotte and Anne by her refusal to seek help or comfort in her last days, yet the devotion she inspired is there in the dog Keeper and in Charlotte's desperate search on the day of Emily's death 'for a lingering spray of heather – just one spray, however withered – to take in to' her (p. 356). Branwell was another problem, but unlike Emily, he was so because Gaskell knew too much. He offers a contrast, the man who had all the advantages, upon whom all the family hopes were pinned, who made nothing of them, while Charlotte, struggling on, used the God-given gift within her. The wasted life is carefully plotted: planning for his future already offset by the good fellowship at 'arvills' and the Black Bull; the failure to get to London (that great Babylon, as Charlotte called it), despite its fascination; and his family's slow realization of the reality, pointed by author's hindsight, so that the Christmas pleasures of 1842 were augmented by Branwell's presence, 'for, till sad experience taught them better, they fell into the usual error of confounding strong passions with strong character' (p. 249). The climatic moment comes when Charlotte, after a visit to Ellen, stirred with memories of Brussels by meeting a Frenchman on the journey, arrives home to find Branwell returned, ill, dismissed and disgraced (p. 280). The scene is managed with a fine sense of the dramatic, reinforced by its truth.

This family group is drawn together for a moment by Branwell's dead talent in a personal recollection from Gaskell's Haworth visit of 1853, which yet poignantly separates Charlotte living from her dead sisters and dead brother. One evening, Charlotte brought out Branwell's portrait (now in the National Portrait Gallery, London) of the three sisters:

> not much better than sign-painting, as to manipulation: but
> the likenesses were, I should think, admirable. I could only
> judge of the fidelity with which the other two were depicted,
> from the striking resemblance which Charlotte, upholding the
> great frame of canvas, and consequently standing right behind
> it, bore to her own representation ... (p. 155).

Here, for a few minutes, the family is gathered, but only one is in the flesh and death is upon her. She stands, the survivor, yet for how long before she too passes the bourn represented by the pillar on the canvas that divides her from Emily and Anne?[52]

The contrast of life and death, of retrospect and anticipation, so intimately bound up with Gaskell's presence as narrator (the biography takes on something of the double time scheme of auto-biography as a result) is one leading theme as Charlotte emerges more and more. A series of contrasts is established, playing between what might have been and what was, between the joy of the past moment and the present sadness. An evening scene in the Haworth sitting-room occurs again and again. Here the sisters had worked and talked, before they

> put away their work, and began to pace the room backwards
> and forwards, up and down ... their figures glancing into the
> fire-light, and out into the shadows perpetually. At this time,
> they talked over past cares, and troubles ... And again, still
> later, this was the time for the last surviving sister to walk
> alone, from old accustomed habit, round and round the
> desolate room, thinking sadly upon the 'days that were no
> more' (p. 166).

They pace through the book, the living circle growing narrower, until Gaskell heard for herself at Haworth how Charlotte would 'come down and walk up and down the room for an hour or so' (p. 508).

Against this threat of annihilation, Charlotte emerges the more strongly, a Christian heroine, restrained, sacrificing, determined in her duty, so that 'no distaste, no suffering ever made her shrink from any course which she believed it to be her duty to engage in' (p. 211). Still the strength of her nature burst through the restraints of duty, for she is seen as titanic, her occupation 'not sufficient food for her great forces of intellect, and they cried out perpetually, "Give, give"' (p. 176). While not attempting a critical evaluation, Gaskell does show how the writer emerged: she was open to the importance of the childhood writings, 'of singular merit for a girl of thirteen or fourteen' (p. 114). The quality of Charlotte's mind is stressed, both in her power of creation in the 'little writings', 'sometimes to the very borders of apparent delirium' (p. 119), and in her early power of analysis. From innate genius and from pressure against circumstances came the artist.

The structure of one particular chapter may be taken as exemplifying Gaskell's skill. The years 1847 and 1848 were the great turning point for Charlotte; if they brought the deaths of Branwell and of Emily, they brought also publication of *Jane Eyre* and the comic revelation to George Smith of Currer Bell's identity. The materials offer full scope for contrast between personal suffering and public success. The chapter (ii, 2) opens and closes with the drear weather of a winter season, Charlotte ill at the beginning, Anne sinking rapidly at the end. The round of duties, parish visiting, the Sunday-schools, are attended to while Branwell declines and their father's health gives them concern in the 'silent stoicism of his endurance' (p. 313). The novels, *Agnes Grey* and *Wuthering Heights* accepted but publication delayed, *The Professor* still seeking a publisher, are there, but scarcely relevant to the primary pattern of their lives, though at intervals, we are reminded, ' "Jane Eyre" was making progress' (pp. 314-15). Yet while the Shadow hangs over the house, escape is possible into the glowing August air, on the moors 'the rich purple of the heather bloom calling out an harmonious contrast in the tawny golden light that, in the full heat of summer evenings, comes stealing everywhere through the dun atmosphere of the hollows' (p. 318). The expansiveness of the writing mirrors at this moment the relief of the friend's visit and the unshadowed world of nature. Then *Jane Eyre* is dispatched and the pace of the narrative quickens as the manuscript is read, accepted and published (speed of telling a reflection of speed of publication, from the novel's dispatch on 24 August to its publication in less than two months). The brief survey of *Jane Eyre*'s reception touchingly concludes with Charlotte breaking the news to her father, who reads it and when 'he came into tea, he said, "Girls, do you know Charlotte has been writing a book, and it is much better than likely?" ' (p. 325). The swing between the outside world and the closed world of Haworth is then once more established, after their brief coincidence in Patrick Brontë's muted words of praise. As interest grows in Currer Bell's identity, Charlotte's brother moves towards his end and Charlotte laments herself: 'Youth is gone – gone, – and will never come back: can't help it ... ' (p. 342). In the consequent visit with Anne to London Gaskell draws on the full humour in the contrast between the authoress whose identity intrigued London and her appearance as one of the retiring Miss Browns (their pseudonym for the visit), who appear only 'shy and reserved little countrywomen' (p. 350). The pleasure of the trip is blotted out by Branwell's death and Emily's final illness: 1848 closes, as the chapter began, at Haworth, sadly and forebodingly:

As the old, bereaved father and his two surviving children

followed the coffin to the grave they were joined by Keeper, Emily's fierce, faithful bull-dog. He walked alongside of the mourners, and into the church, and stayed quietly there all the time that the burial service was being read. When he came home, he lay down at Emily's chamber door, and howled pitifully for many days. Anne Brontë drooped and sickened more rapidly from that time; and so ended the year 1848 (p. 358).

Charlotte's own life closes twice: with her death in 1855 and with her marriage the year before. The shadow of the woman question hovers over the *Life:* it is there in the contrast between Branwell, the man prodigally dissolute in his talent, and Charlotte, as it is between Charlotte and Thackeray, the man brilliant and successful yet ultimately unserious, a mocker, denying 'the better feelings of his better moods' (p. 440). If being a woman put Charlotte at a disadvantage, becoming a wife destroyed her as writer. Faced by the marriage, Gaskell was necessarily cautious. There is no denial that Charlotte was happy (there is every reason to think that, briefly, she was) and as early as 1846 Nicholls is mentioned, 'who, probably, even now, although she was unconscious of the fact, had begun his service to her, in the same tender and faithful spirit as that in which Jacob served for Rachel' (p. 296). But Charlotte's marriage meant the end of the author. For Nicholls, there was no question of her continuing to write once she was his wife. Gaskell uses the proper terms of congratulation in describing the prospective married state:

There is one other letter ... which develops the intellectual side of her character, before we lose all thought of the authoress in the timid and conscientious woman about to become a wife, and in the too short, almost perfect, happiness of her nine months of wedded life (pp. 511-12).

One might suspect, though, a certain contempt in the supposed logic of the process: that a single woman might be intellectual and an authoress, but a married one must 'dwindle into a wife' – after all, even when William Gaskell pocketed the money, he never suggested *his* wife had no business to be author as well. In this marriage the woman was to sink her intellect (and to sink it in Nicholls) and Gaskell rightly closes the main narrative with the marriage ceremony:

> Henceforward the sacred doors of home are closed upon her
> married life. We, her loving friends, standing outside, caught
> occasional glimpses of brightness, and pleasant peaceful
> murmurs of sound, telling of the gladness within . . . And we
> thought, and we hoped, and we prophesied, in our great love
> and reverence.
>   But God's ways are not as our ways! (p. 519)

She was a woman wronged, called an outcast, judged by a lesser standard than male writers, accused of coarseness, denied any lasting happiness, yet with remarkably little rancour or spleen Gaskell has perpetuated 'the memory of Charlotte Brontë' (p. 526).

The trouble *The Life of Charlotte Brontë* gave her has usually been given as the reason Gaskell wanted no biography of herself written.[53] More likely, she did not think her life of sufficient interest. Certainly, she was wearied by the task and even more by the work's reception and consequent fag of the third edition. Before completion, wearied by all its problems, she exclaimed, 'Oh! if once I have finished this biography, catch me writing another!' (421). None the less, in August 1857, in the very midst of appeasement and rewriting she was asking George Smith whether he knew anything of Sir George Saville, some of his friends having 'written to me to write his life' (463). When she learnt of his background she decided against tackling the subject, not because of the problems with Charlotte but because

> he would require a greater knowledge of politics than I either
> have or care to have. I like to write about character, & the
> manners of a particular period – for the life of a great
> Yorkshire Squire of the last century, I think I could have done
> pretty well (469).

The biography had been tougher than she expected and she was never to tackle another, though not as opposed to the genre, as has been suggested. She returned to fiction and with her next novel, *Sylvia's Lovers*, set in Yorkshire, to 'characters, & manners of a particular period'.

6

Sylvia's Lovers (1863): Tragical History

Action is transitory – a step, a blow,
The motion of a muscle – this way or that –
'Tis done, and in the after-vacancy
We wonder at ourselves like men betrayed:
Suffering is permanent, obscure and dark,
And shares the nature of infinity.

Wordsworth, The Borderers, Act III

I

It may be coincidence that Yorshire is the setting of the novel after *The Life of Charlotte Brontë*, but the suggestion that she might write a life of Sir George Saville, and her enthusiasm for 'the life of a great Yorkshire Squire of the last century' as subject, possibly turned Gaskell's mind to that county and to a past age, while the controversies provoked by contemporary characters and 'problem' subjects may have sent her to something she had tried before settling to *Mary Barton* – a tale, 'the period of which was more than a century ago, and the place on the borders of Yorkshire'.[1] This description does not fit *Sylvia's Lovers* and clearly she did not turn back to the actual material of that abandoned work. This novel, though, is her first extended historical fiction – *Ruth* has marked contemporaneity in a 'problem' theme and for all its period detail is set well within the previous fifty years – and it is suggestive that some of the short stories of this period are historical: 'The Poor Clare' (1856), 'Lois the Witch' (1859), and 'The Grey Woman' (1861), while in 1859, about the time she agreed to Smith's terms for a new novel, Gaskell was much involved with the early work of George Eliot and the author's identity. *Scenes of Clerical Life* (1858) – she

159

particularly admired 'Janet's Repentance' – and *Adam Bede* (1859) take us back in time, and Gaskell, thanking John Blackwood for a copy of the latter, remarked that 'I was brought up in Warwickshire, and recognize the country in every description of natural scenery' (533). History was finding play in her imagination.

Sylvia's Lovers, like *Adam Bede*, is set in the 1790s and it could be that Gaskell was partly prompted by Eliot's example to write what is strictly her only historical novel, since *Wives and Daughters*, though set in the 1820s, draws more on childhood memory and partakes rather of the autobiographical novel than a pattern of historical events completed and explicable. Whether George Eliot is a direct inspiration may be doubted, but both novels clearly challenge the kind of historical novel established by Walter Scott. The subtitle of Scott's first novel, *Waverley, or 'Tis Sixty Years Since* (1814) places the action at the same distance from the reader as that of *Adam Bede* or *Sylvia's Lovers*. The events of two generations ago, their shape and consequences determined, are living memory now only amongst the oldest. Scott's subtitle refers to an episode so generally known that it needs no more than pronoun and time-span to identify the Jacobite uprising of 1745 under Bonnie Prince Charlie, which, culminating in military defeat at Culloden and guaranteeing the political stability of Scott's own society, proved a major event central to the fates of all the characters, historical or fictive. George Eliot and Gaskell, while writing of a period of upheaval and great event, prefer to make such things peripheral. For Eliot's characters the harvest and prices are more important than Napoleon's victories in Italy – an emphasis which is part of Eliot's view of history, the continuity of the folk, as she suggests at the harvest supper, its singing of traditional songs being linked by a learned joke into a perspective of harvests that has Homeric society at its further end. For Gaskell, though the great events of history do influence people's lives and one time is not like another, the significance of history is that most of us are not excitingly involved in its great events. Scott was master, as he knew, of the 'Big Bow-wow strain', where Gaskell commands the detailed unfolding of a way of life confined in space and by time, but none the less passionate for that; her drama is of the interior rather than upon the stage of empire.

The French wars play their part in *Sylvia's Lovers*: the press-gang is called into being by the navy's demand for men, and its presence in Monkshaven precipitates the tragedies of Daniel Robson, his daughter Sylvia, and Philip Hepburn, but until the third volume we are almost exclusively confined to Monkshaven. The only exception is Philip's journey to Newcastle and London, and even then nothing happens in the larger world of action. The expedition is important, once Kinraid has been seized and Philip received his message, for the time it allows Philip for thought and decision. Daniel Robson's trial, decisive though it is, is not depicted, as if the novel's centre of consciousness, like the inhabitants of Monkshaven, finding the 'travelling some forty miles ... a most unusual exertion at that time' (p. 326), reluctant to go to York, prefers to stay with the women at Haytersbank farm. Though not bound to Sylvia's point of view (we often go with Philip Hepburn and enter into understanding with other characters) the novel largely concerns itself with those who wait and suffer, whose lives share the nature of infinity. Even Daniel Robson's leadership of the assault on the press-gang's rendezvous, doing rather than suffering, shows him not only as someone having no real authority, but also as someone having no real understanding beyond the isolated event which to him should be self-contained, a blow returned for the press-gang's fire-alarm trick. For him it can have no part of a larger pattern of law and military engagements beyond England, since he is incapable of perceiving such a pattern. It is a tragic complexity, of course, a complexity stemming from the distinctive historical nature of the form, that that pattern does exist and intermesh with individual action. For the women, suffering is permanent, obscure and dark, while Robson's 'blow', an honest piece of revenge, leaves him to wonder like a man betrayed. Only in the third volume – Gaskell possibly needed additional material: though as early as March 1862, before she began on it, she suspected 'the third will be longer than either' (678) – do we move out of England, into the larger action of historical events with Kinraid and Philip at the siege of Acre. Even this is not related to the larger scope of Napoleon's Egyptian campaign (though Napoleon's eventual flight back to France was notorious) and it is perhaps significant that Sylvia learns how Philip saved Kinraid when Kinraid's wife comes to Monkshaven, a reporting of events similar to that used for Robson's trial and execution. This is possibly evidence that the Acre chapter was an afterthought – certainly the coincidence of both men being present would be more acceptable in Clarinda Kinraid's retrospective and partial view alone, though the historical material is not so feebly handled as some commentators would suggest. The historicism of

Sylvia's Lovers is that of life and manners, not of events and institutions, its time-scale allowing accumulation of feeling as well as perspective on events.

The suggestions of historical process and a web which binds as well as connects are laid-in sparingly, but help to enforce the sense of tragedy in an inevitable historical process. The reader, wiser through a standpoint which is broader and advanced in time, can see as they cannot the end to which the characters must come. They may sense some kind of causality, may beat against necessity, but are unable to fathom or control. Gaskell can be mildly ironical about the larger judgment the vista of time gives the reader. When she draws attention to the failure of the vicar of Monkshaven to do anything about 'the discord between the laws of man and the laws of Christ [which] stood before him', she adds that it 'is as well for us that we live at the present time, when everybody is logical and consistent' (p. 72), a salutary reminder that for all our boasted powers we are as muddled in our ways as Dr Wilson was. Our advantage lies only in perspective, which operates on the past alone. We can understand and assess the past because of that distance, but this does not mean that we are capable of coping with our own present more efficiently (p. 71). The pattern only emerges in the course of time; and this pattern, shaped to an already known end, is what *Sylvia's Lovers* offered.

The novel takes us into the minds of others and shows in their different workings modes unacceptable to cold modernity. Yet the shading of those minds colours the events they watch as it determines partly the action those minds initiate. Gaskell is able to play off modern rationality against a penumbra of fate and predestined shaping which, if condemned as superstition in Robson and his coevals, yet has a counterpart in our own sense of the irrevocable mould of history. Our terms are different but are we perhaps linked closer than we think to those figures of the past in seeking meaning? When Daniel Robson, filled with terror and hatred, frequents public houses for gossip about the press-gang,

> probably the amount of drink thus consumed weakened
> Robson's power over his mind, and caused the concentration
> of thought on one subject. This may be a physiological
> explanation of what afterwards was spoken of as a supernatural
> kind of possession, leading him to his doom (p. 268).

Gaskell no more subscribes than her 'modern' readers to the idea of possession, which is established in the subjective minds of the audience to Daniel's fate, yet the word 'doom' enforces the sense that the sequence of events needs explanation and that 'possession' may be as true an explanation (poetically, possibly truer) as any scientific rational one. There is, viewed then or viewed now, in its fullness of thought, act and consequence, an inevitability in what Daniel does that suggests shape, a design that will not allow deviation or escape. The reader recognizes this and contemplates his progress with fear, with pity, but with the dramatic recognition that he cannot intervene in what is already determined.

Elsewhere, the word 'actor' is applied to the characters, with its implications of a 'part' to be played, and we respond at various emotional levels to these actors, from involvement through proximity to objectivity through spatial or temporal distance (as *King Lear* offers us the immediate shock of Gloucester's blinding yet in the objectivity of a dimly historical ancient Britain). Gaskell is well aware of the capacity of art and the imagination to function simultaneously on different levels and the historical novel is a form which peculiarly invites us both to be involved and to be critical:

> At this hour, all the actors in this story having played out
> their parts and gone to their rest, there is something touching
> in recording the futile efforts made by Philip to win from
> Sylvia the love he yearned for. But, at the time, any one who
> had watched him might have been amused to see the grave,
> awkward, plain young man studying patterns and colours for a
> new waistcoat ... (p. 141).

'Might have been amused', but there are tears for things as well. Gaskell reverses the common representation of suffering that seems tragic at the time being perceived as trivial or comic in terms of cosmic proportion; at the end of Chaucer's poem, Troilus from the seventh sphere laughs at the pettiness of his own suffering as it now appears in the scale of universal time and universal feeling. In the long time of history Philip's experience takes on the shape of ideal feeling – of the tragic – stripped as it is by that distance of those everyday details of clumsiness, of unwanted emotion, so many brakes to the ideal feeling and which are so much the stuff of the novelistic world in its mirroring of the natural world. This handling of the long time of history and the short time of immediate experience shows Gaskell resolving the problem set but not solved in depicting John Barton.

Patterns and colours for a new waistcoat are incongruous enough for the grave, awkward, plain Philip; and yet even such trifles may be more serious, whether as tokens or as provocation. The ribbon, Philip's first love gift to Sylvia, is a token of his excess of feeling. The episode is deeply painful, as well as provoking a smile, since the sense of those who have 'played out their parts and gone to their rest' acts simultaneously upon us. And besides, the reader feels Philip's disappointment, first that Sylvia is not there to receive the ribbon and second, in the pain inherent in Sylvia's gift later of the same ribbon as a love-token to Charley Kinraid. However much these people are distanced from us in time, they were bound to a wheel and they suffered. Historical process deepens the experience by insisting we know it in more than one way at the same time – what Gaskell finds touching in its recording, the reader receives simultaneously with the original experience, which is coloured by sadness however ludicrous it may have been in detail. Things fell out thus and thus, and what is stressed by a historical sequence is that they must fall out so. The point is doubly made when Kinraid, bound within a series of events the reader knows already to be completed, lies physically bound in the hands of the press-gang, and turns away from insults: 'Kinraid did not hear or heed. His soul was beating itself against the bars of inflexible circum-stance' (p. 231). It is one of the powers of tragedy, in Greek drama or *Paradise Lost*, that however much we lose sight of the end in the experience of the moment we are aware of the inevitable towards which Eve or Agamemnon moves. As we read we may not be exactly sure of Charley's end or Philip's or Sylvia's, but there can seemingly be no open ending, no chance twist or change, as there might be for Mary Barton or Margaret Hale or even Ruth, whose stories (in whatever tense they are told) still project themselves forward into a variety of possible futures as we read, where in *Sylvia's Lovers* we know the story comes out of a completed past.

The characters themselves are allowed occasional glimpses of the historical process, linked, in Philip's case, to ideas of feeling both powerful and real – feeling, that is, not set aside by passing time as insignificant. Contemplating Alice Rose's life, Philip sees it in pattern as like his and Charley's relationship with Sylvia, a pattern he sees, too, as a justification for his silence about Kinraid's fate:

Then he went on to wonder if the lives of one generation were but a repetition of the lives of those who had gone before, with no variation but from the internal cause that some had greater capacity for suffering than others. Would those very circumstances which made the interest of his life now, return in due cycle, when he was dead and Sylvia was forgotten (pp. 254-5)?

If there is a direct answer to this, it is 'no', since Philip reasons falsely – his betrayal of Kinraid is not excusable as predestined, pattern in itself not justifying a man's actions – but it is a question about the nature of history and our role in the pattern of past, present and future. The greater capacity for suffering does distinguish Sylvia and Philip, is what makes them tragic where Kinraid ultimately is not, what makes them stand out in the apparently repetitive pattern of existence. It is with role and pattern that Gaskell deals in *Sylvia's Lovers*, with the common lot of men who 'till the soil and lie beneath' and with those rare exceptional figures whose suffering still obtrudes when time has smoothed down the features of the past.

II

There is a long gap between publication of *The Life of Charlotte Brontë* (1857) and this novel (1863), the delay being in the writing rather than the conception. In those six years a fair amount of literary work appeared both for Dickens and for George Smith's new venture, the *Cornhill Magazine*, which began in 1860 under Thackeray's editorship. There is surprisingly little evidence for the genesis of the novel. In June 1859, Gaskell contacted Smith, to tell him that Sampson Low had offered £1,000 for a novel in three volumes (558), though she would rather have £800 from Smith than £1,000 from him. Clearly, Smith decided to match the offer, for in October she tells Charles Eliot Norton that the latter sum was to be hers, though not 'a line of the book is written yet', and added despondently, 'I think I have a feeling that it is not worth while trying to write, while there are such books as Adam Bede' (581), though she had earlier promised Smith, 'Oh! I will try & write you a good novel' (563). Even if a line had not been written in October, she seems to have the novel's setting in mind since she adds to Norton that 'Meta, Julia & I are going for a week or ten days to

Whitby tomorrow' (582), where they lodged at Mrs Rose's, a name appropriated for Alice and Hester in the novel. Whitby was cold and stormy, but must have served, since by late December she could tell Smith the novel's title, 'The Specksioneer' (595) or harpooner. Gaskell knew the east coast well and there were reminders enough even in Lancashire of the whaling trade, such as the gate 'hung on whale-jaw posts' mentioned by Samuel Bamford on the path between Manchester and Blackley.[2] Accounts tell of Gaskell pumping Whitby people for information,[3] though whether she was told a local story which provided the main line of the novel is open to doubt: the closing page of the novel is of course no evidence that Gaskell heard the story in fact. The tale's basis has roots in folklore (Samuel Bamford indeed has a similar story of a lover believed dead and unexpectedly returning, though no lie was involved) and Tennyson was to write a variant in 'Enoch Arden', though differences between the versions are more important than likenesses, Gaskell's story having none of the voyeurism or confused morality of Tennyson's tale.[4] The ruined abbey and the steep cliffs, the climb to the church and the moors beyond at Monkshaven all draw on personal experience of Whitby, though Gaskell orientates the town north and south of the river rather than east and west (adding a touch of romance in 'its having been the landing-place of a throneless queen'),[5] while Haytersbank she claimed as a memory of a farm near Sunderland if a memory at all (718).

In March 1860 she tells Marianne that 'so many people are now at work for me, in Yorkshire, that I am sure to have my information sooner or later, without troubling any one further' (603), her daughter having conveyed an offer to look through the *Annual Register* for details, something Gaskell had done '*months* ago'. From the *Register* for 1795 she may have gleaned the gossip at the brothers Foster's table of outrages offered to the king when he was going to open the House of Lords ('violently hissed and hooted, and groaned the whole way; but no violence was offered till he arrived opposite the Ordnance office').[6] The same work provided details (or reminders) of the London Corresponding Society's efforts for Parliamentary reform, the Sedition Act, the arrival of the Princess Caroline as the Prince of Wales's bride, their unborn child later allowing the Monkshaven politicians to exercise themselves on the question whether it would 'be a boy or a girl? If a girl, would it be more loyal to call it Charlotte or Elizabeth?' (p. 178). The *Register* for 1796 recorded the birth of the princess on 7 January, called Charlotte after her grandmother, George III's consort. Such small details as these echo for readers who know the unhappiness of the prince's marriage, the scandals of Queen Caroline, and the early death of Princess Charlotte, placing them beyond the viewpoint of village 'politicians', who do not even know yet whether the royal child will be a boy or a girl.

With so much personal observation and oral information Gaskell had little need to draw on written sources, such as George Young's *A History of Whitby* (1817), indeed seems not to have looked at it even, though its appendix has fascinating details of traditional customs and beliefs, the vessel cups or baskets with a wax image of Christ taken from house to house before Christmas and the fairies Jeanie of Biggerdale and Hob-hole Hob.[7] Indeed, parts of Young suggest minor inaccuracies in Gaskell's account, since *Sylvia's Lovers* opens in October with the return of the first whaler, yet Young gives 8 September as the latest date ever for this event (ii, 567). Factual details like this scarcely matter, though Gaskell took care elsewhere, so that the funeral of the seamen killed by the press-gang takes place in the late afternoon: Young notes that the 'usual hour of burial at Whitby is 3 o'clock, P.M. from michaelmas to lady day' (ii, 611). In a later edition Gaskell revised the information about Daniel Robson's trial (700), though she never adjusted the chronology, which ought strictly to run from 1794, not 1796, to 1800.[8]

One book she did use, to good purpose, was by someone she already knew – William Scoresby (p. 142 above), whose *An Account of the Arctic Regions, with a History and Description of the Northern Whale-Fishery* (1820) provided not only details of the whale industry at Whitby and the ship *Resolution* (commanded by Scoresby's father, i, 307), but also the yarns of Robson and Kinraid.[9] They are not dissimilar from Jem Wilson's tales in *Mary Barton*. In the fascination they have for Sylvia against the scientific geography Philip offers, they show the pull of Kinraid and the imagination against Hepburn's solid unexciting qualities. Kinraid's tale of the iceberg and the whale (p. 106) is a factual matter in Scoresby:

> The crew of one of these Hull whalers having, a few years
> ago, killed a fish by the side of an ice-berg, in Davis' Straits,
> the fins were lashed together, and the tail secured to a boat, in
> the usual way, but by the efforts only of one boat's crew; all

the other boats belonging to the same ship, being engaged in
the capture of two more whales, neither of which were yet
subdued. This circumstance occasioned some altercation among
the crew of the boat, as to the propriety of their remaining by
the dead whale, or of quitting it, and proceeding in an empty
boat, which was at hand, to the assistance of their companions.
The latter measure was carried; but as it was deemed
expedient that one man should remain in the boat, to which none
of them would consent, they were under the necessity of either
remaining in idleness by the fish, or leaving the fish and boat
by themselves. But every one being anxious to participate in
the more active exercises of the fishery, they at length agreed
unanimously to quit the boat connected with the dead fish,
and to proceed to the aid of their comrades. The arrangements
were just accomplished in time; for they had not rowed many
fathoms from the place, before a tremendous crash of the *berg*
ensued, – an immense mass of ice fell upon the boat they had
just quitted, and neither it nor the fish were ever seen
afterwards (ii, 342).

Gaskell follows the precise outline of events, but dramatizes them in
Kinraid's dialect and personality, and by the narrative placing of
detail – Kinraid's emphasis on darkness and steadiness that prepares
while not anticipating the outcome: 'So off we rowed, every man
Jack on us, out o' the black shadow o' th' iceberg, as looked as
steady as th' polestar'. The cold of the water leads Daniel to his
account of his plunge, north latitude 81 (pp. 106-7), again taken
from Scoresby (ii, 360), his apparently exaggerated details of 'my
clothes was just hard frozen on me, an' my hair a'most as big a
lump o' ice as yon iceberg' being largely Scoresby's information how
the sailor's 'clothes were frozen like mail, and his hair constituted a
helmet of ice'. The sense of exaggeration in Robson's tale (though
true enough in essentials) shows how Gaskell modifies or finds a
story appropriate to her characters, and in Robson's second
anecdote, of riding on a whale (pp. 109-11), she not only fits him
with a fine piece of bravado but matches our doubts by an account
on which Scoresby also has reservations. The Dutch harpooner
Vienkes, in 1660, is dashed out of his boat and onto the whale's
back (ii, 366-7). At length, the harpoon disengaging itself, Vienkes
cast himself into the sea and swam, but Scoresby comments in a
footnote that 'Part of the story bears the marks of truth; but some

of it, it must be acknowledged, borders on the marvellous'. Gaskell did not take what came to hand, but stole by line and measure.

Other details, such as the press-gang and the riot, came from tradition and from Admiralty papers,[10] so worked up that without previous knowledge it would be difficult to say where borrowing begins: compare the obtrusive opening of Swift's *Gulliver's Travels* or the more elaborate but undigested borrowings in Charles Reade's *The Cloister and the Hearth*. Even the siege of Acre, though as yet I have not traced the source of her material, does not jar stylistically.[11]

And with this material to hand or being found for her Gaskell plunged into the story itself, writing as always on her familiar long sheets of blue or white paper, to go by the only fragment of the manuscript I know – in a schoolboy's scrapbook magazine, dated 1879, in Manchester Central Library.[12] She began writing 8 April 1860 (910) and reported to Marianne that it was 'hard work writing a novel all morning, spudding up dandelions all afternoon, & writing again at night' (614), but she had done '117 pages . . . *of 570 at least*'. In August, though, she told Charles Eliot Norton that, with the first volume almost finished, she had heard (6 June) that Marianne was seriously ill (631); a long period of convalescence followed recovery, so in December the book was still only about a quarter done (640). She pushed on; in August 1861 she was about half done (667) and by December two volumes were finished, Gaskell offering Smith 'the third also at any time you liked to fix, provided it was not so soon as to hurry it into incompleteness' (670). The manuscript of these volumes was in Smith's hands by the beginning of January 1862 (chapters 1-14 and 15-29 of the Knutsford correspond to the final volume divisions, but chapter 29 is almost certainly the one transferred to volume 2 when it became clear (929) that volume 3 would be too long). The third volume hung fire; partly because she wanted Smith's opinion of what was completed to encourage her, partly because of Manchester conditions. She wanted, if Smith or W. S. Williams had read the manuscript, 'to send . . . a sketch of the third vol: to make you see how everything in the first two "works up" to the events and crisis in that' (675). Clearly, the whole was in Gaskell's mind, but as late as August 1862, with printing of the first two volumes going forward – she sent corrected proofs and revises that month (691, 929) – the publishers had not received and Gaskell seems not to have written any of the third volume. A slightly formal tone appears in letters about this time, which suggests stiffness between author and publisher – one, directed to Smith and Elder, begins 'Gentlemen', instead of her usual 'My dear sir', and points out in hurt tones that printing had begun at Smith's request and he had said it should not inconvenience her; they should have the story as soon as she could finish it (691–2).

What held her back was relief work amongst the mill-workers, hit by the cotton famine of the American Civil War years (1861–5). With the northern blockade no supplies came through and there was a distinct possibility that economics might force England into the war against the North, though liberal sympathies, Gaskell's included, were for the Federalists and negro emancipation. Relief committees were organized and Gaskell was active, whether cutting up calico for shirts to provide sewing for women (681) or raising and dispensing money, co-operating closely with Travers Madge, for instance, at a time when ladies and gentlemen were 'all at work' to relieve the distress.[13] Indeed, over-exertion seems to have contributed to Gaskell's increasing ill-health and sudden death. Still, she did find time for rest and writing in September 1862, though feeling the obligation to go back to Manchester and very hard work, 'which exhausts one both bodily & mentally with depressing atmosphere of both kinds' (697). Finished it eventually was and the novel appeared in three volumes in February 1863, to be followed rapidly by a corrected edition (in both points of detail and an overhaul of the dialect), while by November she was preparing yet another edition, illustrated by George du Maurier, the artist chosen for her next novel, *Wives and Daughters*, on its serialization in the *Cornhill Magazine*.

III

The first volume of the novel ends with Sylvia committed to Charley Kinraid, and Philip at a height of his business career in the Fosters' offer of partnership; the second, after Charley's disappearance and Robson's death, ends with Philip engaged to Sylvia – indeed in Gaskell's original writing, probably ended with Sylvia's breaking to Kester (ch. 28) her acceptance of Philip and determination to stand by that decision. Even transference of the next chapter, 'Wedding Raiment', to be the last of volume 2 does not alter that emphasis on Philip having achieved what ought to be his personal ideal, as the partnership was his worldly one. And the third volume shows the destruction of both his public and emotional life. As with

Ruth, her other three-volume novel, Gaskell seems to have borne the physical format of issue in mind as a factor in the shape of the story. But a comparison between the two novels (and the centrality of the female character and the nature of her personal crisis makes this easy) shows how Gaskell has progressed in her art. There is none of the smudging at vital points, either in terms of plot or character; things not shown to us (Daniel Robson's trial, for instance) are fully accounted for, lightly in terms of detail, but subtly, even painfully, in their effects upon the women who wait, so there are no vague gaps as there was earlier between Ruth departing for London and her arrival in Wales. Gaskell is now also certain how to handle the relationship between subject and mood. A jarring in *Ruth* may be felt between on one hand the idyllic, apparently historical tone of much of the story – located in the old town at the opening, the natural description, the life of the Bensons – and on the other, the 'problem' nature of Ruth's situation, the exposure Gaskell sought to make of a contemporary outrage that would seem better suited to the world of Manchester.

In *Sylvia's Lovers* this harmony of subject and mood is above all in landscape. The natural scene plays its part in the relationship between sea and moorland, between fishing town and farm, between character and action, establishing a world where even the dweller inland is aware of the sea, and where war and the clash of nations make themselves known not only in expensive bread but in the more immediate terms of the press-gang and its preying on the very life-blood of the community, the men who are its sailors. When Gaskell describes Monkshaven and its hinterland, she is already setting the story in motion:

> There was comparative fertility and luxuriance down below
> in the rare green dales. The narrow meadows stretching along
> the brookside seemed as though the cows could really satisfy
> their hunger in the deep rich grass; whereas on the higher
> lands the scanty herbage was hardly worth the fatigue of
> moving about in search of it. Even in these 'bottoms' the
> piping sea-winds, following the current of the stream, stunted
> and cut low any trees; but still there was rich, thick
> underwood, tangled and tied together with brambles, and
> briar-roses, and honeysuckle ... But for twenty miles inland
> there was no forgetting the sea, nor the sea-trade; refuse
> shell-fish, sea-weed, the offal of the melting-houses, were the

staple manure of the district; great ghastly whale-jaws,
bleached bare and white, were the arches over the gate-posts
to many a field or moorland stretch. Out of every family of
several sons, however agricultural their position might be, one
had gone to sea, and the mother looked wistfully seaward at
the changes of the keen piping moorland winds (pp. 4-5).

The very land runs down to the sea rather than inland, so that
Kinraid, having taken his farewell of Sylvia, bursts before Philip's
gaze onto the beach by a valley leading down from Haytersbank. To
Philip, Sylvia might seem to look down to the town and the security
of himself, a landsman, but the reader feels how through Charley's
defiance of the press-gang and the yarns swapped between him and
her father, it is beyond the town that she looks and out to sea and to
romance. Importantly, part of her swing back to Philip and part of
her understanding of the man, even though she did not love him,
comes as she recognizes the truth of Clarinda Kinraid's account of
Philip saving Charley. Philip may be rejected, but she does not doubt
his bravery and admires it in action beyond the seas.

Sylvia is the undoubted centre of the novel. Although *Sylvia's
Lovers* was the last of the novel's proposed titles – *The Specksioneer*
stressed Kinraid, the later *Philip's Idol* emphasized Hepburn – it gives
the right sense of her dealings with other people, a still centre (her
physical situation at Monkshaven unmoved, at least) who by her
very being draws men into this emotional identity. She begins as a
free-natured girl, slightly wilful in her desire for a cloak of brilliant
red rather than the useful grey duffle (not a question of warmth or
durability: the quality is the same, whatever the colour), playful as
she washes her feet before she and Molly put on their shoes for town,
yet already open in her nature – an openness unconscious and
possibly uncontrollable. When the whaler comes in she accepts
naturally the joyful handclasp of the girl who calls out, 'She's o'er
t'bar! She's o'er t'bar! I'm boun' to tell mother!' (p. 29). The contrast
with Philip is clear enough. He takes on himself the position of moral
guardian and Sylvia understandably resents his asking how she
knows such a girl, as she did his insisting that it was the grey duffle
she wanted, not the red. Her resentment is as understandable as his
wish to show love by the affectionate care he hopes will one day be
his right. Philip's tenderness is clear, however unwelcome. He is a
lover able already to draw so much pleasure from her mere presence

that when he is to accompany her home he anticipates 'so keenly the pleasure awaiting him in the walk that he was almost surprised by the gravity of his companion' (p. 35). Charley Kinraid's role as yet is more covert. Molly Corney has already hinted (boasted, rather) that Charley is more than cousin to her and Sylvia, drawn by the death of the seaman and Kinraid's heroic stand against the press-gang, feels that the harpooner is Molly's by right. She accepts readily enough the proposal to go and see the fashionable cut of cloaks at church the day of the seaman's funeral, an occasion which she cannot anyway treat with the simple levity of Molly's excuse for going and where she and Kinraid are brought into physical proximity. Her emotional responsiveness has already been established by handclasp and faint when the whaler came in. Touched by the service and burial, her sensibility expands. Sylvia is not yet fully aware, indeed, is never fully aware on the rational level, though she is to feel more in years to come and feel more intensely, but she is open to impressions. Because more finely attuned she is aware of the implications of relationships and actions, suffers more than ordinary folk, and in suffering is set apart. What the ordinary character collapses under or does not notice, the tragic character bears.

This tragic sensibility is linked to a whole train of personal and communal associations, established by Gaskell in the first part of the novel. These give the reader a sense of Sylvia's difference in kind from others and of the dark end towards which her whole life tends. They also show the passional, at one point close to mystical, expansion of Sylvia herself, by which experience and memory become part of her living self. Links of association are already being forged when Sylvia returns from the Corneys' farm after settling Sunday's expedition with Molly. She sees her mother, 'watching for her, with her hand shading her eyes from the low rays of the setting sun; but as soon as she saw her daughter in the distance, she returned to her work, whatever that might be' (p. 64). There is no overt emotion here, only posture and quiet action, but 'Sylvia, without any reasoning or observation, instinctively knew that her mother's heart was bound up in her', and Gaskell hints at Sylvia's future life, takes us indeed into the aftermath of the main tale, the long but empty part of her story, when that picture of her mother standing there will rise up, 'the remembrance of which smote Sylvia to the heart with a sense of a lost blessing, not duly valued while possessed' (p. 65). The incident says something about the Robson family, as it says something about Sylvia. Molly's mother would not stand so and Molly would not understand or recall such undemonstrative affection. That it is offered and that Sylvia is open to it, forms her capacity to love greatly and suffer intensely, even if feeling is not expressed by gesture or sound. It is a family that concentrates its love. Gaskell's technique of memory here allows her to anticipate by a shaft of intelligence that shows a story completed, a glimpse of Sylvia as someone who will fall into neglect, her life to be suffering rather than joy, the historical novel's stretch of time being used for pathos, and so colouring this early our response to Sylvia's story that has still to unfold in its detail.

In the churchyard the sight of Kinraid, and Sylvia's response, are already qualified for the reader by that illumination, however fitful, of her future. Gaskell stresses the presence of experience within time through physical detail that links into the life of the community. The continuous stretch of history, forward and back, like Carlyle's image of it in *Past and Present* as Ygdrasil, the World Ash, its roots in past and branches in future, develops in the complex of the funeral scene. The description of that Sunday shows a scheme of present (pause, tranquillity before winter comes on), future (coming winter and death of the old), and past (the old themselves, ready to depart, yet whose lives have been the life of Monkshaven) (pp. 66-7). The old people are part of the generations whose feet have worn the steps to the church, and Sylvia's life, rendered vivid by particularity, is part of those generations. The communal ritual of burial in which she takes part grips her, and in responding she develops her own individuality. From the curiosity of a child at the funeral, Sylvia moves to join in communal mourning. Then, though, most import- antly for the sense of her personal tragedy, there is a shift to her single consciousness. Rather than her being subsumed into the historical process of community, of joining those feet on the steps, she passes beyond to a more personal awakening, a leading from above that gives a vision of life, so that she realizes, however momentarily, 'the enduring sea and hills forming a contrasting background to the vanishing away of a man' (pp. 79-80).

She has the capacity for inner life that finds literary expression in the evangelical awakening emphasized by George Eliot in *Scenes of Clerical Life* and *Adam Bede*. If Sylvia is not strictly a moral being, her emotional self partakes of what Eliot characterized as 'that recognition of something to be lived for beyond the mere satisfaction

174

of self, which is to the moral life what the addition of a great central ganglion is to animal life'.[14] In so far as any one of us can recognize that, so far do we become individual and therefore ahistorical, tending towards the great comic or tragic figures, St Theresa, Odysseus, Cleopatra, Dorothea Brooke, Sylvia Robson. Such recognition is beyond Molly, whose life therefore, however vivid in detail, interests us that much less (and is the easier for her), especially since Sylvia's moment of vision, which has taken in Charley Kinraid, her lover, as well as enduring sea and hills and the vanishing away of man, alerts us to the pattern of her days as one which moves her towards the intensity and isolation of the tragic.

Philip, though Kinraid is established as an object of emotional interest through Molly and the funeral, is the first of Sylvia's lovers. Philip's complexity is that he occupies the place in the action where we might expect to find the villain, and yet there is no villain in the novel. His situation is the more painful because he is loving, intelligent, successful at business, with talents that would have made him a great merchant in a larger sphere. His attempt to live by his lie about Kinraid's disappearance destroys all he has tried to build up; Philip, ostensibly so unemotional, is caught between his passion and his moral code and destroyed by restraint. For all his physical drabness he can inspire love – Hester is carefully used to show that – and Sylvia comes to recognize the power of the man: even in his lie he has done it to obtain an object beyond himself. His love may be egoistic but at least it is intense, engrossing him wholly as Sylvia's love and hatred engross her, as Kinraid's passion never could him. Even Philip's self-justification of his lie, that Kinraid is a light o' love, is tied in with the truth of his own constancy (p. 244). There is a complex suspension of judgment about this point, since Philip's decision to lie (more properly, remain silent and so suppress the truth: another instance of his restraint) does not make him unfeeling – his heart goes out to Sylvia when he sees her grief over Charley's supposed death. He feels not jealousy but sympathy, though

for all his pity, he had now resolved never to soothe her with the knowledge of what he knew, nor to deliver the message sent by her false lover. He felt like a mother withholding something injurious from the foolish wish of her plaining child (p. 249).

Judgment is only possible at the end; even then its danger is stressed by the false judgment of posterity upon Sylvia. Philip assumes the parental role, presumes to judge Kinraid ('false lover'), yet, though so temperamentally opposite, unsuited emotionally as partners, he and Sylvia exist beyond judgment, matched in possessing depth of being. In this, at least, they are like Samuel Richardson's Clarissa and Lovelace, those moral opposites who yet are the only opponents worthy of each other in their world, as Philip and Sylvia are the only ones capable in theirs fully and permanently of suffering, uniting their lives in what is obscure and dark.

Kinraid, already the hero of the press-gang attack, is first seen by Sylvia at the graveside, more like an imminent corpse than a lover. Charley is able to pay more attention to her at that moment, than she to him. Apart from the act's solemnity, in which she is so wrapped 'that she had no thought to spare at the first moment for the pale and haggard figure opposite' (p. 74), he knows, as she does not, that his affections are free. But if Sylvia has no thought for him, he is already an object of fascination, of romantic idealism, and she speaks to him tenderly, though wondering at her own temerity. She has an impulsive desire to love and serve – when her mother sends sausages to the convalescent Kinraid, Sylvia wants to wrap them in a fine damask napkin and, though daunted by her mother's forthright objection, she gathers 'two or three Michaelmas daisies, and the one bud of the China rose' (p. 91) to lay in the fold of the towel as tribute for this romantic figure. Kinraid has the qualifications of a hero: brave, determined, acting rightly and suffering for it, with all the dash and charm Philip so singularly lacks. He can tell stories, show himself off to advantage, and he lives a full animal life into which fine moral distinctions never enter. It is one of Gaskell's delicacies that she feels no need to establish early on the moral standing of Kinraid's action or nature. Kinraid does nothing wrong so far as Sylvia is concerned, whatever we might suspect if he had married her. Against him is Coulson's account of how Charley wooed his sister, who died within six months when Charley broke off to pursue another girl, 'that he played t' same game wi', as I've heard tell' (p. 203). But we do not know that Charley would have treated Sylvia the same (he does come back), even if he marries soon enough once Sylvia can no longer be his. And the force of Coulson's vehemence as witness is mitigated when he himself is able to marry within a year of having declared his passion for Hester Rose and been rejected.

At the New Year's Eve party, Sylvia is naturally drawn to the good looks and liveliness of Kinraid, so marked a contrast to Philip's. Yet, as Kinraid's marriage makes clear, his emotional life is shallow by the side of Sylvia's. Because we are aware of Sylvia's capacity for suffering in the early glimpse of her later life, doubt already clouds the idea of a successful union between Kinraid and Sylvia. Kinraid takes another wife because like most men he is ordinary and, frustrated in one direction, he will take another. He easily forgets and passes into the stream of time, out of Sylvia's life into the ordinary and unrecorded flow of history, whereas she and Philip are not so easily absorbed into everyday reality, figures tragically unable to accommodate themselves to circumstances.

I said earlier that Sylvia is part of the generations of history, and in that typical; I have also suggested that she is tragic, and in that sense exceptional. She is of the continuum of history and yet tries to resist events – above all in turning on Philip. 'I'll never forgive yon man, nor live with him as his wife again. All that's done and ended' (p. 404). She partakes of two kinds of experience. She is human and can no more escape from process than anyone else, yet she also sets her face against what has happened and in her 'greater capacity for suffering' (p. 255) moves out of the cycle. In this she is unlike the typical hero of Walter Scott, who comes to accept that, history having a current, he must conform or break. Usually only minor characters, like the nobly tragic Mac-Iver in *Waverley*, persist in their old ways and fare disastrously, while the heroes, notably Waverley himself, accept political reality. Sylvia, even in defeat, remains at the centre of the novel, and yet seems to resist history, to appeal against its movement. She remains true to past experience, because it still exists for her, while her separation from the community, until she is reported as a dark solitary figure, underlines her tragic status.

Sylvia establishes herself through her capacity to suffer. The way such experience can isolate and preserve a character, as art preserves, isolates, makes exceptional, is suggested when Bell seeks to alert Sylvia to danger by the story (fiction within fiction) of the deserted Nancy. It is not the moral that Sylvia sees, the repeated pattern of history that should apply the tale as a warning to herself, but the tragic singularity of the suffering girl: ' "Poor crazy Nancy!" sighed Sylvia. The mother wondered if she had taken the "caution" to herself, or was only full of pity for the mad girl, dead long before'

177

(p. 199). Sylvia's inability to take Nancy as a 'caution' or to react as though she no longer suffers is allied to her own imaginative capacity, one mark of the tragic, to keep suffering alive even at the cost of possible happiness.

With Kinraid gone from her life and Philip dead – forgiven, but too late – Sylvia is left alone. The conclusion shows within the framework of the narrative the verdict of history; from the reader it provokes the response to tragedy. She remains 'a pale, sad woman, allays dressed in black', though fading from people's memory, known if at all as part of 'the tradition of the man who died in a cottage somewhere about this spot – died of starvation, while his wife lived in hard-hearted plenty not two good stone-throws away' (p. 530). So much for history, which distorts and discards. One man, old when the bathing-woman, purveyor of tradition, was young, denied the story. But what meaning does history have when we must enter a vigorous protest against it? The perspective has gone wrong. Let Kinraid, who is no part of the tradition, pass into history and be forgotten. We have shared Sylvia's drama and if after its close the critics write the wrong review then we protest that history is wrong but tragedy is right. The action is momentary, fading as the memory of man, but the suffering partakes of the nature of infinity.

7

Wives and Daughters (1866): The Echoing Grove

[the genius] of Mrs. Gaskell strikes us as being little else than
a peculiar play of her personal character.

Henry James on *Wives and Daughters*

I

In publishing what proved to be her last novel, Gaskell agreed to its
serialization, a method she had resisted after *North and South* despite
Dickens's blandishments and George Smith's promptings, except for
comparatively short pieces like 'My Lady Ludlow'. Since an author
was paid for the serialization as well as volume publication, rewards
were greater, yet even with Smith, whom she liked, Gaskell seems to
have been reluctant to consider offering any longer work for his
Cornhill Magazine, partly perhaps because of an antipathy to
Thackeray, editor from its founding in 1860 until he retired in
March 1862. In a letter, about October 1859, when the new magazine was seeking contributors, Gaskell reverted to her feelings about
Thackeray's silence at the news of Charlotte Brontë's death and
added that 'my only feeling about not doing any thing you ask me
for the Magazine is because I don't think Thackeray would ever
quite like it' (576). This did not mean she utterly refused (she
declares she'll put aside these feelings if possible), and she submitted
the cunning trifle 'Curious if True' for the second number (February
1860), following it with 'Six Weeks at Heppenheim' (May 1862)
and the splendid 'Cousin Phillis' (November 1863 to February
1864). *Sylvia's Lovers* had been designed from the first, though with
never a doubt that Smith was to publish it, as a three-volume novel.
Yet by 1864 Gaskell was ready to change her mind. There may have
been three reasons for this. First, she needed as much money as

179

possible, since she was planning to buy secretly a house as a place of retirement for herself and William and a home after their deaths for her unmarried daughters; it was here, at The Lawn, Holybourne, in Hampshire, that on 12 November 1865, the novel still unfinished, she was to die in the midst of tea-time conversation. Double-payment for serial and book publication was a strong motive, then. Second, she published 'Cousin Phillis' in four episodes in the *Cornhill* without trouble from the demands of the method – things being easier than with *North and South* because she finished the work before publication began and (more importantly) because the greater length of the *Cornhill* episodes over those in *Household Words* meant she did not have to 'make effects' in the way Dickens wanted.[1] Third, Thackeray gave over being editor in March 1862 and (under the nominal headship of G. H. Lewes) Frederick Greenwood, for whom she had no antipathy, became the *Cornhill*'s effective editor. Her second contribution, 'Six Weeks', appeared close on Thackeray's resignation.

Gaskell's first thought had been for a different story. Setting out her various projects to Smith in September 1863, she mentions the never-written 'Life and Times of Madame de Sévigné', the travel sketches that became 'French Life' (*Fraser's Magazine*, April-June 1864), the progress of 'Cousin Phillis' – and a tale called 'Two Mothers', 'in my head very clear' (712). Presumably she gave Smith further details, because its only other mention is in the letter (May 1864) outlining *Wives and Daughters*, where she says, 'I threw overboard the story of the "Two Mothers" because I thought you did not seem to like it fully – and I have made up a story in my mind, – of country-town life 40 years ago' (731). It is tantalizing to have title and no idea of the lost book. The rest of her letter shows the new novel clear in her mind:

> a widowed doctor has one daughter Molly, – when she is
> about 16 he marries again – a widow with one girl Cynthia,
> – and these two girls – contrasted characters, – not sisters but
> living as sisters in the same house are unconscious rivals for the
> love of a young man, Roger Newton, the second son of a
> neighbouring squire or rather yeoman (731).

She proceeds to deal with Osborne's secret marriage, Roger's engagement and expedition, and his brother's death, though not the final outcome: 'You can see the kind of story and – I must say – you may

find a title for yourself for *I* can not. I have tried all this time in vain'
– the familiar trouble dogged her to the end.

The outline shows a number of minor changes were made as the
concept grew, not only in the Hamley name (from Newton), but
also in matters of status: Squire Hamley is very definitely a squire
rather than a yeoman, fiercely proud of birth and line, for there have
been Hamleys in the county from before the Conquest (' "Nay," said
Miss Browning, "I have heard that there were Hamleys of Hamley
before the Romans" ' (p. 43)), while Lord Cumnor of the Towers
comes from people who were merchants in James I's time and only
granted their title in Queen Anne's. Other initial uncertainties
(interesting but not critical to the novel's success) are indicated in
the manuscript and both serial and volume issues: the Cumnors, for
instance, begin as Tories, for 'there was a great Whig family in the
county who, from time to time, came forward and contested the
election with the rival Tory family of Cumnor'.[2] The political
opposition of Hamley and Cumnor which plays a part in the Squire's
tetchy isolation was something only fully realized during process of
composition (by chapter 6 Gaskell was adding the detail in manuscript of Squire Hamley's newspapers – 'one, an old established Tory
journal').[3] Yet such is Gaskell's essential grasp of the movement of
her story and skill in handling detail that no sense of jar or
disruption is felt beyond the need to correct a couple of words as she
would have done had she lived to oversee publication of the
completed work.[4] Already, though, the central relationships – Molly,
Cynthia and Roger, Mr Gibson and his second wife – are worked
out,[5] and it was with this outline alone seemingly that she began to
write.

The manuscript shows she worked on rapidly and without much
trouble (unless parts of it have been copied out again, which seems
unlikely) by the evidence of erasures and rewriting. Serialization
began in August 1864, so she must have written fast between her
letter to Smith in May and that date, though clearly she was not
far ahead at times during publication. At the beginning of March
1865 she had sent the copy for April and May, and when she died in
mid-November the story ran on for two further episodes, ending
with the January 1866 issue. She had hoped to write much in Paris in
March 1865 (she moved about a good deal during this period of
composition, including Cambridge, Fryston – home of Lord
Houghton – and the newly purchased house); but staying at Mary

Mohl's in the Rue du Bac she was overcome by the stuffy heat of the apartment and the unaccustomed mealtimes (nothing between 11 a.m. and 6 p.m.), suffering some kind of collapse. She had undoubtedly never fully recovered from that strain of relief work during the cotton famine, and at all times was liable to suffer when writing intensively. In April she had scarcely progressed beyond the July episode. By May she could report that the August 1865 number was written (750, 751, 758).

Space was still a problem. It seems Smith or Greenwood had set the conclusion for about December 1865, though not with Dickens's absoluteness. Early on, Gaskell estimated the length as 'I *believe* about 870 pages of my writing; but it is so difficult to tell. I could make it longer; I have so much to say yet; but oh! I am so tired of spinning my brain, when I am feeling so far from my story!' (746). The manuscript (now in the John Rylands University of Manchester Library) comes out at 920 pages,[6] a small number of sheets having extra material on the back. She might lament in May 1865 that she had '*such* a quantity of story to get in', when faced with drawing things together, but some latitude was allowed. At this point she had written the August number and declares that it 'is to last till after the December No;' an ambiguous remark since she goes on to say she has 'four more numbers to write' (758), so making it unclear whether the four numbers, ending with December's, were to conclude the novel or whether she really was to continue *after* December. Certainly the novel was designed to end *about* that time, and she had written enough for a January episode to appear after her death. In a letter tentatively dated 31 October 1865, from The Lawn, she says, 'I am going to finish my story while here if I can' (781-2), an indication of how near completion she felt herself to be. It is safe to assume that the novel if completed would not have gone much beyond January, so that very little is lost, and the drift of the story (Molly's and Roger's engagement, with their marriage or the certainty of it) may be taken as the true conclusion.

II

Gaskell wrote on the familiar foolscap sheets, mostly blue of various shades, without chapter division (provided, with chapter titles, in proof). The manuscript has the compositors' names on it, but almost no other printing house signs. Only at one point, the end of Squire

Hamley's humiliating row with Mr Preston at the drainage works (ch. 30) does she write: 'Please, end of a chapter',[7] while someone in blue pencil has written 'Qy chapter' at the point where chapter 51 now begins (after Molly's painful interview with Cynthia). In writing, Gaskell clearly kept the basic serial length in mind and there is a sense of episodes which naturally pause to provide the end of a chapter.[8] The occasional false starts or passages, which are then struck out, enforce the point that this is the original manuscript and not a fair copy, since Gaskell continues after the crossing-through or turns over the page and begins again on the back.[9] This excised material is either expanded or else repositioned: in both cases evidence of the skill with which Gaskell focused on passing detail while bearing the grand design in mind. An example of the first is in chapter 21, 'The Half-sisters', when the party which includes Molly and Cynthia are about to play vingt-un. The description of the game, Cynthia's lack of money, and the conversation with Mr and Mrs Gibson on return home all seem to be an expansion from a deleted paragraph designed to take the action rapidly forward:

> . . . *very sorry to go in for anything so slow.*'
> Cynthia had not got her purse with her, and borrowed from
> Molly. But she gambled extremely – put on very high stakes
> without any regard to probability, so much was she attending
> to her neighbour's conversation, and advising him about his
> cards. The end of it was that when the game was over she
> was five or six shillings in Molly's debt. Molly never thought
> twice about this till after nine days had elapsed, when wanting
> some change she asked Cynthia for repayment. Cynthia went
> very red, much to Molly's surprize as she happened to know
> she had received five or six pounds from Mrs Gibson, as
> payment of a dividend – Mr Gibson having relinquished all
> claim to his wife's fortune as has been said before.[10]

This would do well if we didn't now see how Gaskell has filled it out with the home conversation about the Hamley sons and the seemingly casual mention of Mr Preston's visit, which enforces the 'blackmail' theme, though here only hinting at it by Cynthia's abruptness in going to her room and by her mother's embarrassment.[11] Another example of this expansion, the laying of plot groundwork through brief exposition followed by close presentation of conversation and psychological detail, is the handling of the scandal that involves Molly. In chapter 47, Molly was to be confronted by her father immediately after Mrs Gibson's reading of Cynthia's letter, presumably with news that the gossip had reached him. To save what might be a truncated or clumsy narrative, Gaskell delayed the confrontation by detailing the return of the Cumnors (providing Lady Harriet to rescue Molly) and the buzz of gossip that forces Miss Browning to do her duty by Mary Pearson's child and tell Mr Gibson, however unpleasant the consequences.[12]

An example of the second, treatment of excised material – its repositioning because some other concern must be fully allowed play, the architectonics demanding that each movement be properly prepared for and developed – comes at the end of chapter 21. Gaskell began by writing what is virtually the opening of chapter 25, 'Hollingford in a Bustle', but running her pen in rapid circles through each line, turned over the page and began the sequence of chapters 22, 23 and 24 which takes us back to the Hamleys and fleshes out the irritable relationship between the Squire and Osborne. Coming again to the preparations for the Easter ball (ch. 25) Gaskell did not turn back and copy out what she had written before (possibly the portion of manuscript was out of her hands by this time), so that we have lost the Brownings' hopeful preparations for another visit by Lady Harriet, who they were determined should not catch them unawares again.[13]

Amidst the concern for and control of the whole design and her constant domestic and social preoccupations, where writing was only one more piece of busy-ness, difficulties of local detail were dealt with as best she could. In December 1864 she wrote to Smith asking for 'one more printed copy of all I had written, as I had not one either in MSS or print, and have forgotten all the names' (740). This perpetual trouble gives Miss Browning the Christian name variously of Sally, Dorothy and Clarinda; the second Mrs Gibson starts uneasily as Mrs Brown (this once only), but her married name of Kirkpatrick occasionally drops into being Fitzpatrick. Where necessary Gaskell left blanks, trusting to herself, William Gaskell, or Smith to fill in at proof stages: 'in the last piece sent . . . there is a word omitted in describing the band at the Ball: – I did not know what instrument to put in; and wise people tell me "CLARIONET".[14] Earlier, not recalling Molly's mother's maiden name, she left a blank after 'Mary' but no one could fill it up, though a later blank was plugged when Miss Browning doubted Mr Preston to be a 'match for Mary Pearson's daughter'; other blanks are filled at random or else the name recalled and inserted in the manuscript.[15] Where necessary other 'wise people' yielded information: the rare plant Mr Gibson gives to Lady Harriet, *Drosera rotundifolia*, was a blank in the manuscript; young Coxe's ignorance of the difference between 'apophysis and epiphysis' was a total blank, while it was no doubt Cambridge friends who told her that it was in Oxford that the examinations are called 'Schools', 'a high wrangler' being the aim at Cambridge, not a First. The proposed course of Osborne's university career (largely and ironically achieved by the slower Roger) is expanded into something more precise than a casual expectation that he will 'do great things at college'.[16] The expansion is not just information, however, for it makes Osborne's failure the more painful: 'he quite hopes to get a fellowship at Trinity. He says he is sure to be high up among the wranglers, and that he expects to get one of the Chancellor's medals' (p. 71). The confidence of Osborne, echoed through his adoring mother, makes concrete the bitterness of his actual career.

Other details show an awareness of minor effects: the reality of such details as Molly 'tying up the long sea-green stalks of bright-budded carnations', which began simply as 'tying up the carnations', the scene visualized and expanded in midflight, for Gaskell crosses out the word when no further than 'carna'; while Mr Gibson, enraged by Coxe's love-letter, determines to replace Shakespeare in the surgery by Bacon's Essays, which immediately becomes Johnson's Dictionary, a more basic humiliation of the foolish Coxe; and Molly's reading at the Hamley home is changed from *The Heart of Midlothian* to *The Bride of Lammermoor*, perhaps hinting more closely at Osborne's love entanglement through the loves of Ravenswood and Lucy, a more romantic affair and therefore more in tune with Molly's idealism than poor Effie Dean's illegitimate child.[17] Psychologically, changes show an awareness of what is proper to a character. We may regret the disappearance of Miss Browning's exclamation of 'Goody Grope!' into the tame 'Goodness me!', but there is no doubt about the inappropriateness of an elderly spinster talking of washing her lace 'as tenderly as if it had been a new-born babe' and it was crossed out in manuscript.[18]

III

Some of these details are no doubt minor, and not likely to affect our reading of the novel as a whole. Yet they do, through the only manuscript we possess of a novel by her, show the command Gaskell now had of her medium, and her awareness of effects both large and small, even under the stress of keeping up with the serial publication. She might be unwell, harassed, pressed for space, house-hunting, yet she never lost sight of the needs of the novel itself and wrote with a determination that it should be as complete as possible. The pace is established at the beginning, in many ways leisurely, and the laying out of the story maintains that pace, Gaskell not needing to huddle up the ending as she had had to do with *North and South*. Henry James, in his review of the novel (the *Nation*, 22 February 1866), noted and defended this way of working, for if the reader might be tempted to ask 'of what possible concern to him are the clean frocks and the French lessons of little Molly Gibson' he will find they are a means to the 'realization' of Molly, Gaskell's central idea, and 'have educated him to a proper degree of interest in the heroine'.[19]

This accumulation of detail, the web or texture of the novel, is essential to its existence. The establishment of Hollingford, the routine of people's lives, the moment-to-moment trivia of their existence, once called up, forms the basis of their fictional existence. The intermeshing of individuals which comes from a close knitting of their ordinary routines (here beginning in and at all times intertwined with love) finds early expression in Molly's fantasy, recognizable from personal childhood memory, of a constant link with her father, centre of her young world, by a chain as long as his longest round in medical practice, for her to pull when she wanted him, 'and, if you didn't want to come, you could pull back again; but I should know you knew I wanted you, and we could never lose each other' (p. 27). The idea, a pleasing fancy founded in affection, takes some of its force by Molly's quiet selflessness ('and, if you didn't want to come, you could pull back again'), which only asks for knowledge of love, not for its demonstration in physical presence. The sense of security in her relationship, that a chain does exist, makes the intrusion of Mrs Kirkpatrick, with its rude breaking of threads, the more painful, especially when Gibson finds he has assumed a chain very different from that offered by Molly. This web is woven in the community of Hollingford and the surrounding countryside: we never go beyond Hamley Hall or Ashcombe – London and France exist only by report, while the Africa of Roger's expedition is no more than a dim rumour.

Hollingford is generally held to be another re-creation of the Knutsford of Gaskell's childhood, apparently confirmed by 'Chesterford', its original name in the manuscript, soon disguised as Hollyford, and then fixed as Hollingford. A closer look suggests (in the latter part, at least) that this is rather the Midlands of Warwickshire and schooldays in Stratford – two miles outside Hollingford, Molly can see 'the blue range of the Malverns' (p. 533), while Aimée, travelling to find her husband, takes the Birmingham coach from London. Warwickshire words ('scomfished', 'unked') may further suggest the setting. If establishing the exact location may seem unimportant, this physical separation of Knutsford and Hollingford serves to stress that Gaskell is not evoking, however skilfully, a single place she knows, but is creating time and place, even if at the back of it there may be experience and reminiscences of her own. To use scenes and even a period of time which she has lived through may help her to see and so create, but Hollingford is not Knutsford and Molly Gibson is not the young Elizabeth Stevenson.

The period of the novel is that of Gaskell's youth, certainly; it is set before 'the passing of the Reform Bill' of 1832 (p. 3). There is a fairly easily calculable chronology, from about 1822 when the story opens and Molly is twelve, while the main action, beginning about 1826, occupies just over two years. This sequence is disturbed by Osborne's son, according to his birth-certificate, being born in 183- (p. 660) and nearly two years old at this time. But this is a minor blemish (the age is right for the overall scheme) in the general control of the action. Molly was born roughly in the same year (1810) as Gaskell, so no doubt memory serves in establishing a sense of period through hints, allusions and commentary – we are in the years before Catholic Emancipation (1829) began to be talked of, though Byron is dead (1825).[20] The period setting is not far from the world of George Eliot's *Felix Holt* (1866) and *Middlemarch* (1870-1), both placed about the time of the 1832 Reform Act, and overlaps in part with that of *Vanity Fair* (1848), which runs from about 1813 to 1840.[21] Gaskell, however, is not here concerned with the dynamics of history, though like Thackeray and Eliot she is aware of a world removed from her own in customs and costumes.[22] Other references remind us of our own new age, since we are reading of days before railways, before Muscular Christianity, when memories are still fresh of the French Revolution and the Regency crisis (pp. 3, 30, 304), while real figures such as Sir Astley Cooper the

187

surgeon and the biologist Geoffroi-St Hilaire appear briefly. Eliot offers a quasi-scientific analysis of the pressure of circumstance upon individuals; Thackeray, the portrayal of manners. Gaskell differs from both, since her past, of which she insistently makes us aware, has two functions: to allow the action to be completed and contemplated from the satisfaction of distance which shows the whole; and to take advantage of sympathies for an age which while past hovers yet in the memory of many readers and so charges events with our own feelings for childhood and youth.

The culture that was Gaskell's, the accumulation of a lifetime, is fully in evidence, even though often in no more than muttered fragments or faint whispers, so that the novel is often an echoing grove. She was confident enough to write quotations from memory, so that James Shirley's 'Only the actions of the just/Smell sweet and blossom in the dust' (p. 253) came as 'The sainted memory of the just/Smells sweet and blossoms in the dust' before being corrected in proof. Yet clearly she possessed Shirley's verses, as she possessed Shakespeare ('smiling at grief' or Lady Cumnor looking like Lady Macbeth in black velvet), calling up such things at will from the store; falling into half-quotations (as she sometimes indicates an intensification of language by enclosing it in inverted commas to give it the status of quotation) and this mosaic colours the work. If Lady Cumnor and Lady Macbeth are no more than momentarily alike, yet a childhood song, long before copied out into one of those manuscript music books, will come at need and sound ironically as Cynthia sings 'Tu t'en repentiras, Colin ... si tu prends une femme' (p. 311), 'such a pretty, playful little warning to young men', as Mrs Gibson calls it, blissfully unaware that the listening Osborne is already married and to a French girl.

More complexly, when Mrs Hamley dies the decline of Squire and his estate finds expression in the reduction of his establishment and the decay of possessions which take on a metaphoric force:

> The whole stable-establishment had been reduced; perhaps
> because it was the economy which told most on the enjoyment
> of both Squire and Osborne ... The old carriage – a heavy
> family-coach bought in the days of comparative prosperity
> – was no longer needed after Madam's death, and fell to pieces
> in the cobwebbed seclusion of the coach-house (p. 288).

This – and it is part of a much longer analysis of what was wrong at the Hamleys' – seems to accelerate process (as the forest springs around Sleeping Beauty's castle) and though there is no direct verbal echo it catches the mood of and might be suggested by Gaskell's favourite modern poet, Tennyson, in 'Mariana':

> The rusted nails fell from the knots
>   That held the pear to the gable-wall.
> The broken shed look'd sad and strange:
>   Unlifted was the clinking latch:
> Weeded and worn the ancient thatch
>   Upon the lonely moated grange.

The possibility is strengthened by Molly's earlier awareness, when reading Osborne's poetry, of a stillness so intense that the house 'in its silence ... might have been the "moated grange"' (pp. 92-3), Tennyson's own moment of stillness having its starting-point in Shakespearean allusion.

There are larger units of allusion at work and a fine example of creative reworking (not a deliberate process, for the most part) is the first two chapters, where Molly as a child of twelve visits the Towers for the first time, falls asleep on Mrs Kirkpatrick's bed, is forgotten and, after ordeal by dessert with the Cumnor family, is rescued by her father. This summary itself may suggest some of the fairy-tale parallels and whole cloud of folk associations that permeate this section, from the opening 'rigmarole of childhood' that places it for the adult reader in those early days and announces it as a prelude to the narrative and to Molly's life. The rigmarole of 'In a county there was a shire' imitates 'This is the key of the kingdom./In that kingdom there is a city./In that city there is a town' and so on to house, room, bed and on the bed a basket with flowers.[23] Perhaps Gaskell might have ended the novel by following the poem through its reversals again from the flowers in the basket, the basket on the bed and so out to the shire in the county. Story-telling is established, as is the world of a child's wonder, secure, often puzzled, yet fenced around by the certainties, however arbitrary, of the adult world. The excitement of closed gardens being opened, of sleeping under trees and being found by ladies who talk over her, suggest tales of faerie and of elvish queens, of Goldilocks and the three bears. Clearly these echoes need tact in their recognition and interpetration, yet, though not wishing to overemphasize the connection, the Miss Brownings returning in separate vehicles from the Towers, each thinking Molly 'was with the other' (p. 17), recalls Mary and Joseph returning from the Temple (this sets up no parallel role for Molly, except as child and the lost one). These patterns of childhood, of form (rhymes and tales) and of content (children's adventures), mirror Molly's childhood world of stories and her world of childhood experience. All this is the subtlest of webs, vibrations set up in the mind that is close to Gaskell's own world of tales, poems, folk belief, literature and art, which allows her to refer to Poole's painting of Solomon Eagle in *Mary Barton*, *Pickwick Papers* in *Cranford*, the song 'Leezie Lindsay' in *North and South*, or ghost stories in *The Life of Charlotte Brontë* with an ease that springs from a memory not only stocked with but naturally possessing and rejoicing in all these things. They are not dead tokens but living impulses.

The security given Molly by her father, which she would wish to make more sure by the chain, is the certainty of happy childhood, where even discomfort can be resolved by the return home. It is the breaking of this security by her own father and the disturbance, emotional and mental, which sets Molly on an adolescent quest, an intensified version of the common passage from childhood to the adult world, begun in the passionate outburst at the proposed marriage, proceeding through rejection of Osborne, and the growth of respect for Roger into love. The quest's resolution would be the recognition, which Molly has virtually achieved by the story's end, that life is a flux. After childhood, permanency is only retrievable in its tales.

IV

The opening adventure at the Towers is the prelude, a recurrent feature of the novels: *Mary Barton*, *Ruth*, *North and South* all have this short, seemingly dispensable yet integral lay-out of themes: in miniature it establishes Molly, presents her father and Hollingford society, and introduces the careless character of Mrs Kirkpatrick, who never tells a lie, yet finds it easier not to think what is truth. Molly is impelled from the passivity of her familiar environment (the innocent victim of Master Coxe's passion) to the Hamley friendships that demand more of her than the naturally accreted affection for her father. On her visit she finds a family role open to her, though with no implication of acting or pretence. She is the daughter that the Hamleys lost, the confidante in love of her sons that Mrs Hamley needs, and a sister to Roger and Osborne, who treat her as an equal when forced to accept her knowledge of the latter's marriage. A more active response is demanded, yet she is still in no sense a fully passional character; her feelings are sympathy and affection, filial love for Mrs Hamley. Then her father comes with his news, determined by his love for Molly, which is to alienate her and drive her into areas of fiercer passion.

Gibson is an honest man, faithful to Mary Pearson, his first wife, yet visited by memories (scarcely more than hints, yet effective in mystery) of Jean, the love of his life. An intelligent man and successful doctor, he is part of the life of the mind that Hollingford offers. By the best standards (or those of Mrs Kirkpatrick, who thinks them the same thing) he is vulgar with bread and cheese lunches and drinking tea from his saucer. He thinks himself old enough to look back on his past emotions with a regret qualified by the certainty that he is serenely beyond them. If, in choosing a new wife, he had had less love for Molly or more, things might have turned out better. As it is he accepts the consequences of his own action, ironically negated as it is by Coxe's departure, bears with the new Mrs Gibson (his only savagery is when she breaks professional confidence about Osborne's health), and makes the best of a bad job. If life is a comedy to him who thinks, a tragedy to him who feels, Gibson is lucky.

The second Mrs Gibson is something of a chameleon, a shape-changer (we may take the hint from the variety of her names: Hyacinth Clare, Mrs Kirkpatrick, Mrs Gibson), whose nature is coloured by her surroundings and who has no values that she consistently holds to. To argue with her is to wander in the maze of subterfuges from truth that she lays out, so that while she may lose a skirmish, ultimately she wins the field like a bush-fighter or guerilla, as she vanishes before a frontal assault and twists and turns in the pursuit, so that her adversary overruns her. She is careless – of exact truth, of people's affections and wishes – concerned to gain comfort, easily jealous as of Lady Harriet's friendship with Molly, preferring even after an uncomfortable visit to the Towers or a scolding to tears by Lady Cumnor that only she shall be thought intimate with the noble family. But she is not evil; she has not the sustained energy for it. Lady Agnes and Lady Harriet have escaped damage and her jealousy shows itself in special attention to Molly, which is unwelcome rather than vicious, even when it is to ensure that Molly and Lady Harriet shall not meet (pp. 411-12). Most of Mrs Gibson is surface. She has manners, but lacks the values (evident amongst the Cumnors) on which such a system is based, and her trivial observance displays the trivial mind.

She makes her husband and Molly extremely uncomfortable, but the effect is comic. Yet there are hints that she is not able to conceal unpleasant truths from herself, so that beneath the silliness there is a capacity for pain, however limited, to which we can respond. Pinned down by Gibson over Osborne's health (pp. 441-2), she laments, 'I wish I'd never married again', and if policy and egoism limit her wish to marriage in general rather than complaint of Gibson in particular, she senses that she has not found the escape that she had hoped for. Teaching had been a tedium where only those many little indulgences, innocent in themselves, sustained her, such as 'the dirty, dog's-eared delightful novels from the Ashcombe circulating library, the leaves of which she turned over with a pair of scissors' (p. 148) – less innocent may have been the distraction Preston offered. She is nearest to pathos, not unmingled with her own hysterical relief, in the proposal scene. It begins typically when, realizing the possibility of an offer, she feels herself blush 'and she was not displeased at the consciousness'. With Gibson's entrance comes 'a conviction of her willingness to accept a man' who an hour before was simply 'one of the category of unmarried men to whom matrimony was possible' (p. 118). Gaskell shows in quick juxtaposition their reactions to Gibson's proposal: how both stand back and recognize their reactions. Gibson is aware that the question of the wisdom of what he has done came 'the instant that the words were said past recall', while her response is a pathetic breakdown in tears, 'it was such a wonderful relief to feel that she need not struggle any more for a livelihood' (p. 120). Though unintentional, it is not inappropriate that the novel breaks off with Mrs Gibson left to dream about her daughter and her clothes.

The daughter, Cynthia, is a more toughly independent character, able to deal with her mother, aware of what is truth, yet cursed with a shallowness of feeling which she recognizes, regrets, and yields to. Judgment of her is through herself; it is one of the subtleties of the writing that the author never condemns, hardly comments upon her nature. It emerges from the harshest critic of all, who bitterly reflects upon her own ability to analyse but not to act. Psychologically we feel the truth of a shallowness that comes from deprivation – the child forced to be independent, sent away to school, scarcely allowed home,[24] so that the inability to feel deeply may be seen as a product of an original need for self-defence.

There is an originality here,[25] in the suspension of authorial judgment and in the real value of Cynthia. In the end she is an unsatisfactory companion for Molly, but she is lovable and loving so far as she can be. Gaskell prepares her arrival carefully (part of the modulation of reference to characters throughout, increasing as an entry is approached, the gap increasing between mentions as they pass from the action). Mrs Kirkpatrick was established as a mother on Molly's first visit to the Towers, but Cynthia begins to be mentioned on Clare's visit that leads to Gibson's proposal. Despite invitations, she did not come herself, nor to her mother's wedding, and Molly's questioning of Mrs Kirkpatrick produces no useful information, only her own use as a mirror for her prospective step-mother's romance with Mr Gibson ('But I like the dark-haired, foreign kind of beauty best – just now' (p. 146)). The details of Cynthia's physical appearance, so reluctantly given by her mother, are recalled at the wedding, when Mr Preston points to the portraits of French court beauties and finds her likeness in that of Mademoiselle de St Quentin. Like Molly's, our expectation is aroused by Cynthia's imminence. She proves to be charming and it is only with acquaintance that her faults emerge; at first even what would be flaws in others, seem natural:

> Cynthia was very beautiful, and was so well aware of this fact
> that she had forgotten to care about it; no one with such
> loveliness ever appeared so little conscious of it. Molly would
> watch her perpetually as she went about the room, with the
> free stately step of some wild animal of the forest – moving
> almost, as it were, to the continual sound of music (p. 250).

All this – 'free', 'animal', 'music' – suggests a plasticity not bound by restraint of convention. Yet what is natural in Cynthia is contradicted by her concealment, her duplicity in the secret understanding with Roger and continued involvement with Preston, all of which can be seen again as defences of someone left to fend for herself as a child. She can gain love, yet except as daughter or sister (and then only to kin by marriage), she seems scarcely capable of returning it. She smiles on all men alike, and after overwhelming Preston, Roger

193

Coxe, finds refuge in marriage with Mr Henderson, who offers Cynthia love enough and security enough but who won't bother her with passion or seriousness as Preston or Roger would – ' "I don't like people of deep feelings," said Cynthia, pouting. "They don't suit me. Why couldn't [Roger] let me go without this fuss? I'm not worth his caring for!" ' (p. 700). Cynthia is right: she and Roger are quite unsuitable, but she has had her diversions on the way. It is a relief to see her happily settled (she would be capable of suffering) with her dandyish Mr Henderson and feel that the pain Roger has suffered can only draw him and Molly closer.

Molly grows up through experience which is both painful and sustaining. She begins as the princess *lointaine*, guarded by her father, sent into a strange country to avoid the puppyish infatuation of Master Coxe. The love that Gibson feels for her and she returns is a guarantee of the rightness of his action, but she is at a stage when adolescent life begins to take form of its own, ready to receive impressions from outside familiar circles. She is agitated by the suggestion of Squire Hamley that her father might marry again, though this is scarcely more than a passing shadow. As so often, however, it is one of Gaskell's key-notes which prepare the reader. In the comedy of circumstances – comedy in the larger sense – Gibson, who has no such idea when Hamley makes his rough jest, is led by Miss Eyre's prolonged absence and by the slovenly lunch laid before Lord Hollingford (pp. 113-14) to turn his thoughts to 'a sensible, agreeable woman of thirty or so'. There is comedy in the disparity between image and Clare's reality. But the comedy is for the reader, not for Gibson in his marriage, still less for Molly, who feels betrayed by the news which now seems like something long designed, an exclusion from the security of her father's confidence. It is part of Molly's adult sense of an alienating world that when Gibson confesses his marriage plans she suddenly finds criticism of her beloved father and is able even at that moment to recognize that silence may be better than a reaction of impulse.

The move from Hollingford to the Hamleys is in some sense the physical representation of Molly's move from the Eden of childhood into the fallen world of adult experience, though I wouldn't press this analogy too far, any more than the idea of Mrs Gibson as the wicked step-mother. Gaskell uses these configurations of folk- and fairy-narratives, but is not bound by them. Brought under the loving influence of Mrs Hamley, Molly easily falls in with the mother's idealization of Osborne, the brilliant son who takes after her in delicacy and beauty. Molly, a willing partisan, delights in accounts of his career and his poetry, partly because this sharing gives pleasure to Mrs Hamley. This is Molly's first real experience of a woman's influence on something more than the level of Betty or Miss Eyre. If anything its power and sympathy make the idea of a new mother in Mrs Kirkpatrick more difficult, for Mrs Hamley can be a mother without breaking in on the Hollingford home and at the same time directs Molly towards the wider shores of love in the ideal image of Osborne. Molly thinks not of marriage (Squire Hamley blunders here, though he is right in Molly's intimate involvement with his family), but rather of a partisanship as much given to Mrs Hamley as to the son who is the outward manifestation of her need for love and sympathy.

When the sons are expected (Roger arrives first) Molly is skilfully placed in stillness, so she overhears the arrival and the formation of a family group while Osborne is most in her mind (she is reading one of Osborne's poems), unaware of the disaster that is overtaking Osborne:

> The house was so still, in its silence it might have been the
> 'moated grange'; the bomming buzz of the blue flies, in the
> great staircase window, seemed the loudest noise indoors. And
> there was scarcely a sound out-of-doors but the humming of
> bees, in the flower-beds below the window. Distant voices
> from the far-away fields where they were making hay – the
> scent of which came in sudden wafts, distinct from that of the
> nearer roses and honeysuckles – these merry piping voices just
> made Molly feel the depth of the present silence. She had left
> off copying, her hand weary with the unusual exertion of so
> much writing, and she was lazily trying to learn one or two
> of the poems off by heart. . . . Suddenly, there was the snap of
> a shutting gate; wheels crackling [MS cranching] on the dry
> gravel, horses' feet on the drive; a loud cheerful voice in the
> house, coming up through the open windows, the hall, the
> passages, the staircase, with unwonted fulness and roundness of
> tone . . . through the undraperied hollow square of the hall
> and staircase every sound ascended clear and distinct; and
> Molly heard the Squire's glad 'Hallo! here he is!' and Madam's
> softer, more plaintive voice; and then the loud, full, strange

tone, which she knew must be Roger's. Then there was an opening and shutting of doors, and only a distant buzz of talking (pp. 92-3).

The description has something of what Barbara Hardy in another context has called 'sensitive scenery',[26] its silence suggesting Molly's suspended yet receptive state. Molly then goes down, after a proper interval, to be drawn into the family misery over Osborne's university failure and to see Roger for the first time.

Roger, who gives 'the impression of strength more than elegance', has a solid reality, that seems unlikely to defeat the fervent admiration Molly has for the chevalier, Osborne. At dinner, when the Squire in his disappointment and anger at news of Osborne's failure calls for a bottle of Osborne's favourite wine, one of only six bottles left, to drink Roger's health, Molly makes at least a gesture, in placing her palm over the glass, 'an open mark of fealty to the absent Osborne' (p. 98). She has taken him as her lord, moving in an ideal world where Osborne is concerned, with that sense of the higher life common in adolescence. When Osborne does arrive, though, she is already in a process of reassessment, after her father's news and Roger's sympathy for her despair, which is to take her from adoration of Osborne (or rather, his image) to love of Roger. By this process Gaskell charts the development and maturity of Molly, her judgment already keen enough in assessing her mind-made image to feel a kind of relief when her first meeting is deferred, 'she was so much afraid of being disappointed' (p. 190). And then Osborne comes on her unexpectedly, so she has no chance to prepare a response until the first impression is established. The disgust with bullocks, the fastidious fatigue, the languor and fragility are all part of the Osborne conveyed by Mrs Hamley; yet the reality is something different from Molly's creation.

There is no great revulsion. Before the end of the afternoon 'she had reinstated him on his throne in her imagination' (p. 192). But it is now as poet she sees him, not the chevalier 'sans peur et sans reproche'. Before she knows Osborne has a wife, the process of disqualification has begun. Molly demands something more vigorous, both mentally and physically. Osborne's lassitude and petulance are partly excused by the reader's knowledge of his marital problems and of his threatened life, yet the painfulness of his life is overshadowed by the pain he gives his father, who shuts himself away with his grief and ill-temper, bewildered as a squirrel in a cage (p. 296).

The painfulness of Gaskell's finest moments is often the pain of regret in lost opportunity, of 'if only', and this pain she conveys in Osborne's death, where Molly is called on to subdue her grief to alleviate the Squire's despair. As Molly approaches Hamley Hall so a light throws its beam towards her, 'spotting the silver shining with its earthly coarseness' (p. 642). Osborne lies in the old nursery: in some sense the relationship of infant to father has been restored, for in death Squire Hamley has acted newly made father to his child ('the Squire would let none on us touch him; he took him up as if he was a baby' (pp. 641-2)). But mixed with love and grief is also anger and disappointment. To lose an infant is sad; to lose someone with whose life you have been long associated is an untangling that tears away whole areas of one's own existence.

And so Molly comes and in silence slips to his feet and there 'they sate, silent and still, he in his chair, she on the floor; the dead man, beneath the sheet, for a third' (p. 643). In its suggestion of grief by frozen attitudes, themselves symbols of the emotion they represent, it has something of the power of Keats in the fallen gods of *Hyperion*: 'Long, long those two were postured motionless,/Like sculpture builded-up upon the grave/Of their own power' (i, 382-4). Molly, emotionally and structurally, is the link between the living and the dead, as this tableau reminds us: she links the Squire to his wife, to Osborne, to his own dead daughter Fanny, and more importantly in this moment she keeps him alive and brings to him a living daughter and heir in Aimée and her son, as she will give herself to the Squire in the unwritten but certain marriage with Roger. From the passive-feeling child, surrounded by the patterns and security of childhood narratives, she moves through an adolescent ideal of romance to a strength which gives sympathy and love. In finding out some of the ways in which people strive to become fully themselves, she is brought to a reality which is more painful because more complex and less certain in its outcome than tales suggest and with which she comes to terms.

In choosing an epigraph from Henry James's review of the novel on its posthumous publication I wanted to enforce the deeply personal nature of Gaskell's writing, as well as to hint why she is not in the end a writer of the highest order like Dickens or George Eliot. If we try to value Gaskell too highly, we shall only do damage by an inflated view. She is at times perhaps too personally involved in her own creation; she has not the great artist's power of 'anonymity', of the withdrawal of self, that allows the full creation of unpleasant characters or the free play of evil.[27] Gaskell finds it difficult to think of anyone as actively bad, so that Mrs Gibson, for instance, is never vicious or productive of evil. This in turn means that a dynamic drive is lacking.[28] Technically, *Wives and Daughters* is the greatest of her novels. Unlike *Sylvia's Lovers*, most nearly an achieved tragedy, it does not falter in tone as that novel does at the Siege of Acre. There is a sustained control of the narrative flow, in which characters are prepared for and the background both natural and social is detailed and dramatically effective. Yet occasionally we may feel that Gaskell is fulfilling her own wish, expressed in a letter to George Smith in 1860: 'I wish Mr Trollope would go on writing Framley Parsonage for ever. I don't see any reason why it should ever come to an end' (602). Though *Wives and Daughters* clearly was to finish, the drive towards a conclusion can seem missing. Playing over the novel is Gaskell's own character: her humour, her understanding of people and situations, her reading, her memories – all these combine to make the novel a summation, however unintentional, of her writing career, all combine to make the echoing grove of personality.

Yet if James is right in his analysis, there is something more still to *Wives and Daughters*. There is a seriousness in Molly's presentation as a study of growth to maturity, the more difficult to handle because it involves process and impressions of transition from one state to another: from childhood through adolescence to the adult. In this, Gaskell is again the heir of the Romantics, above all of Wordsworth, both the poet of the *Lyrical Ballads* and of *The Prelude*.[29] The novel is great not because it challenges direct comparison with, for instance, the social analysis and interaction of history and character that *Middlemarch* excels in, but because it charts the course and progress of human feeling and reveals, as did its author herself, the unique personality.

8

The Short Stories

'My dear Scheherezade'

Charles Dickens to Elizabeth Gaskell, 1851

From her first published short story, 'Libbie Marsh's Three Eras' (1847), to the end of her career, Gaskell produced about thirty tales. She was a natural story-teller. Dickens's tribute to her as the fascinating narrator of the Thousand-and-One-Nights, though part of an attempt to placate her after he had written up one of her ghost stories as 'To Be Read at Dusk', suggests how he valued her as a contributor. There are her own accounts of telling tales among friends – with the Howitts at Heidelberg in 1841, 'the most frightening & wild stories we had ever heard, – some *such* fearful ones – all true' (44); or those ghost stories the proposed telling of which shook Charlotte Brontë, or the tales the Winkworths heard. Even the novels show a tendency to self-contained or inset stories; her characters are inveterate story-tellers. The often separate existence of such stories from the novel in which they came to be embodied is suggested by an independent manuscript version of the ghost story in *Sylvia's Lovers* (ch. 38).[1]

Besides her delight in these tales, they had obvious advantages. Being short – a comparative term: some, like 'My Lady Ludlow' and 'A Dark Night's Work', as long as *Cranford*, are really short novels or novellas – they could be written more easily in terms of time and concentration than the novels. Many are occasional pieces, for Travers Madge's Sunday School magazine, for Dickens's Christmas numbers of *Household Words*, called forth by circumstances to which she could respond more easily than the demand of a full-length work. They all (except 'The Moorland Cottage') appeared in periodicals and were, to some extent, ephemeral, hence repetitions of theme or motif from story to story, even rewriting of the tale itself, as though a trial run had suggested possibilities in the material which could be exploited once the issue of a magazine had passed into oblivion of a year or two. *Cranford* has its origin in 'The Last Generation in England'; 'Half a Lifetime Ago' was first published as 'Martha Preston'. Significantly, the earlier version of each appeared in the United States, so the readership of the versions would overlap very little.

There were two other practical considerations. Too much has been made, perhaps, of the tyranny of the three-volume novel as a form in the Victorian period, yet for a writer who wanted to work in fictional forms that did not easily extend to this length, periodical publication was increasingly available in magazines like *Household Words* and the *Cornhill*. Though Gaskell had problems with *North and South*, other tales by her were published serially by Dickens ('Lizzie Leigh', her first contribution for him, appeared in three parts, while 'My Lady Ludlow' extended over fourteen numbers – comparable with the troublesome *North and South*'s twenty), proof that there was nothing in her nature or her kind of fiction anti-pathetic to serialization, though experience might make her bitter. The variety in her stories indicates how far she could let the nature of the tale determine its best length, though there are those that seem spun out or huddled to a conclusion. When enough material accumulated Gaskell gathered what she thought worthwhile into volume form; five collections appeared in her lifetime.[2] In 1859, the wish to get Meta abroad after her broken engagement led Gaskell to reprint a collection (*Round the Sofa*) against her better judgment, and the publisher, Sampson Low, aggravated her dissatisfaction in a forced deal by attempting to pass it off as an original collection. Yet this bargain points up the other advantage of these stories: they brought in cash quickly and when it was needed. For a household often pressed for money, any addition to their general resources was welcome. In Germany in 1859 Gaskell could offer Dickens three stories, receive the money, and so extend the tour. The amount earned was substantial: if we take the thirteen stories published in *Household Words*, for which figures are now easily available,[3] she earned between 1850 and 1858 £241 4s. 6d. (quite apart from payments for *Cranford* and *North and South* during the same period), about £27 a year from this source alone. There was also the advantage, when she came to take it, that short stories could be sold twice over, once to the magazine and again to a publisher in volume form – this was one copyright that Gaskell wisely reserved to herself.

Themes and interests in the short stories are akin to those of the novels, yet here more sharply focused by concentration of form; even the lengthy 'A Dark Night's Work' centres upon a single sequence of events, a small group of people, rather than the socially complex ramifications of *Wives and Daughters*. Gaskell's earliest efforts were basically Sunday-school stories, with a clear moral (though often she felt the need to hedge round the concluding tag with humorous irony, as though to separate it from the story for the sophisticated or to apologize for something embarrassing to her but demanded by the form). The theology and comfort of stories like 'Bessy's Troubles at Home' and 'Hand and Heart' are of the simplest, their modern interest lying in details of life and feeling rather than the assurance of God as loving refuge; yet insistence upon a power greater than the individual's finds its extension in stories like 'The Moorland Cottage', where Maggie's idealism preserves to her a sense of the higher in life, so fatally lost to her brother. Such enlarging of the spirit, part of the Romantic as it is of the Christian tradition, is linked again and again in the stories with the inner development in woman, while so often the man (a brother or a lover) is caught by the world, where an inherent selfishness enlarges and engulfs him. In the world of Molly Gibson, God may largely have disappeared, yet the ability to see beyond self and to strive beyond (Cynthia can *only* see) is a true development from the Sunday-school fiction.

The Romantic tradition is central, for the 'fluxes and refluxes' of feeling that Gaskell so often and so subtly traces are those Wordsworth speaks of in the 1800 'Preface' to *Lyrical Ballads*, while his championing of low subjects and common speech (something distinct from vulgarity) helped make industrial and other subjects possible in their own terms, without the genteel fictionalizing that Frances Trollope still found necessary. Libbie Marsh and even Bessie are interesting in themselves. Wordsworth had shown the way to break out of the mechanical restrictions of plot; instead, character begins to dominate in telling a story, and an organic relationship developed between incident and feeling. In 'Libbie Marsh's Three Eras' each era is both an event in the life of the crippled boy, Franky, and an emotional experience in Libbie's life dependent on that event. Libbie moves in terms of the development of feeling, not simply in the accumulation or resolution of events. There is no discovery of wealth or lost heir or husband – the voyage of exploration is within. In some stories, Gaskell moves into the very territory of Wordsworth: 'Half a Lifetime Ago' and 'The Half-Brothers' might be subjects for Lyrical Ballads. The use of objects – the cottage in 'Half a Lifetime Ago', for instance – calls on the emotional or symbolic power of things drawn from long and close association with their human owners, like Margaret's ruined cottage in *The Excursion* (bk 1), and on the way the process of ordinary lives, as in 'Michael', becomes bound up with place beyond any sense of the mercenary. In taking ideas of betrayal, devotion, love that is greater than the obvious satisfactions of marriage and children – Susan Dixon's love for her idiot brother in 'Half a Lifetime Ago' does not take away the hardness of sacrifice – Gaskell concentrates upon the Wordsworth who created 'Michael', who urged that 'We have all of us one human heart'; she ignores, the more obviously for the direct comparison of material possible between 'Half a Lifetime Ago' and 'The Idiot Boy', the comic romance which Wordsworth finds in Johnny's night errantry. For Gaskell perhaps, though Wordsworth no more than she denied seriousness of feeling, idiots are too nearly tragic; to Betty Foy's untroubled love for her idiot boy, Gaskell adds in Sarah Dixon the strain of looking after a recalcitrant irrational being and the emotional suffering of love denied.

The line of feeling that runs through an individual's whole life is strongly evident in the stories. Memories are constantly drawn upon, to renew and strengthen through past experience – 'that blessed mood,/In which the burthen of the mystery/ . . . /Of all this unintelligible world,/Is lightened' – or by contrast to emphasize how dayspring hopes are choked up, especially the aspiring spirits of the woman, whose social position denies her the freedom of the man. Dreams of the past may be springs of life or they may be hauntings that only prove the deadness of the past – they have a logical extension in the ghost stories, most notably in 'The Old Nurse's Story', for the dead and the living may both haunt scenes of their past.

The stories are surveyed here in three main groups: first, the earliest tales and isolated examples published in a variety of magazines; second, those written for Dickens, published in *Household Words* and *All the Year Round;* and third, contributions to the *Cornhill*, culminating in Gaskell's greatest short story, 'Cousin Phillis'. The stories are uneven in quality, though even the weakest have points of interest. The temptation is to think of them only as incidental to the novels and so to stress the ways they anticipate or reflect work done better there. This is often true, but there is a fruitful interplay in Gaskell's *oeuvre*, of which the stories form a major part.

Three stories were published in *Howitt's Journal* between June 1847 and January 1848.[4] 'Libbie Marsh's Three Eras' (June 1847) shows the orphan Libbie drawn by sympathy and love into the lives of Franky Hall, a young cripple, and his shrewish mother, whom she wins over through the only being Mrs Hall treats with tenderness. Each 'era' is a stage in Franky's brief life and in Libbie's movement from self-pity to involvement with others that brings happiness in sharing life with Margaret Hall after Franky's death. For Franky, whom she first sees as a shadow cast on the blind opposite, Libbie buys a pet bird on Valentine's Day, a day made variously significant by the idea of sweethearts, by Libbie's own plainness, by its being her own birthday which, since her mother's death, 'had been the dreariest of all the year because the most haunted by memory of departed happiness' (i, 465). Happiness returns in action. The second era is a Whitsun outing with the Halls and the third, Franky's funeral. Linked in with these is the wooing and marriage of Anne Dixon. In small space, Gaskell effectively integrates this undertheme and gives a sense of reality to her story by details: of Libbie's flitting (yet 'hardly a flitting after all', since 'instead of a cart-load of drawers and baskets, dressers and beds, with old king clock at the top of all, it was only one large wooden chest to be carried after the girl' (i, 459)); of Manchester people's frank comments (Margaret Hale, later, at least has the advantage of beauty); and of the Dunhams Park jollity, with the mistake of the early meal, even while we see the shadow on Franky, openly recognized without mawkishness as death. Gaskell's higher purpose is apparent in the workpeople raised up by their holiday amidst nature: 'I can catch the glance on many a face, the glancing light of the cloud of glory from heaven, "which is our home"' (i, 478). Only when she comes to the explicit moral does the tone, intimate and 'comfortable', hesitate and Gaskell become jokingly self-defensive.

The second story, 'The Sexton's Hero' (September 1847), challenges accepted definitions of the hero. Set on Morecambe Bay, the sexton tells of early life amidst a wild set of young fellows and the rivalry with Gilbert Dawson (increased by their interest in the same girl), which culminates in a challenge to fight that Dawson in conscience refuses. The sexton, having married his Letty, returns late one night across the Bay and as the inrushing tide threatens, Dawson rescues them at the cost of his own life. Atmosphere is dramatically handled: as the couple cross the sands, night and sea close in:

> it were growing darker and darker above and around us, all but one red line of light above the hills. . . . We were longer than we should ha' been in crossing the hollow, the sand was so quick; and when we came up again, there, against the blackness, was the white line of the rushing tide coming up the bay! It looked not a mile from us; and when the wind blows up the bay it comes swifter than a galloping horse (i, 497).

Dawson's herosim, of conscience, of action, of magnanimity, is answer enough to those who framed the question: What is a hero? and the story ends with the brevity of a parable as the Sexton 'turned to his work; and we, having rested sufficiently, rose up, and came away' (i, 501).

More ambitious in its variety of tones, but less successful, is the seasonal 'Christmas Storms and Sunshine' (January 1848). The rivalry of the two families, whose heads work on opposing news-papers, is mildly satirical, never caricature. Gaskell, amidst a comedy of insult and competition, yet shows Mary Hodgson's loving nature and accounts even for Mrs Jenkins's sourness by her childlessness. The central seriousness is in the Hodgson child's attack of croup, with Mrs Jenkins coming to the rescue, stirred by carel singing: 'she began to think over long past days, on softening remembrance of the dead and gone, on words long forgotten, on holy stories heard at her mother's knee' (ii, 200). The families end by taking Christmas dinner together; though lightweight, there is a pleasingly comic sense of detail and an understanding of the realities of life – Mary takes her husband his dinner, in the cold and carrying a crying baby, but he 'had made his appetite up for a potato-pie, and (literary man as he was) his body got so much the better of his mind, that he looked rather black at the cold mutton' (ii, 197).

Two stories for Travers Madge's *Sunday School Penny Magazine* – 'Hand and Heart' (1849) and 'Bessy's Troubles at Home' (1852) – are neat exemplifications of Christian heroism in humble life. Gaskell herself brusquely repudiated the latter as 'complete rubbish', telling Marianne that the 'children who like Bessy's Troubles are great geese' (845). Yet both show a realistic sense, as in the stench of a room where three boys have slept without ventilation (iii, 551). Young

Tom in 'Hand and Heart' is never priggish, while there is sympathetic comedy in Bessy's lesson that scheming for other people without considering their wishes may be selfishness. It is Bessy's sister, Mary, slow and awkward, who is the real heroine and whose scalding convinces Bessy that she must never 'neglect the work clearly laid out for [her] by God or man' (iii, 534).

Three items in *Harper's New Monthly* have been ascribed to Gaskell.[5] The common link is the magazine's association with Sampson Low, English publisher and agent for many American works and for whom in 1857 Gaskell undertook an English edition of Maria Cummins's *Mabel Vaughan* (footnoting Americanisms like 'a good time'; altering words like 'sick' to 'ill'). The American appearance of 'The Doom of the Griffiths' (January 1858), acknowledged Gaskell's by republication in *Round the Sofa*, seems to have involved some jiggery-pokery by Low (488). 'An Incident at Niagara Falls' (June 1858), feeble though it is, has Gaskell's name attached, and is in fact one of the additions she made to *Mabel Vaughan*, 'always with the kindly-granted permission of the authoress'.[6] 'The Siege of the Black Cottage' (February 1857), then, is the really dubious item. A well-to-do farmer's wife explains how, without wealth or beauty, she married so comfortably. Alone in an isolated cottage she defended herself and a large sum of money from Shifty Dick and Jerry; the local farmer's son is so taken by her spirit and determination that he marries her. The story turns more on plot than character, Bessie's situation gives rise to little analysis of feeling, and I would think the attribution doubtful though not impossible. 'An Incident at Niagara Falls' shows the danger of attribution by mere 'feel'. This routine anecdote, of a young man rescuing two Irish labourers trapped on an island at Niagara's brink and his refusal of reward beyond the sale of walking sticks from branches he retrieves from the island, is no addition to Gaskell's reputation. It is is difficult to see why she wrote it into Cummins's novel, except perhaps to relieve the evangelical idealism of the original; presumably Low submitted it to *Harper's*. 'The Doom of the Griffiths', work of the 1830s (488), is altogether superior. Cursed for treachery, the Griffiths shall never prosper and after nine generations the son shall slay the father. Its power lies in the struggle of Owen, last of the Griffiths, to avoid the doom laid on him: he seeks, in face of dire provocation – his own son's accidental death – not to be the death of his father. The prophecy is of course fulfilled, but through the father's anger rather than the son's. Owen's father-in-law believes that Owen fulfilled the prophecy in revenge rather than by accident, and so fixes the way the world will see the tale's pattern, a similar irony to that at the end of *Sylvia's Lovers*. The power, apart from Owen's struggle to avoid fate, lies in the young man's relationship with Nest, whom he secretly marries, and scenes of Welsh life and landscape with the valley of the Griffiths's estate and the village wedding where Owen meets Nest. The ending, in which Owen, Nest, dead child, and dead father are lost in the 'tossing darkness' of the sea, is rapid, too rapid perhaps, but presses home the helpless frailty of men gripped by a curse.

'The Moorland Cottage' (1850), published as a small book designed for the Christmas trade, is related in size and purpose to the Christmas books of Dickens and of Thackeray ('Our Street', 'The Rose and the Ring'). Its idealism and melodramatic ending at sea off the Welsh coast link it both to the 'Sunday-school' tales and to *Wives and Daughters*. Dickens's Christmas Books all have a seasonal connection (slight enough with *The Battle of Life*) and tend to represent the Christian spirit through goodheartedness and guzzling; Thackerary and others, imitating the idea of a small gift book, often jettisoned the seasonal linking. There is no obvious Christmas sense in 'The Moorland Cottage', but there is a Christian sense. In contrasting the growth of Maggie and her brother Edward, Gaskell shows their gradual separation as he grows more worldly, ending with forgery and well-deserved death at sea, while she, constricted in worldly terms, finds love and sense of higher purpose through the influence of Mrs Buxton, an invalid like Mrs Hamley. The parallel development of girl and boy is a favourite theme of Gaskell's; and the higher nature of the girl, more passionate, aspiring, unworldly, is a common pattern of Victorian fiction. Gaskell uses it again in *Ruth*; Dickens contrasts Tom and Louisa in *Hard Times*, as George Eliot does Maggie and Tom Tulliver in *The Mill on the Floss*. Despite plot likenesses and even coincidence of names, it is useful to see here, rather than direct influences, a common Victorian fascination with a theme. The moral situation of 'The Moorland Cottage' is far more complex than that of the 'Sunday-school' tales: there is Edward's corruption; Maggie's love and her knowledge, when Edward's freedom is only to be had by breaking off her engagement, that she cannot give up Frank; and her choice to go to America to keep Edward on a true path. The story might have been better for a quiet ending; the crisis has been moral rather than physical. But there is a sense that a grand finale is needed. The emigrant ship goes up in flames; Edward selfishly tries for the boats and is drowned (a decided satisfaction); Maggie is rescued by Frank, aboard in disguise and already heroically at work ridding the ship of its gunpowder. There is the satisfaction of a happy ending and many fine incidental details, not least when Edward, still true to his vocation as attorney, even when accepting his passage money from the man he has cheated, 'proposed to draw up a legal form of assignment' (ii, 364).

The last in this group, 'Mr Harrison's Confessions' (*Ladies' Companion*, Spring 1851), is in the comic vein of *Cranford*, serialization of which began late in 1851. Harrison, the young doctor, new to Duncombe, a village which like Cranford is 'in possession of the Amazons', finds himself innocently a philanderer, having taken the advice of Morgan, his senior in partnership, on the proper professional manner. His interest and growing love from the first is for Sophia, the vicar's daughter, but he variously finds himself tangled with his housekeeper, with Caroline Tomkinson (compromisingly kneeling before her with his stethoscope), and with Jemima Bullock, who he gets on well with, finding out 'that we mutually disliked each other, and were contented with the discovery' (v, 452). Much turns on mistaken conversation, of the Pickwick/Mrs Bardell kind; the Dickensian influence is strong, both in depicting Sophia, who first appears with 'the light coming from above on her head' (v, 417-8), and interestingly in Miss Horsman, a rare Gaskell villainess, whose innocent questions scarcely conceal her venom. She is the more disturbing because her motivation can only be inferred as sexual frustration. Serious elements lie in the death of Sophia's young brother (from croup) and Harrison's success in saving the arm of a gardener that Morgan was firm for amputating. At the end Sophia is saved by Harrison's new medicine and all is set for their happiness; the marriage of the would-be brides is a pat rounding-off, only Miss Horsman not being matched. Gaskell is moving towards *Cranford* very clearly, in her balancing of comic, even farcical, with the serious, but she has not yet hit the full pathos of situation, nor discovered how to project a character like Miss Jenkyns who, severe in forms, is yet responsive to human need.

Gaskell might refuse George Smith a story for the *Cornhill* as not good enough, though 'good enough for Dickens' (595), and agonize about sending another story in 1859 when Dickens was unpopular and quarrelsome,[7] yet between 1850 and 1863 the bulk of her short stories (some twenty in all) went to him. Even after *North and South,* two considerable stories – 'My Lady Ludlow' and 'A Dark Night's Work' – ran successfully as serials without sign of trouble. The whole range of her work is represented. One especially interesting group is the contributions to the extra Christmas numbers of *Household Words* and *All the Year Round,* where Dickens commissioned stories and (first with 'The Seven Poor Travellers', 1854) provided a frame to introduce them, a device Gaskell took up for *Round the Sofa* (1859), where the circle at Mr Dawson's house hear Margaret Dawson tell the story of 'My Lady Ludlow' and are then each assigned as narrator one of the reprinted pieces.

Dickens, gathering contributors in 1850, urged Gaskell to write for his new periodical and she was given pride of place in the first issue of *Household Words,* immediately after Dickens's opening announcement, a compliment indicative of his admiration, but one that few besides Gaskell could relish, since (with rare exceptions) contributions were anonymous. 'Lizzie Leigh' (March–April 1850), like its successors 'The Well of Pen-Morfa' (November 1850) and 'The Heart of John Middleton' (December 1850), is a tale of common life, of suffering and subdued triumph. It opens mysteriously with a deathbed forgiveness and Mrs Leigh's determination to find in Manchester the daughter who has been cast off for sin. Yet the mystery is pursued through character rather than suspense, details that illuminate the life of these country people – the farm, the coming marriage of 'our Jenny', the Bible reading. Anne Leigh recalls how she fancies having heard her daughter's voice,

> and I've stolen down, and undone the latch before now, and looked out into the still, black night, thinking to see her – and turned sick and sorrowful when I heard no living sound but the sough of the wind dying away. Oh, speak not to me of stopping here, when she may be perishing for hunger like the poor lad in the parable (ii, 211).

In Manchester, Gaskell manipulates a tight plot of connection between Susan, the girl Anne's son falls in love with, and the child abandoned by Lizzie and raised by Susan. In the small space of the story such coincidence seems allowable, though the child's death is an unnecessarily high price for Lizzie to pay. The women – Anne, Lizzie, and Susan – are bound together by love, and the losing of one object of love leads and helps in the search for another. In the characteristic ending, Lizzie finds a chastened happiness, of service to others and sharing the joy from which her sin bars her in its fulness.

The sadness so often part of Gaskell's work is the primary effect of 'The Well of Pen-Morfa'. Nest Gwyn, the village beauty, puts out her hip when she slips on the frozen freshet by the well. A cripple for life, she is deserted by her fine lover, though her mother implores him at least to save her life by visiting until she is strong again. The women are strong and faithful, where the man is slack. Nest's pride keeps her within doors lest she is pitied. Only at her mother's death is she called out again, by the Methodist David Hughes, whose challenge of love she responds to by taking half-witted Mary Williams to live with her, who 'loved her back again, as a dumb animal loves its blind master' (ii, 263), an oddly resonant image of interdependence, the second term suggesting Nest's own darkly wandering nature, completed only by someone crippled like herself. Duty in love is enforced by Nest's death at the well, thirty years later. More effective is the narrator's opening account of a woman, once the beauty, returning to Pen-Morfa pregnant, bringing up her crippled child alone - unconnected directly with the main tale, it yet provides an image for it: the woman driven, after betrayal, to direct her best affections into channels that outwardly seem unrewarding and for the giver even are often harshly demanding.

In 'The Heart of John Middleton', Gaskell boldly and success-fully assumes a male role as narrator: John himself, a man ignorant, yet struggling with himself to be worthy of the woman he loves. In John and his Nelly an opposition is dramatized between Old and New Testament - between vengeance and love. From mere ignor-ance he moves, like Caliban learning language, successively through the blood wrath of Jehovah and the hysterical fanaticism of Dissent. When his enemy is delivered into his hands, it is image, memory, the whole trail of meaning that he has followed, that saves him. As he goes to fetch the constable he comes to a stream like that long ago where he saw his wife first and now his child stands by the brook with a message from his wife: the golden thread in the black coarse web of life is unbroken, spun on in the child, and he takes it for his guide. Gaskell moves beyond Sunday-school resolutions by making the Biblical language and imagery part of John's character, not a separable message.

209

Quite different in style and mood is the patchy 'Morton Hall' (November 1853), where reconciliation between Royalist Mortons and Puritan Carrs comes in the third of three loosely connected episodes. The link is family and house, not plot, the whole framed by the comic old maid Bridget, whose role as narrator allows the reader ironic pleasure in seeing more than can her ignorance while it points towards the possibility of a happy ending despite the sequence of decline in aristocratic fortune inevitable in the historical pattern. The Mortons' decay is emphasized by changing landscape; even Bridget can remember a road with hedges between Morton and Drumble (Manchester) where now stand only houses that make Morton a suburb of the great town. The disastrous marriage of Sir John Morton with Alice Carr, the Puritan holder of a sequestered estate, is finely managed: even knowing him false, her heart can stop beating, 'not for fear, but because she loved Sir John even yet' (ii, 455). His arrival to break up her entertainment of Puritan ministers is enforced by echoes of Ulysses' return (punishment of the maids) and of Sleeping Beauty as the hall is locked up with the feast spread still on the tables. His cruelty to his 'mad' wife is avenged when the Morton pride kills Miss Phillis and Master John, though the presence and loyalty of faithful Bridget and her sister give pathos to what might only be irritating or stupid. The advance of Drumble is not lost at the end, when young Cordelia marries a mill-owner, Carr, descendant of the Puritan purchaser of Morton Hall; landscape and the new ways have swallowed up Morton. Gaskell, however drawn to the past, never pretended that it could be retrieved except imaginatively; reconciliation comes in new generations, not in restoration of the old.

This theme is pursued also in 'My French Master' (December 1853), framed by reminiscences of early life and its pleasures, which set off the main episode of M. de Chalabre, a refugee from the French Revolution. He teaches French to maintain himself, yet is accepted as still the gentleman. There is fun in the way, helping a country-woman over a stile, 'taking up the silk-lined lapel of his coat, he spread it on the palm of his hand for her to rest her fingers upon; instead of which, she took his small white hand in her plump, vigorous gripe' (ii, 509). With the restoration of 1814 M. de Chalabre returns to France as though twenty years were nothing. All is lost, though, and in England again he accepts that he is a French teacher and nothing else. To enforce this, he marries Susan Dobson,

his landlady's daughter. His own daughter's marriage to the purchaser of his estate (Gaskell slyly brings in Mary Mohl as would-be
matchmaker) is a neat rather than satisfying ending.

Two pieces utilizing French material, which hover between fiction
and journalism, offering stories as pendants to the historical thread,
may conveniently be mentioned here. 'Traits and Stories of the
Huguenots' (December 1853) sketches briefly opposition to government harassment and, with the revocation of the Edict of Nantes,
offers 'some of the traditions which I have heard and collected'
(ii, 492); no one seems yet to have identified the sources more
closely. The anecdotes are of love, suspense, and loyalty, doubly
interesting to Gaskell for her own belief in religious freedom and for
her acquaintance with people like the Martineaus, descended from
these refugees. The other piece, 'An Accursed Race' (August 1855)
is a curiosity, an account, adapted from Francisque-Michel's *History
of the Accursed Races of France and Spain,* of the Cagots, a people
denied all civil rights virtually until the nineteenth century, and
held to be lepers, inwardly if not outwardly. Gaskell confines herself
almost entirely to the French material and shows a preference for
stories like the rising of the oppressed Cagots of Rehouilhes against
their neighbours, who 'were conquered and slain, and their ghastly,
bloody heads served the triumphant Cagots for balls to play at
ninepins with!' (v, 222).[8]

Gaskell's three most characteristically Wordsworthian stories may
be grouped together. 'Half a Lifetime Ago' (October 1855) originally
appeared in *Sartain's Union Magazine* (vol. 6, February 1850), the
later version being considerably expanded and made more dramatic
by showing rather than telling; the relationships become more
complex and the ending is changed significantly. In both the heroine
– the eponymous Martha Preston of the earlier version, Susan Dixon
in the later – has to choose between her lover and her idiot brother:
no easy choice, where love has a real power over her. Wordsworth
had laid open the affection of Betty Foy for her idiot son, but Betty
had no competing interest, no husband to lose if she clung to the
helpless boy; and Gaskell moves in the realism of fiction by making
the young brother wild and physically violent at times. 'Martha
Preston' opens like Wordsworth's story of Margaret and the ruined
cottage (*The Excursion,* bk 1) as the narrator offers to tell what he
knows of the woman, 'while the noonday hum of busy insects in the
wood mingles with the hum of the bees' (p. 133). There are telling

observations: Martha's mother so active that she prefers to do tasks herself rather than teach her daughter and who dies 'quickly, sharply as she had lived'. But the later version is vastly superior, whether in the initial sketch of Susan's isolation (the end of the narrative projects beyond this opening) or in significant connections. Young Willie's care becomes Mrs Dixon's deathbed charge on Susan, and the relationship between her, Willie and Michael Hurst – the youth brought to serve for a year on the farm by Dixon's reputation as 'statesman' – is meticulously complicated by Susan's power over Michael, Michael's over her, the occasional brutality of Michael to Willie and yet the ease with which he wins the boy to his side after Susan has sprung to the defence. Out of this complex of feeling there is no easy way. Even when Susan taunts Michael over his vaunted dancing – 'Does it help you plough, or reap, or even climb rocks to take a raven's nest?' (v, 285)[9] – it is to keep him at a distance just because she feels his charm and power. After the fever that deprives Willie of his wits, Michael is still prepared to marry Susan, if the boy is sent to Lancaster Asylum. Even when she rejects Michael, Susan still hopes he may return: it is not an easy piece of heroism and though the old servant approves, her words are unconsoling: 'thou hast done well. It is not long to bide, and then the end will come' (v, 311). But for Susan the biding is long enough. When the fits are on Willie and she has wrestled with him,

> she would sally out to taste the fresh air, and to work off her
> wild sorrow in cries and muttering to herself. The early
> labourers saw her gestures at a distance, and thought her as
> crazed as the idiot brother who made the neighbourhood a
> haunted place (v, 316).

In 'Martha Preston', the woman, after her brother's death, rescued the son of her tepid lover; Gaskell tightened this up by Susan finding Michael's body in the snow, banishing sentimentality in death, the reconciliation being between disappointed sweetheart and widow.

'The Half-Brothers' is a slighter, though effective, piece.[10] The despised elder brother, whose dying mother has linked her new-born son to his love, shelters the younger in a snowstorm on the fells, warming him at the cost of his own life. Although not published until 1859 (*All the Year Round*, Christmas number, as 'The Ghost in the Garden Room'), 'The Crooked Branch' in setting and situation belongs here. Nathan Huntroyd, a northern farmer whose proper pride is in his land, marries late, and the couple's one child, Benjamin, is the darling of their age. If Nathan's integrity is like that of Wordsworth's Michael, then Benjamin's progress is that of Luke. Fallen into evil courses in the city, after long silence – believed dead – he comes to rob his parents. They know what he has done and, stunned, paralysed (the mother, sight already failing, goes blind), they are forced to testify in court what their son bade his accomplice do to his own mother – 'for to hold th'oud woman's throat if she did na stop her noise' (vii, 258). The power lies in the unspoken recognition by Nathan and his wife Hester that they bear responsibility, however unintended, for their son's crookedness; and in the refusal, justified yet in conflict with their love, of further money, which makes so painful (to them, to the assize court, to the reader) the exposure of filial callousness. Nathan's refusal to pay more is a decision beyond anything Wordsworth requires of Michael, and Gaskell extends, consolidates what she has learnt in the terrible irony of Hester's consolation in the Bible:

> Eh! but thatten's a pretty story i' the Gospel about the
> Prodigal, who'd to eat the pigs' vittle at one time, but ended i'
> clover in his father's house. And I'm sure our Nathan'll be
> ready to forgive him, and make much of him – maybe, a deal
> more nor me, who never gave in to's death. It'll be liker to a
> resurrection to our Nathan (vii, 238).

Horribly, Benjamin does rise from the dead, but it is death he brings to his own mother.[11] Gaskell's hauntings can be the more terrible for not being supernatural.

The supernatural appears directly in 'The Poor Clare' (December 1856): Lucy is unknowingly cursed by her grandmother and haunted by a malicious double – she describes to her lover how in 'the great mirror opposite I saw myself, and right behind, another wicked, fearful self, so like me that my soul seemed to quiver within me, as though not knowing to which similitude of body it belonged' and as he seeks rational explanation in nerves, he sees behind her at that instant 'another figure – a ghastly resemblance, complete in likeness so far as form and feature and minutest touch of dress could go, but with a loathsome demon soul looking out of the grey eyes, that were in turns in mocking and voluptuous' (v, 361, 362). The plot, though skilfully involved, seems uncertain of focus and the story is finally unsatisfactory. Interesting, however, is Gaskell's integration of the apparition with a Christian sense that the curse, having given the devil his chance, can only be cancelled by an equivalent in active good.

Equally unsatisfactory, if in different ways, is the plot of 'My Lady Ludlow' (June-September 1858). Scheherezade's presence is strong: the long interpolated tale of Clement and Virginia's love in the French Revolution, fine though it is, is introduced on the flimsiest grounds, and characters elsewhere are brought in as much for their stories (Miss Galindo's disappointed love, for instance) as for their part in the main action. The narrative moves by a series of stories and story-tellers: Margaret Dawson opens with her education in Lady Ludlow's household, and unfolds the stories of people she encounters there. The clash between the old aristocratic ways of Lady Ludlow and the new evangelicalism of the clergyman Mr Gray, wanting a Sunday-school and a revival of Christian behaviour, provides the dynamic of the piece and is never lost to sight; yet though Lady Ludlow, spokesman for old ways, is brought to display the natural humanity and sense of justice that rise above all niceties of mere manners, a feeling remains of the theme being dissipated, despite Margaret Dawson's modest disclaimer that it is 'no story'. For all Gaskell's obvious homage here to *Scenes of Clerical Life* (and the discovery that Dissenters, even those who make their fortune as bakers, are human) aim and tone are uncertain.

Gaskell's last regular contribution to *Household Words*[12] was 'The Sin of a Father' (November 1858; retitled 'Right at Last' on republication), a neat mystery story, where the obvious crime (a servant's theft) is a blind; disappointment that detection seems so easy is compensated by the true discovery that the problem of marriage is to do with personality rather than money. It was Gaskell's last contribution only because Dickens quarrelled with Bradbury, Evans, his printers, in 1859; *All the Year Round* in format and policy and staff differed only in name and legal technicalities. Gaskell, unhappy about the quarrel and Dickens's embarrassingly public separation from his wife, felt obliged to supply a story for which she had received advance payment, the superb 'Lois the Witch'. Yet this does not explain why her other two major contributions to *All the Year Round*, 'The Grey Woman' and 'A Dark Night's Work', both written after establishment of the *Cornhill* and amongst her best work, should have gone to Dickens, unless we abandon (as I think we must) the popular idea that Gaskell gave him only her inferior work in the 1860s.

'Lois the Witch' (October 1859) is a tragedy in a historical setting: the death of Lois, accused at Salem, is inexorably accepted and made more poignant by her own recognition of witchcraft and the possibility that she even might unknowingly be a witch. Except for Captain Holdernesse (and he will not deny absolutely), no one doubts the possibility of Satanic intercourse and only the narrator can speak with the voice of modern understanding. Importantly, that understanding is not of eighteenth-century rationalism, dismissing such things with scorn, but of nineteenth-century Romanticism, prepared to enter imaginatively into a way of thinking and feeling apart from its own. However wrong these people were (and their own confession of error is quoted at the end), they are not hypocrites or aliens – even Parson Tappau, mixed though his motives are, believes and trembles. The story draws on elements of the romance technique of Hawthorne,[13] a writer Gaskell was conscious of explicitly in the presence of his ancestor Hathorne as a character and implicitly in Prudence, whose impishness is a distorted image of Pearl's in *The Scarlet Letter*. The curse of Hannah, and Manasseh's visions are fulfilled, yet rather because of an imaginative fatalism in the characters than because Gaskell is playing fast and loose between scepticism and belief. Whatever she read or remembered, the only true source for the historical material, which shows Gaskell's fruitful pillaging, is Charles W. Upham's *Lectures on Witchcraft* (1831) – the colony's situation (the minute-men of Essex, withdrawal of the charter, the Canadian expedition), Cotton Mather and his sermon, the words of the eye-witness that the girls 'began to tumble down like swine' are all there.[14] The story itself is Gaskell's invention. Coming an orphan from England to a strange land, amongst those whose forms of religion are not hers, Lois finds herself isolated enough without the trap of a family where the children lean to insanity – Manasseh's religious and erotic mania, Faith's hysterical fixation on Pastor Nolan, Prudence's manic-depressive precocity – and whose mother is prepared to use Lois as the means to keep her son's sanity, if it is the only way. The family's hysteria is compounded by the larger yet still enclosed hysteria of New England, and innocently Lois antagonizes both those who might have spoken for her and those who will speak against her. She prefers the Book of Common Prayer to extempore praying, seems to pursue Manasseh when his mother is against the alliance yet will not help him when Grace Hickson humbles herself (a proud, ill-willed humility), terrifies and thwarts Prudence, and appears to have the affection of Pastor Nolan that Faith craves. Accused in the meeting house, Lois bewildered as she is, rises to the tragic dignity of one who knows what awaits her and will do what she must:

> Sirs, I must choose death with a quiet conscience, rather than
> life to be gained by a lie. I am not a witch. I know not
> hardly what you mean, when you say I am. I have done
> many, many things very wrong in my life; but I think God
> will forgive me them for my Saviour's sake (vii, 199).

Bitterness is left to Hugh Lucy, who comes from England to claim her, the light that gleamed for Lois across the sea and was the last temptation to the lie: he is the voice of the normal world, by which we judge events and the pity of it.

In 'Morton Hall' Bridget and Ethelinda believed their names were black-marked in the book at Rome of those 'to whom the Papists owed either grudges or gratitudes' (ii, 446), and 'The Grey Woman' (January 1861) draws on folk traditions of such implacable enemies, whose secret network defies law. There is an element too of chapbook tales like 'Bluebeard' and 'Mr Fox', [15] where wives are lured into marriage by women-killers – in more than one sense. Gaskell herself drew on an English variant for the ramshackle 'The Squire's Tale' (*Household Words*, Christmas 1853), where she failed to reshape tradition: if the Squire, his income derived from highway robbery, not his supposed southern estates, made merry on the old lady's ginger-wine before doing her in, it seems improbable he would succumb to remorse as he does. Now, however, in 'The Grey Woman' there is not the comic delusion of old maids like Bridget or the fabled realm of Bluebeard, but modern Europe. The Grey Woman herself is wooed and married almost against her will by M. de la Tourelle. Cut off from her family, isolated in her husband's chateau, Gaskell builds up her growing fears and helplessness from her entry there: 'in the gloom of an autumnal evening, I caught my own face and figure reflected in all the mirrors, which showed only a mysterious background in the dim light of the many candles that failed to illuminate the great proportions of the half-finished salon' (vii, 315). It is yearning for family contact that leads her to go for a letter in her husband's rooms during his absence: in the dark she hears men approaching, hides beneath a table, and discovers her husband to be leader of a band of robbers. To retain her sense she bites her hand and hears her husband's laughter

> as he kicked something heavy that they dragged in over the floor, and which lay near me: . . . I don't know why – I can't tell how – but some feeling, and not curiosity, prompted me to put out my hand, ever so softly, ever so little, and feel in the darkness for what lay spurned beside me. I stole my groping palm upon the clenched and chilly hand of a corpse! (vii, 327).

She escapes only to be pursued by an implacable foe who seems to have agents everywhere: even Amante, her faithful companion, is found and murdered despite every precaution. Her consolations are the birth of a girl, who 'seemed all my own', and Dr Voss, who becomes her second husband; by now there is no need for disguise – 'my yellow hair was grey, my complexion was ashen-coloured' (vii, 359).

When Dickens inserted the work 'Dark' in Gaskell's title and produced the melodramatic effectiveness of 'A Dark Night's work' (January–March 1863),[16] a deliberate low-tone was vitiated. The original hints more effectively at the after-vacancy of action, when 'we wonder at ourselves like men betrayed'. Wilkins is a man betrayed by himself. His accidental killing of his partner and erstwhile chief clerk, Dunster, is the night's work that destroys his life and threatens his beloved daughter Ellinor and faithful servant Dixon – the deed is not so dark as Dickens wanted to make it, though relief for Ellinor only comes after the killing, literally, 'comes to light'. Wilkins's violent action in striking Dunster is the blow of irritation against someone become necessary to him through his own increasing inefficiency. His is an inner destruction. The blow does not ruin him in the eyes of the world, which judging by appearance finds it easy enough to attribute the confusion of his business affairs to the peculations of Dunster rather than the criminal irresponsibility of the gentleman-like attorney. Dunster's death and secret burial (an echo, perhaps, of George Eliot's Dunstan Cass in name, though the death and finding of the body, superficially alike, only serve to stress differences between this tale and *Silas Marner*), though a shared secret between Ellinor, her father and Dixon, serves to cloud their love, involved as they are in the guilt of concealment.

Wilkins brings on his crisis by delight in the world's trappings and Gaskell traces equally skilfully the world closing upon the other man central to Ellinor's 'night', Ralph Corbet, who rather than risk shame prefers to cleave to his career and (honourably enough in the world's view) abandons Ellinor. Though a sensible youth, he has a shallow nature: after a year's separation Ellinor meets him 'with great shyness, for she remembered well how they had parted, and thought he could hardly have forgiven, much less forgotten, her passionate flinging away from him' (vii, 428). He, naturally enough, has long forgotten and never thought forgiveness needed. Gaskell finely shows the accretion of worldly interest that builds Ralph's career, so that from his first impulse of love he comes to the sense of his father's enquiries 'as to how much fortune Miss Wilkins would have; how much down on her marriage; what were the eventual probabilities' (vii, 446). Prudence, of course; and part of Ralph's tragedy is his being no worse than others – certainly not than Ellinor's father, indeed, except in love for Ellinor – yet spinning a web of daily events to engineer a career which inevitably wraps him round as he grows older. In his final encounter with Ellinor, as the judge who tried Dixon for Dunster's murder, Ralph helps her and may feel momentary regret in comparing her with his fine wife, but he has had his chance. His affections were subdued to his intellect, so that when Ellinor was ill, the house, lacking her management, strikes unfavourably on Ralph's perceptions, 'which were critical rather than appreciative' (vii, 496); and Gaskell makes us aware of how his better feelings for Ellinor are *conscious* rather than intuitive – liable therefore to be swamped by the stronger persuasion of his career:

> But, when he came down in the morning, and saw the faded Ellinor flash into momentary beauty at his entrance into the dining-room, and when she blushingly drew near with the one single flower freshly gathered, which it had been her custom to place in his button-hole when he came down to breakfast, he felt as if his better half was stronger than temptation, and as if he must be an honest man and honourable lover, even against his wish (vii, 500).

Ellinor is betrayed emotionally. How shockingly is prepared by Gaskell in describing Ellinor recovering from the deaths in her childhood of mother and baby sister, 'hardly letting herself love any one for some time, as if she instinctively feared lest all her strong attachments should find a sudden end in death' (vii, 413). Her father uses an image that expresses the potential and the tenderness of Ellinor's love: disappointed of a confidence from her about Ralph, he reflects that 'the young man had done wisely in not tearing open the rosebud of her feelings too prematurely' (vii, 434). The complex - of youth, beauty, tenderness wrenched prematurely, of emotion and physicality, inevitable flowering damaged by anticipation - is rendered ironic by our knowledge that Ellinor already is open to Ralph, though no overt understanding exists between them. She accedes to the engagement being broken off, because she understands what Ralph wants. Although he does not know the truth, she is haunted by it and feels that whatever the grounds for separation, marriage would anyway be impossible. When she moves with the faithful Miss Monro to East Chester, she hopes to go 'into an unhaunted dwelling in a free, unknown country' (vii, 523). The eventual revelation of the crime shows Gaskell's care in placing detail that seems of the surface, yet is vital. The railway is first mentioned when Ralph is to marry Miss Beauchamp (vii, 529) - it seems scarcely more than an aside, a reminder of the time-scheme. Then Ellinor goes back to Hamley: the railway is forty miles off, though the line is being surveyed. When she is in Italy and inaccessible (here, postal delays, like the Roman Carnival and the steamboat accident, show Gaskell drawing on her Italian travels), the action is taken to begin the cutting that reveals the body: the convergence of the twain. Ellinor finally achieves happiness with Livingstone, who if something of a cipher yet serves seven years and yet seven for his Rachel - but the gap in time can never be closed up. Ellinor's wrinkles speak of 'our carver's excellence,/Which lets go by some sixteen years' and in doing so insist that this story is profoundly human and because human, profoundly difficult.

The stories contributed to the Christmas numbers may puzzle us, quite apart from absence of specifically festive elements, by their grimness or sadness, unless we remember firstly that they were always part of a series, by various hands and overseen by Dickens, so guaranteeing variety of mood; and second, that there can be a pleasure in the terrifying and melancholy when a round of stories is told by the Christmas fire.[17] Gaskell's first contribution, 'The Old Nurse's Story' (Christmas 1852), is a splendid ghost story. Its combination of realism and common sense in the narrator with the perpetual re-enactment of Miss Furnivall's ill-deed and the threat to the child Rosamund place it in a class with 'The Turn of the Screw'. There is a pleasing matter-of-factness in the nurse's acceptance of the organ music produced without player – 'I thought it was rather pleasant to have that grand music rolling about the house' (ii, 430) and a subtle intensification of terrors as the climax approaches: the little girl trying to lure Rosamund into the snow and death, the 'great bronze chandelier' that 'seemed all alight, though the hall was dim', and even as Miss Furnivall tries to undo in age what was done in youth, her phantom self appears and urges on the act of hate (ii, 444-5).[18] 'The Squire's Story', Gaskell's second contribution, already discussed, was feeble indeed by comparison (one suspects her writing because she felt she must rather than wanted to) and it was not until 1858 that she contributed again. 'The Manchester Marriage' is a return to her vein of domestic realism, though it shifts rather from the likely dilemma of Alice Openshaw, faced with the return of her sailor husband when she is settled in a second marriage, to Norah's loyalty. Frank Wilson, the first husband, is dealt with rather cavalierly (and conveniently) by drowning, though the opening upon the honest, no-nonsense Mr Openshaw of situations and feelings beyond any in his philosophy is neatly done. For *All the Year Round* Christmas numbers, Gaskell wrote 'The Crooked Branch', discussed above, and finally 'Crowley Castle' (1863).[19] Dickens remarked of this story that Gaskell 'has a way of rather abusing her strength by making her victims unjustly unhappy sometimes',[20] and certainly Theresa is unhappy in both her marriages, to the vile Count de Grange and to Marmaduke Brownlow (after his wife has been poisoned by Theresa's maid). The maid, Victoria, regards this as a bond of gratitude, a shared secret, though Theresa is scarcely even guilty in wish, much less in expression. Yet Theresa dies, paying for childish spitefulness.

'Curious if True' (February 1860), Gaskell's first contribution to George Smith's new *Cornhill Magazine*, is a lively *jeu d'esprit*. Its treatment of Charles Perrault's fairy-tale characters,[21] at their party on 18 August near Tours, is highly sophisticated – unless we recognize the joke, the idea that these creations have not been held in the timeless amber of their stories but changed like ordinary human beings would be coarse, even offensive. The fun is in recognizing, as the narrator does not (his claimed descent from Calvin indicates how far he is imaginatively from the world of Mother Goose), these people under their disguises, like the Marquis whose servant had 'boots half-way up his ridiculously small legs, which clattered as he walked along, as if they were too large for his little feet' (vii, 265). A rational mind pursues the logical development of Puss in Boots or Bluebeard's widow (still treasuring memories of her first husband), yet the real appeal is from and to the imagination steeped in the fantastical reality of the tales, as Gaskell hints in a poetic moment: while the narrator waits for each gate in the chateau to be unlocked

> I could almost have fancied that I heard a mighty rushing
> murmur – (like the ceaseless sound of a distant sea, ebbing and
> flowing for ever and for ever), coming forth from the great
> vacant galleries that opened out on each side of the broad
> staircase, and were to be dimly perceived in the darkness above
> us. It was as if the voices of generations of men yet echoed
> and eddied in the silent air (vii, 262).

Gaskell is true to the voices of the generations.

A second story, 'Six Weeks at Heppenheim' (May 1862), appealingly uses material from Gaskell's German visits and has the satisfaction of a happy ending, but the woes of Thekla and her loyalty to a feckless lover produce irritation rather than sympathy. More interesting is the narrative's movement towards the grape harvest and the bucolic society observed by the English narrator as evening draws on in the vineyard, with distant voices singing the German harvest-hymn ('We plough the fields and scatter') and the pastor's blessing, after which 'they once more dispersed, some to the village, some to finish their labours for the day among the vines' (vii, 398).

This sense of community distinguishes 'Cousin Phillis' (November 1863–February 1864), the evening psalm led by Pastor Holman amidst his men and fields being one of many observations that lead this, amongst Gaskell's finest stories, to be called an idyll. The depiction of country life in 'Cousin Phillis', directed, purposive – Holman is a farmer for five days and minister on Saturday and Sunday, – a life undisturbed by town or industry, uniting labour and prayer, enforces this idea. Holman's quotation of Virgil's *Georgics* shows a passional consciousness, shared by his daughter Phillis, of the world in which he shapes his existence, its values confirmed by a continuity:

> At a certain point, there was a sudden burst of the tawny
> ruddy evening landscape. The minister turned round, and
> quoted a line or two of Latin.

221

'It's wonderful,' said he, 'how exactly Virgil has hit the enduring epithets, nearly two thousand years ago, and in Italy; and yet how it describes to a T what is now lying before us . . . ' (vii, 17).

For neither Gaskell nor Holman, though, does this continuity belong to a world of literary pastoral, where sun shines and sheep feed without care. Virgil's poems are concerned with the tasks of agriculture, as Holman, stressing their reality, emphasizes later:

> he insists on choice of the best seed, and advises us to keep the drains clear. Again, no Scotch farmer could give shrewder advice than to cut light meadows while the dew is on, even though it involve night-work. It is all living truth in these days (vii, 86).

Virgilian parallels impinge upon events in the tale: the storm during haymaking, when Holdsworth and Phillis are thrust into physical closeness, hints at Aeneas in the cave with Dido, as the journey to Canada and the wife there suggest the establishment of a new empire in Italy. These are only hints, though, not parallels, suggestions of an appeal to the reader's sense of tears in the nature of things – of things as they are. For if pastoral or even idyll suggest permanence, reading the story shows again and again how flux is the greater principle. Virgil is not English, but an Italian, and however much his poetry and Horace's comes alive for Holman by Holdsworth's talk of the country in which they lived and wrote, their Italy is not modern Italy (the literary succession of Virgil, Dante, and Manzoni is a historical clue – again, not one emphasized – to process within the tale). To fail to recognize change invites disaster and the Holmans intensify their pain by thinking still of Phillis as their child when she has made the inevitable, the necessary, transition to a woman. The desire to hold, to render permanent, is constantly thwarted: by Phillis's embarrassment at Holdsworth's sketching her portrait or earlier by her inevitable human movement when she has seemed naturally framed and held, like a work of art:

> Now I turned, as Mr Holdsworth had done, to look at her again out of the window: she had just finished her task, and was standing up, her back to us, holding the basket and the basin in it, high in the air, out of Rover's reach, who was giving vent to his delight at the probability of a change of

place by glad leaps and barks, and snatches at what he
imagined to be a withheld prize. At length she grew tired of
their mutual play, and, with a feint of striking him, and a
'Down, Rover! do hush!' she looked towards the window
where we were standing, as if to reassure herself that no one
had been disturbed by the noise; and seeing us, she coloured all
over, and hurried away, with Rover still curving in sinuous
lines about her as she walked (vii, 48).

Holdsworth and Paul have looked at her as though she can be
viewed with the unembarrassed stare we give a work of art; but the
aesthetic poise is broken in upon by awareness in the object and the
embarrassment that comes from finding oneself observed when
unconscious of others' gaze. This persistent movement casts a shadow
over the optimism of Phillis's final exclamation, after she has 'faltered
out her wish for change of thought and scene', and then cries, 'Only
for a short time, Paul! Then – we will go back to the peace of the old
days. I know we shall; I can, and I will!' (vii, 109). I think Gaskell
means us to feel uneasy at least about the possibility of anything so
simple as a return. The determination is in Phillis and no doubt she
can find happiness. But there is no hint that the happiness will be in
return to a lover – not even in a second-best marriage to cousin Paul,
whose future wife has been named already. Yet the openness of our
response here is part of the tale's strength, since the knowledge ('I
know we shall') is Phillis's, not her author's, the ending challenging
rather than resolving.
  'Cousin Phillis' superficially repeats the familiar pattern of a
woman brought to love by a man who then abandons her. In other
stories the man is culpable or else, like Kinraid in *Sylvia's Lovers,* if
faithful enough, shallow by comparison with the woman. Gaskell's
originality and power lie in the way she transforms such elements, in
a story where no one is guilty except with good intention and in
which the narrator is not simply a mouthpiece or commentator but
plays his own part in the painful course even by trying to save Phillis
from pain. Paul, working for the railway engineer Holdsworth – the
railway is another sign of change, as with passing reference to the
Penny Post – discovers his mother's relatives, the Holmans, who in
their simplicity of life make him feel 'as if I were somebody in the
Old Testament . . . being served and waited upon by the daughter of
the host' (vii, 11), though he is not to be a Jacob and labour to win

Rachel. The strength in Phillis and her father is both physical and moral, stressed by the daughter's assurance and maturity when set against the older but still adolescent Paul's. That strength is tested severely: it bears up, the story does not end in the tragedy of death, but fable-like the oak suffers more in the storm than would the reed.

Holdsworth is a pleasing young man, less serious than the Holmans, but intelligent, entertaining, able to bring his own experience alive in the imagination of others. His love for Phillis is real enough, as is hers for him. He meets Phillis in a garden, shares his knowledge of mechanics with her as well as her father, and by silent worship expresses what he feels:

> As we had passed to the orchard, Holdsworth had admired
> and spoken about some flower which he saw; it so happened
> he had never seen this old-fashioned kind since the days of his
> boyhood. I do not know whether he had thought anything
> more about this chance speech of his, but I know I had not –
> when Phillis, who had been missing just at the last moment of
> our hurried visit, re-appeared with a little nosegay of this same
> flower, which she was tying up with a blade of grass. She
> offered it to Holdsworth as he stood with her father on the
> point of departure. I saw their faces. I saw for the first time an
> unmistakable look of love in his black eyes; it was more than
> gratitude for the little attention; it was tender and beseeching –
> passionate. She shrank from it in confusion, her glance fell on
> me; and, partly to hide her emotion, partly out of real
> kindness at what might appear ungracious neglect of an older
> friend, she flew off to gather me a few late-blooming China
> roses (vii, 61).

But it is love through gesture, through look, not through declaration; nothing has been said by Holdsworth or Phillis that commits them to the future, and it is here that Paul tries to help. Holdsworth told him before going to Canada of his love for Phillis; Paul has seen the nosegay and, feeling rather displaced in the Holmans' interests, has reflected rather ruthfully that Phillis's belated gathering of flowers for him 'was the first time she had ever done anything of the kind for me' (vii, 61).

Distressed by Phillis's decline after Holdsworth's departure, Paul makes Holdsworth's declaration for him. He produces temporary happiness and, as he can anticipate in telling his story, greater misery:

'He had never spoken much about you before; but the
sudden going-away unlocked his heart, and he told me how
he loved you, and how he hoped on his return that you might
be his wife.'

'Don't,' said she, almost gasping out the word, which she
had tried once or twice before to speak; but her voice had
been choked. Now, she put her hand backwards; she had quite
turned away from me, and felt for mine. She gave it a soft
lingering pressure; and then she put her arms down on the
wooden division, and laid her head on it, and cried quiet tears.
I did not understand her at once, and feared lest I had
mistaken the whole case . . .

She lifted up her head and looked at me. Such a look! Her
eyes, glittering with tears as they were, expressed an almost
heavenly rapture – her colour vivid and blushing . . . So it was
all right then, and my conjecture was well-founded (vii, 73-4).

Of course Paul is right, which makes it the more terrible when
Holdsworth writes from Canada that he has married someone else.
There was love, but never having declared it he need not worry to
change the object of his affections; there was love, but if it had never
been acknowledged, Phillis would have recovered from her decline.
Instead, she has to bear, in silence, grief the worse for the joy she had
found, until her anxious father berates Paul, and in defending him
Phillis collapses physically. None of them is to blame: not Holdsworth, not Phillis, not Holman, not Paul. It is the absence of anyone
culpable, which forces us to turn back and feel the suffering alone,
that makes the story so painfully true – and in having Phillis live,
Gaskell recognizes the girl's strength and a common enough harshness of life.

The Holman farm is idyllic enough, but even there the cycle of
the year moves on, returning yet never to the same point and never
to rest – the two hay harvests are alike, yet different, the change
wrought by time absolute in the storm at the first that brings
Holdsworth and Phillis together and in the letter which Paul receives
during the second that announces the marriage and the lovers'
eternal separation. Phillis will recover and farm-life may – will –
resume, yet Phillis can no more become again what she was before
she met Holdsworth than she could become a girl by leaving off
aprons and reverting to pinafores. Here Gaskell displays supremely

her control of events and character, her power in handling and exploring emotion, her portrayal of society and individual, that make her outstanding amongst the nineteenth-century short-story writers.

9

Miscellaneous Writings and the Letters

I Miscellaneous Writings

Like most writers, Gaskell produced a variety of pieces that reflect occasional requests, particular interests, or the chance to earn some ready money. Some, like the sonnet 'On Visiting the Grave of My Stillborn Little Girl',[1] clearly came from a private impulse that did not allow publication; verse, indeed, was not a natural medium, as her one collaboration with William Gaskell reminds us. 'Sketches Among the Poor. No.I' found no successor, despite the title's promise (i, xxii-v).[2] Written in couplets, its material is reminiscent of George Crabbe's poems of 'The Village' and 'The Borough', anticipating Elizabeth's future interests in memory and the contrast between country childhood and town life.

Once she was authoress of *Mary Barton*, Gaskell's name could be a useful property, no doubt the main reason for Sampson Low inducing her to edit Maria Cummin's *Mabel Vaughan* (1857; p.205 above), while the Preface contributed to the English edition of C. Augusto Vecchi's *Garibaldi at Caprera* (1862) explains that any profits are to go at Garibaldi's request to schools

> which the Philanthropic Association of Ladies at Turin are
> seeking to establish in the Neapolitan dominions, at the
> instigation of Garibaldi, who believes that the best method of
> raising the character of the people is by conferring on them the
> benefits of a wise system of female education (p.vii).

The cause was one with which Gaskell would be sympathetic and no doubt she readily lent her aid. Other pieces have been attributed to her:[3] a report on Emerson's Lectures in Manchester and a Letter of Enquiry, both in *Howitt's Journal* (vol ii, December 1847, the latter a very dubious attribution), and the puzzling 'A Few Words about "Jane Eyre" ', which seems to quote or draw on a letter by Gaskell. More interesting, whether hers or not, is a review of *Lancashire Lessons* by W. T. M. Torrens (*Reader*, vol 5, 25 March 1865), an account of the Lancashire Cotton Famine during the American Civil War, the review speaking of the Manchester situation from personal experience.

The first interesting piece is the description of a day spent from the Byerleys' school at Clopton Hall in Warwickshire, included by William Howitt in *Visits to Remarkable Places* (1840). A delight in the macabre is clear in the account of Charlotte Clopton's premature burial, her corpse seen by torchlight in the ancestiral vault 'in her grave-clothes leaning against the wall; and when they looked nearer, she was indeed dead, but not before, in the agonies of despair and hunger, she had bitten a piece from her white round shoulder!' (i, 506). The thrill is carried directly into the life of the schoolgirl-explorer when she and a companion lift the lid of a chest; 'What do you think we saw? - BONES! - but whether human, whether the remains of the lost bride, we did not stay to see' (i, 507), the girlish imagination stimulated here by reading of Samuel Rogers's tale of Ginevra, who disappeared on her wedding day, having crept into such a chest to hide for a joke and perished within it.[4] The same curiosity in disappearances and discovery (often linked biographically to the disappearance of Gaskell's own sailor brother, but equally part of her interest – and her age's – in ghosts and mysteries) is strong in her first article for *Household Words* (June 1851), 'Disappearances'. Ostensibly in praise of the modern police force, a particular interest of Dickens himself, it is a string of anecdotes, including one of a lawyer who never returns from a rent-collecting expedition; fifty years later his murder is confessed by a dying man (ii, 414), an episode that may have been recalled in part for 'A Dark Night's Work'.[5]

Material for Gaskell's articles comes from disparate sources. 'The Schah's English Gardener' (*Household Words*, June 1852) she claimed to have met; Mr Burton seems lacking in her own natural curiosity, though his situation was dispiriting enough. One senses he was not fond of such delicacies as sour goat's-milk with ice and was repelled by the savagery of executions where men, suspended upside-down, had one leg and one arm removed. A certain ingrained Europeanism, even Englishness, is well conveyed in Burton's opinion that the 'slave-like obeisance' of the Persian salaam was 'unfitting a European' and in his mildly comic outrage that Persians 'ate their peas and beans unshelled, rather then take any unnecessary trouble; a piece of piggism which especially scandalised him' (viii, 593, 598, 596, 601).

Exuberantly drawn from summer holidays in the Lake District, 'Cumberland Sheep Shearers' (*Household Words*, January 1853) shows something of the background on which Gaskell drew in short stories like 'Half a Lifetime Ago' as well as the more joyful side of Lakeland life in the close observation of the shearers, astride their benches, competing in 'a sort of rural Olympics' (iii, 460). Woven into the account is a love episode between shearer and buxom girl amongst those folding the fleeces. References to the ancient world and a classical peasantry link this piece to the comparative method of 'Modern Greek Songs' (*Household Words*, February 1854). Ostensibly a notice of Claude Fauriel's *Chants Populaires de la Grèce* (*Folk Songs of Modern Greece*, 1824-5), which she may have come across through the Mohls and certainly knew through Felicia Heman's version of 'The Message to the Dead', mentioned specifically in the article,[6] the piece is very typical of the reader's digest approach in many *Household Words* articles. It summarizes and links anecdotes, Gaskell herself providing modern or English comparative examples – experience of a Greek family in England, an analogy between the Klephts (freebooters) and Robin Hood, the personification of the plague in Scotland 'as a blind woman, going from house to house, giving death to all whom she touches; but, as she can only grope along by the sides of the walls, those escape harmless who keep in the middle of the streets' (iii, 472, 484, 489). It is an effective piece of popularization, in the best sense, of a book not readily available in English.[7]

Even more tenuous is the link between Victor Cousin's book on Madame de Sablé and 'Company Manners' (*Household Words*, May 1854). Cousin's study is the springboard into French manners and the best way to promote even in England that peculiarly French institution, the *salon*. Gaskell purports to be seeking the lost art of Sabléing (her own coinage) or how *tenir un salon*. The piece is an amusing theory of how to bring about relaxed conversation with reminiscences of gipsy teas that triumphed over formal dinners. The only other contribution to Dickens's publications (apart from 'Traits and Stories of the Huguenots' and 'An Accursed Race', already discussed) is 'An Italian Institution' (*All the Year Round*, March 1863) on the Camorra, the secret society that demanded its percentage for 'protection' on all transactions in Naples; the subject fascinated Gaskell enough for her to write a second piece on it, never published.[8] Gaskell was keenly alive to the irony that its tyranny was no worse than that of the Bourbon kings of Naples and more efficient as a system (vi, 535). Gaskell recognized that though the Bourbons were gone the Camorra had not; her final comments open up the vision of a whole nation undermined, since the 'more active the measures taken, the more does the extent of the disease manifest itself' (vi, 540).

In introducing Vecchi's book, Gaskell wrote of Garibaldi as one 'who by his valour and his patriotism had enabled Italy to lift her head once more among the nations of Europe, and opened out to her the prospect of a fresh career of glory' (p. vi). No doubt a similar liberal enthusiasm made her wish to commemorate 'Robert Gould Shaw' (*Macmillan's Magazine*, vol 9, December 1863), who 'gave up his life for what he believed to be right – deliberately risked, and cheefully laid down, a prosperous, happy, beloved, and loving life' (p. 113). Shaw, whose family Gaskell had met in Paris in 1855, raised and led the first Negro regiment of the American Civil War, despite opposition in the North itself, with 'the truest moral courage' marching out of New York 'amidst the jeers and scoffings of the "roughs," and the contemptuous pity of many who should have known better' (p. 114). Garibaldi triumphed in life, Shaw in death, killed and buried with his 'niggers', his sacrifice one which Gaskell prized (again, heroism not clear to many) to do-away the crime of slavery. She raised her memorial to him, as Boston was to raise the St Gauden memorial in 1877, unveiled by Henry James's philospher brother William who 'could almost hear the bronze Negroes breathe'.[9]

To *Fraser's Magazine*, edited by an old Manchester acquaintance, J. A. Froude, Gaskell sent 'Shams' (vol 67, February 1863) and the splendid 'French Life' (April-June 1864). This latter shows her continued preoccupation with France, as do the pieces in the *Pall Mall Gazette*, identified by J. G. Sharps.[10] Two regrets must be that 'French Life' was not extended to take in her second Italian visit (712) and that the planned book on Mme de Sévigné was never written; the visit to Vitré and Les Rochers (vii, 634-41) are the earnest of a classic amongst the lost books of the world. The diary form of the articles allows Gaskell to converse about modern arrangements (flats, concierges, dress, mealtimes), the English housewife being particularly alive to the small amount of butter eaten (vii, 612) – she who had in desperation once urged Marianne to bring butter from London (636). But variety is the great pleasure of the accounts, a delight in the absurdities of human nature, whether of Mme de Villette who as the climax of her receptions 'would desire her *femme de chambre* to hand round the heart of Voltaire, which he had bequeathed her, and which she preserved in a little golden case' (vii, 607) or of the lady who amused herself of a morning by pulling a cord by her bedhead at which all seven wardrobe doors flew open to display her gowns (vii, 618). There is the horror of Mme de Gange's murder (a reminder of Gaskell's strong stomach) and concern in noting Protestant and Catholic involvement in social work (vii, 664-7, 654-7). Perhaps this is the nearest we can come to the fascination of Gaskell's conversation as it ranges over the Reign of Terror, French hostesses, and the last fairy on the Isle of Man (vii, 646, 642, 663).

II Letters

> Don't you like reading letters? I do, so much (to John Forster, 17 May 1854).

If Gaskell had had her way the pleasure of reading her letters would largely have been denied us. She urged Forster in that just quoted to burn it and all others from her, as she vainly urged Marianne to do. The loss would have been serious indeed, since in the reassessment of Gaskell that has proceeded steadily since about 1960 the one great discovery (because of material previously unavailable) has been the letters, published in 1966 by J. A. V. Chapple and Arthur Pollard. Whatever qualifications one may have about the edition – the 'unfortunate happy' discovery of many leters during printing, that throws out the chronological sequence; over-light annotation; incompleteness; unsatisfactory indexing – its excellencies are clear: above all, allowing the letters to be read. They are essential sources (as the use made of them in this study shows) for Gaskell's life and literary activities. In them something is captured of the fleeting substance of that culture in Manchester and beyond, of which she was a vibrant centre. She followed Southey when he declared that 'in letter-writing I love to do nothing *more* than just say what is uppermost'.[11] The results catch the mind in flux (one of the essential paradoxes of art); she could jokingly characterize one of her own letters and capture even in jest what makes them valuable to us - 'Oh! I am afraid this letter is going to be what Dr Holland once called a letter of mine "a heterogeneous mass of nonsense". But that was before I wrote Mary B - he would not *say* so now' (286). Humour, an understanding of the world and a pleasure in the understanding, the sense of a busy involved life all appear in the letters. She is colloquial, often delightfully slangy, making her correspondent aware of a voice, suiting style and content to her recipient. We can follow her working out ideas, breaking down in attempts to explain things, full of anecdote, quotation, and delighted reference - a mind alive, seizing often the moments left her in the busiest of lives ('wine time' one is headed (12), when the ladies are in the drawing-room and the gentlemen still at table), and able to convey that life to us. She shows none of the consciousness of a writer like Alexander Pope that his letters may be for publication - Pope indeed edited his for print - and there is rarely that rough shaping of material to be polished later, as Charles Lamb can be seen drafting some of the *Essays of Elia*.[12] Amongst nineteenth-century letter writers she is outstanding; none of the qualifications here that I make on her as a novelist. She outpaces for sheer interest (not biographical importance, be it noted) Dickens and Thackeray, is colloquial where George Eliot is often in her best dress - only Jane Welsh Carlyle matches her. In a typical letter to Marianne, Gaskell's repetition and inconsequence show she uses the form to convey assurance and information, yet even the mosaic forms a pattern, regarded the right way, to show the loving careful mother:

My dearest Polly,
  This won't be an elegant letter but I will write on any scrap of paper to set you at ease. I wish I could have afforded to let you go to Portsmouth but you see I can't. You may get those songs Papa says, as I told you yesterday. Your note this morning was *very* nice, darling. Remember Miss Chorley's hours, *after* 12 *before* 2 - The man came (M. Hallé's man Hinxman) to tune the piano yesterday - it was more than $\frac{1}{2}$ a note *flat*, besides being altogether out of tune - and he says it is all but ruined by being so shockingly tuned. It will take 4 tunings this next month, & cost *two guineas*, - something about the frame &c., - and so I must scrubble up money for that.

Pray burn any letters. I am always afraid of writing much to
you, you are so careless about letters. No news. Meta is going
to Alderley at 4 this afternoon. Papa to dine with Mrs
Schwabe. I can't go, have had & have one of my atrocious
head-aches. As far as I know Susanna is going to London
today .... 'Scripture readers' are men, sent & paid by a
London society to any clergyman who applies for them to help
him to read the bible in his parish. There was one at
Boughton you may remember. They read & act under the
clergyman's direction. The black kitten is lost. *The children have
never missed her, so you must take no notice.* I have no time for
more. Only be happy love & enjoy yourself. I wish you'd say
if you've been to Mr Bowman again (274-5).

I began with Plymouth Grove and in this letter end where I began.
In a true sense Gaskell's work, as her life, centres on her home and
while I have been careful to avoid mere biographical connections
between life and work, fully to understand Gaskell - she is not a
difficult author, though often a subtle one - demands we begin to
understand her culture and its context.

Notes

CHAPTER 1   Elizabeth Gaskell

1 *The Letters of Mrs Gaskell*, ed. J. A. V. Chapple and Arthur Pollard (Manchester, 1966), p. 81. References to this edition indicated in text by a single number in brackets (always the page reference); in notes as *Letters*.

2 Details from *Sale Catalogue: Re the late Miss M. E. Gaskell, 84, Plymouth Grove, Manchester* (Auctioneers, Geo. H. Larmuth & Sons). Copies in Manchester Central Public Library.

3 See Edgar Holland, *A History of the Family of Holland*, ed. W. F. Irvine (Edinburgh, 1902); and Bernard Holland, *The Lancashire Hollands* (London, 1917). See also Sir Henry Holland, *Recollections of Past Life* (London, 1872).

4 Elizabeth Gaskell, *My Diary*, ed. Clement Shorter (privately printed, 1923), p. 28; *Letters*, pp. 8-10. Aunt Lumb's house was called The Heath (one of the auctioneers' many errors).

5 Phyllis D. Hicks, *A Quest of Ladies: The Story of a Warwickshire School* (Birmingham, 1949), pp. 80-2; see below p. 187 on the setting of *Wives and Daughters*.

6 See E. Holland, *History*, p. 71; H. Holland, *Recollections*, p. 8; and George Head, *A Home Tour through the Manufacturing Districts of England in the Summer of 1835* (London, 1836) (facsimile reprint, 1968), pp. 339-42.

7 Reproduced in A. B. Hopkins, *Elizabeth Gaskell: Her Life and Work* (London, 1952); Arthur Pollard, *Mrs Gaskell: Novelist and Biographer* (Manchester, 1965); Winifred Gérin, *Elizabeth Gaskell: A Biography* (Oxford, 1976).

8 Manchester Central Public Library; volume inscribed and dated 12 June 1827.

9 See e.g. John Forster, *Life of Charles Dickens* (1872-4), ed. J. W. T. Ley (London, 1928), p. 298; and *A Schoolmaster's Notebook*, ed. Edith and Thomas Kelly (Chetham Society, 3rd Series, vol. 8) (Manchester, 1957), pp. 1-3.

10 [Joseph Priestley], *An Appeal to tme Serious and Candid Professors of Christianity* (London, 1771, 3rd edn), pp. 4, 5.

11 Priestley, *Appeal*, p. 18.

12 *History of the Corruptions of Christianity*, quoted by Basil Willey, 'Joseph Priestley and the Socinian Moonlight', *The Eighteenth-Century Background* (1940) (Harmondsworth, 1972), p. 183.

13 Historical information in this section drawn from Earl Morse Wilbur, *A History of Unitarianism* (Cambridge, Mass, 1952).

14 The term first used in 1672/3; given currency by Stephen Nye's *A Brief History of Unitarianism* (London, 1687).

15 Charles Lamb, *Letters*, 2 vols (London, 1950), i, p. 328 (to William Wordsworth, 19 October 1810).

16 See Willey, *Eighteenth-Century Background*; Joseph Priestley, *Autobiography* (1805), ed. Jack Lindsay (Bath, 1970).

17 Priestley, *Appeal*, p. 22.

18 See Robert Southey, *Letters: A Selection*, ed. Maurice H. Fitzgerald (London, 1912), p. 385 (15 October 1824); and Mary Moorman, *William Wordsworth: The Later Years 1803-1850* (London, 1965), p. 106.

19 F. D. Maurice, *The Kingdom of Christ* (1837), 2 vols (London, Everyman, n.d.), i, pp. 139-40. Maurice was a Unitarian turned Anglican.

20 S. T. Coleridge, *Notebooks*, ed. Kathleen Coburn (London, 1957), vol. 1, sect. 467.

21 L. Tyerman, *The Life and Times of the Rev. John Wesley*, 3 vols (London, 1871), i, p. 180.

22 Basil Willey, 'Samuel Taylor Coleridge', *Nineteenth-Century Studies* (1949) (Harmondsworth, 1973), p. 10.

23 William Turner of Newcastle had entertained him and his sister Harriet to tea; James Drummond and C. D. Upton, *The Life and Letters of James Martineau*, 2 vols (London, 1902), i, p. 11.

24 Drummond and Upton, i, pp. 24-5.

25 Drummond and Upton, i, p. 287, quoting from his article 'Personal Influence on Present Theology: Newman-Coleridge-Carlyle' (*National Review*, Oct 1856; reprinted in *Essays*, vol. 1).

26 James Martineau, *Endeavours after the Christian Life* (London, 1843), pp. 1-2. The quotation from S. T. Coleridge's *Biographia Literaria* (London, 1817), ed. J. Shawcross, 2 vols (London, 1907; 1969), i, p. 60, is in context of Wordsworth's 'The Female Vagrant', but as Willey (*Nineteenth-Century Studies*, p. 20) says, it epitomizes Coleridge's distinctive quality as critic.

27 *Memorials of Two Sisters*, ed. Margaret J. Shaen (London, 1908), pp. 218, 216; the common attribution to Mozart is spurious.

28 Martineau, *Endeavours* ('The Besetting God'), pp. 19-20.

29 Brooke Herford, *Travers Madge: A Memoir* (London/Manchester/Norwich, 1867), pp. 23, 26.
30 *The Religion and Theology of Unitarians* (London, 1906), pp. 139, 140.
31 Herford, p. 23.
32 F. W. Newman said their books were not displayed by booksellers and added that 'no Romish hierarchy can so successfully exclude heretical books, as social enactment excludes those of Unitarians from our orthodox circles' (*Phases of Faith* (London, 1850), 1860 (facsimile reprint, Leicester, 1970, intro. U. C. Knoepflmacher), p. 49).
33 Herford, p. 151.
34 See Owen Chadwick, *The Victorian Church*, pt. 1 (London, 1966, 3rd edn. 1971) for Bishop Lee.
35 See Chadwick, pp. 349ff; and *Letters*, pp. 256-7.
36 Shaen, p. 26.
37 Newman, *Phases*, p. vi.
38 I. Giberne Sieveking, *Memoir and Letters of Francis W. Newman* (London, 1909), p. 106.
39 Sieveking, p. 104; see *Letters*, p. 88.
40 Sieveking, p. 44.
41 Newman, *Phases*, p. 28
42 F. W. Newman, *Personal Narrative in Letters* (London, 1856), pp. 47, 31.
43 Newman, *Narrative*, p. 84.
44 Newman, *Phases*, p. 62; Shaen, pp. 57, 25.
45 Newman, *Phases*, pp. 174-5, 133.
46 Newman, *Soul*, pp. 99, 4, viii; the earlier book was the one generally admired by Newman's friends, who felt that if it were unknown, *Phases* would make people 'think him cold and hard, with extraordinary powers of intellect, but without the capacity for deep religious feeling' (Shaen, p. 58).
47 For further discussion of Newman, see Willey, *More Nineteenth-Century Studies* (London, 1956); and see *Letters*, pp. 109, 124.
48 Herford, pp. 125, 185; Herford himself, main source of my account, was a leading Unitarian – indicative of the love felt for Madge.
49 Gaskell, *My Dairy*, pp. 35, 39.
50 C. E. Norton, *Notes of Travel and Study in Italy* (1859) (Boston, 1881), pp. 239-40, describes Manning in 1857, the year of Gaskell's own visit to Rome.
51 The episode derives from *The Apology of Theophilus Lindsey, M.A., on Resigning the Vicarage of Catterick, Yorkshire* (4th edn., London, 1782): Oldfield's Soliloquy is p. 221fn.
52 E.g. *Sylvia's Lovers*, p. 527: 'all that the blessed Christ . . . had said of the Father, from whom He came'.
53 H. Holland, *Recollections*, p. 12.

54 *Wives and Daughters,* p. 500; from *Lessons for Children* (London, 1808), pt 2, p. 91, a work interesting if only because it teaches children of 5 years the difference between words and concepts.

55 Herford, p. 93; about 1850.

56 *Bygones Worth Remembering* (1905), 2 vols (London, 1915), ii, pp. 231, 232.

57 Newman, *Phases,* p. 2 and *The Soul,* p. 159; Shaen, p. 35; Herford, p. 54.

58 *Schoolmaster's Notebook,* p. 1.

59 McLachlan, 'Cross Street Chapel in the Life of Manchester', *Memoirs and Proceedings of the Manchester Literary and Philosophical Society* (Manchester, 1942), lxxxiv (1939-41), p. 32.

60 McLachlan, 'Cross Street Chapel', pp. 3, 36.

61 'On Female Studies', *A Legacy for Young Ladies* (London, 1826), pp. 42-53.

62 *Anna Jameson: Letters and Friendships (1812-1860),* ed. Mrs Steuart Erskine (London, 1915), p. 211; *Ruth,* p. 212; Shaen, p. 22.

63 Barbauld, *Legacy,* p. 52.

64 Lamb, *Letters,* i, p. 228 (dated 1802).

65 *Sylvia's Lovers,* p. 491; *North and South,* p. 266.

66 *Sylvia's Lovers,* p. 260; compare 'The Heart of John Middleton' (ii, p. 391), where pedlars' books include the *Seven Champions, Pilgrim's Progress, Paradise Lost,* and Byron's *Narrative* – and see 'Half a Lifetime Ago' (v, p. 280).

67 *North and South,* p. 32; see *The Spectator* (no. 94, 18 June 1711).

68 Quoted e.g. *Letters,* p. 33, *North and South,* p. 500, Maria Cummins, *Mabel Vaughan* (introduction).

69 *Wives and Daughters,* p. 311; MS music-book, dated June 1827, in Manchester Central Public Library (the song is dated August 1828).

70 *Ruth,* p. 208: 'it was with an exquisite pang of delight that, after a moment of vague fear ("Oh, mercy! to myself I said,/If Lucy should be dead!") she saw her child's bright face of welcome'.

71 Geraldine Jewsbury, *Letters,* ed. Mrs Alexander Ireland (London, 1892), p. 78.

72 Herford, p. 160.

73 'French Life', viii, p. 663; *Ruth,* pp. 68, 173-4, 190, 306.

74 *Life of Charlotte Brontë,* p. 501; *Letters,* p. 172; Charles Dickens, *Letters,* ed. Walter Dexter, 3 vols (London, 1938), ii, pp. 359-60. 'To Be Read at Dusk' appeared in *The Keepsake for 1852;* available in *Reprinted Pieces* and Charles Dickens, *Selected Short Fiction,* ed. Deborah A. Thomas (Harmondsworth, 1976).

75 Details from *The Autobiography of Sir Charles Hallé* (1896), ed. Michael Kennedy (London, 1972), pp. 122-41.

76 Fanny Lewald, *England und Schottland*, 2 vols (Brunswick, 1851-2), ii, p. 617.

77 *Letters*, p. 218; *Cranford*, p. 131; see E. H. Gombrich, 'Raphael's Madonna della Sedia', *Norm and Form* (London, 1966); *Ruth*, p. 152.

78 *Catalogue of the Art Treasures of the United Kingdom. Collected at Manchester in 1857*, n.d. or place.

79 H. Holland, *Recollections*, p. 209. Other details from *Recollections of the Table Talk of Samuel Rogers*, ed. Alexander Dyce (2nd edn, London, 1856), pp. 155-6; *National Gallery: Descriptive and Historical Catalogue of the British and Foreign Pictures* . . . (81st edn, London, 1913); Shaen, p. 41.

80 *Mary Barton*, p. 68; illustrated in T. S. R. Boase, *English Art 1800-1870* (Oxford, 1959), plate 66B (and see p. 214).

81 *Letters*, p. 580; the story, from Aesop, Gaskell could have remembered from *The Monitor*, a gift anthology compiled by Mrs H. Gregg (Liverpool, 1804), p. 25, her copy of which is in Knutsford Public Library (Hopkins, p. 29).

82 Shaen, p. 57.

83 Gaskell knew Nasmyth and his works at Patricroft well (see Shaen, p. 134).

84 *William Langshawe, The Cotton Lord*, 2 vols (London, 1842), i, p. 203. H. Holland, *Recollections*, p. 212, mentions the laboratory. The Literary and Philosophical Society, of which Dalton was President from 1817 until his death, preserved his original equipment and notebooks until their destruction by enemy action, 1941.

85 Head, *Home Tour*, p. 78.

86 Barbauld, *Legacy*, p. 50.

87 Lewald, ii, p. 540.

88 Shaen, pp. 19, 15, 22.

89 Kate O'Meara, *Madame Mohl: Her Salon and Her Friends* (London, 1885), p. 24, quoting from Mary Mohl's *Madame Recamier*.

90 O'Meara, pp. 111, 170.

91 M. C. M. Simpson, *Letters and Recollections of Julius and Mary Mohl* (London, 1887), p. 91; this work includes a photograph of one of the drawing-rooms.

92 O'Meara, p. 51.

93 *Letters*, pp. 925-6; see also E. T. Dubois, 'Madame de Sévigné et l'Angeleterre', *XVIIe Siècle* (1971), pp. 75-97 and Arthur Tilley, *Madame de Sévigné* (Cambridge, 1936). Gérin, *Gaskell* (p. 225) misleadingly suggests that Gaskell wished 'to introduce' Sévigné to the English public – and in details of the Brittany visit incorrectly makes Vitré and Les Rochers the same place.

94 O'Meara, p. 245.

95 Shaen, p. 170; used in 'A Dark Night's Work' (vii, 562) to impede Ellinor's return to England.
96 Henry James, *William Whetmore Story and His Friends*, 2 vols (London, 1903) (facsimile reprint, n.d. [1957]), i, p. 12.
97 *Letters of Mrs Gaskell and Charles Eliot Norton 1855-1865*, ed. Jane Whitehill (London, 1932), p. 99.
98 *Gaskell/Norton Letters*, p. 59.
99 James, *Story*, i, p. 354.
100 MS letter, Unitarian College, Manchester (in keeping of John Rylands University Library of Manchester).
101 MS Minutes of Memorial Fund, pp. 56, 49 (Manchester Central Public Library). For Story, see James, *Story*, ii, p. 61.
102 MS letter, Unitarian College, Manchester, to R. J. Gordon (in John Rylands University Library of Manchester).
103 H. McLachlan, *The Unitarian Home Missionary College 1854-1914* (Manchester and London, 1915), pp. 14, 32, 34; see *Letters*, pp. 758ff. William Gaskell tutored e.g. the Winkworths in History, Composition, Chemistry, German and Music (Shaen, p. 11).
104 W. E. Adams, *Memoirs of a Social Atom*, 2 vols (London, 1903), ii, p. 390. Hopkins (p. 45) quoting this accidentally includes part of Adams's tribute to another teacher.
105 *Two Lectures on the Lancashire Dialect* (London, 1854), pp. 9, 8; added as explanatory supplement to 5th edn (1854) of *Mary Barton*. Gérin (*Gaskell*, p. 89) quite wrongly suggests these lectures were specifically on the novel's use of dialect.
106 Jewsbury, *Letters*, p. 383.
107 Gaskell, *My Diary*, pp. 5, 8, 14, 9; perhaps Gaskell thought as she wrote, as we might in reading, of Coleridge's 'Frost at Midnight'.
108 Gaskell, *My Diary*, pp. 22, 25, 35, 37.
109 *Gaskell/Norton Letters*, p. 68.
110 *Letters*, pp. 523, 524, 57, 11, 57.
111 Gérin, *Gaskell*, p. 75.
112 *Life of Charlotte Brontë*, p. 457.
113 See Thea Holme, *The Carlyles at Home* (London, 1965), especially chs 2, 3 and appendix.
114 *Family Expositor*, 6 vols (London, 1739), i, pp. i-ii; Gaskell, *My Diary*, p. 40.
115 Samuel Bamford, *Passages in the Life of a Radical*, 2 vols (London, 1844), i, p. 277; ii, pp. 19, 239; i, p. 8.
116 Samuel Bamford, *Early Days* (1848), 2 vols (Manchester and London, 1859), i, p. 192.
117 Bamford, *Passages*, i, p. 124.
118 Bamford, *Passages*, i, pp. 139ff; compare Elizabeth Stone's comic use of the ceremony in *William Langshawe*, i, pp. 288ff.

240

119 Bamford, *Early Days*, i, p. 128.
120 [T. W. McDermid], *The Life of Thomas Wright, The Prison Philanthropist* (Manchester, n.d.) [1876], pp. 12, 16.
121 McDermid, p. 72; and see [Henry Morley], 'An Unpaid Servant of the State', *Household Words*, iv (1852), pp. 553ff
122 Frontispiece to Knutsford, vol. v; Gérin, *Gaskell*, facing p. 206.
123 *Gaskell/Norton Letters*, p. 116.
124 Jewsbury, *Letters*, pp. 383-4.
125 Shaen, pp. 23-4.
126 *Letters and Memorials of Jane Welsh Carlyle*, ed. James Anthony Froude, 3 vols (London, 1883), i, 321.
127 Jewsbury, *Letters*, pp. 93-4; see also Susanna Howe, *Geraldine Jewsbury: Her Life and Errors* (London, 1935).
128 [Florence Nightingale], *Letters from Egypt* (privately printed, 1854), pp. 1, 13.
129 Shaen, p. 24.
130 J. G. Sharps, *Mrs Gaskell's Observation and Invention* (Fontwell, Sussex, 1970), pp. 554-62; the outline only is in *Mary Barton*, ed. Stephen Gill (Harmondsworth, 1970), appendix 1.
131 *Letters*, pp. 288, 566, 594; the book of her own she could re-read was the least moral, *Cranford*.
132 Details drawn from *Letters*, pp. 484, 65, 430, 431, 581, 774; and see Anne Lohrli, *Household Words* (Toronto, 1973), p. 128. Similar information can be gleaned from the letters about the short stories.
133 Gordon Haight, *George Eliot: A Biography* (Oxford, 1968), p. 266. For *The Mill on the Floss* Eliot received £2,000 for an edition of 4,000 copies, plus 30 per cent on every copy above that number (p. 318).
134 *Autobiography and Letters of Mrs Margaret Oliphant*, ed. Mrs Harry Coghill (London, 1899) (facsimile reprint, Leicester, 1974), p. 44. But see also what she says (p. 70) about never having fought for higher prices.

CHAPTER 2 *Mary Barton* (1848) and *North and South* (1855); Industry and Individual

1 *Mary Barton*, p. lxxiii.
2 *Manchester as It Is* (Manchester, 1839), p. 11; Leon Faucher, *Manchester in 1844: Its Present Condition and Future Prospects* (London and Manchester, 1844; facsimile reprint, 1969), p. 15 (the often illuminating or dissenting footnotes supplied by the anonymous translator). See also Edward Baines, *History of the Cotton Manufacture in Great Britain ... and a View of the Present State of the Manufacture*, (London [1835]), especially pp. 360, 362, 395. For a general survey of the county and Manchester, see Edward Baines, *History, Directory,*

and Gazatteer (sic) *of the County Palatine of Lancaster*, 2 vols (Liverpool, 1824-5; facsimile reprint, 2 vols, Newton Abbott, 1968); for the Industrial Revolution and further reading see T. S. Ashton, *The Industrial Revolution 1760-1830* (1948) (revised edn, London, 1968), E. J. Hobsbawm, *Industry and Empire* (1968) (Harmondsworth, 1969); old but still useful is J. L. and Barbara Hammond, *The Town Labourer* (2nd edn, London, 1925).

3 Quoted Faucher, p. 10.

4 Baines, p. 222; also pp. 186-7, quoting Erasmus Darwin's poetic version of weaving (*Botanic Garden*, 1791).

5 Baines, pp. 243-4.

6 *Manchester as It Is*, p. 11.

7 *Sketches in the Life of John Clare*, ed. Edmund Blunden (London, 1931), p. 47.

8 Faucher, p. 40 fn; Lyon Playfair, *Report on the State of Large Towns in Lancashire (Health of Towns Commission)* (London, 1845), p. 123; see also John Burnett, *Plenty and Want* (Harmondsworth, 1966), especially ch. 3 ('The Town Worker'), and for the debate on conditions, *The Standard of Living in Britain in the Industrial Revolution*, ed. Arthur J. Taylor (London, 1975).

9 Jane Welsh Carlyle, *Letters and Memorials*, ed. James Froude, 3 vols (London, 1883), ii, p. 116. Carlyle in preparing these letters was discovering how much Jane had needed his love and how little she had received.

10 Lewald, *England und Schottland*, 2 vols (Brunswick, 1851-2), ii, pp. 559-60.

11 *Mary Barton*, pp. 68-70; compare the similar contrast for Birmingham of an omitted section in Dickens's *The Old Curiosity Shop* (1841), ed. Angus Easson (Harmondsworth, 1972), p. 705.

12 Burnett, *Plenty and Want*, p. 17; Lewald, ii, p. 577 questions how a household can be maintained when the housewife, out all day, returns exhausted. Gaskell turns this ignorance to comic effect (*Mary Barton*, pp. 136-7).

13 Faucher, pp. viii, vii.

14 *Report of the Road and Street Cleansing Company* (Manchester, 1843), p. 4; and see Geraldine Jewsbury, *Letters*, ed. Mrs Alexander Ireland (London, 1892), p. 126.

15 MS Visiting Committee's Reports: Deansgate District, p. 107 (M126/2/3), Manchester Central Public Library.

16 Playfair, pp. 38, 39, 41fn.

17 A. T. H. Waters, *Report on the Sanitary Condition of Certain Parts of Manchester* (Manchester and Salford Sanitary Association) (Manchester, 1853), p. 16.

18 *Report of the Committee of the Manchester and Salford Sanitary As-*

sociation for the Year 1861 (Manchester), pp. 12-13.

19 Compare Faucher, p. 27: 'After a hasty meal, men, women, and children sally forth to saunter in the streets, or to lounge in the beer-houses'; see also pp. 28, 48, 49 (and translator's qualification, p. 49fn.).

20 Faucher, p. 41.

21 *The Condition of the Working Class in England* (1845) (London, 1969), pp. 79-80.

22 Lewald, ii, pp. 539-40, 560 – though she also notes (ii, 560) that those who have made money enough don't live in Manchester.

23 The point is made by e.g. M. W. Flinn, 'Social Theory and the Industrial Revolution' in Tom Burns and S. B. Saul (eds), *Social Theory and Economic Change* (London, 1967), p. 13.

24 John Forster, *Life of Charles Dickens* (1872-4), ed. J. W. T. Ley (London, 1928), p. 540; on education see e.g. Flinn, 'Social Theory', particularly pp. 14-16. Dickens expressed his views clearly to the Metropolitan Sanitary Association (May 1851); see *Speeches of Charles Dickens*, ed. K. J. Fielding (Oxford, 1960), p. 129.

25 Playfair, p. 126 and fn.

26 Faucher, pp. xiii, xiv (translator's preface).

27 Joseph Perrin, *The Manchester Handbook* (Manchester, n.d.) [1859], pp. 101-7.

28 Faucher, pp. 53, 55.

29 Jewsbury, *Letters*, pp. 238, 239 (Peel Park is now partly the site of Salford University; public library and art gallery continue on the site). Lewald (ii, pp. 539-40) touches on the closeness of fields and the public park.

30 E.g. Dickens (see Forster, p. 785).

31 G. F. Pardon, *The Manchester Conductor* (Manchester, 1857), pp. 58-9 (a handbook produced particularly for visitors to the Great Art Exhibition of that year).

32 See e.g. R. J. White, *Waterloo to Peterloo* (1957), ch. 15 and Bamford, *Passages in the Life of a Radical*, 2 vols (London, 1844), i, 164ff (the central incident is pp. 199-226). For a more detailed account, see Joyce Marlow, *The Peterloo Massacre* (London, 1969).

33 Perrin, p. 41.

34 For full and excellent discussion, see E. P. Thompson, *The Making of the English Working Class* (Harmondsworth, 1968); he also has a section on Peterloo, pp. 734-68.

35 Faucher, p. 25fn.

36 Flinn, 'Social Theory', p. 14.

37 *Poor Man's Advocate* (21 January 1832), p. 3b (facsimile reprint, New York, 1969).

38 *Poor Man's Advocate* (21 January 1832), p. 4b; the writer is silent on

the imposition this could be for the new hand.

39 Compare Patrick Brantlinger, 'The Case Against Trade Unions in Early Victorian Fiction', *Victorian Studies*, viii (1969).

40 No doubt this reflects historically the disappearance by and large of such ceremony; as outward show rather than the inner meaning of such organizations, its abandonment suggests their real growth.

41 Frances Trollope, *The Life and Adventures of Michael Armstrong the Factory Boy*, 1840 (serialized 1839–40) (facsimile reprint, London, 1968); all references are to this edition.

42 See Brantlinger, pp. 37, 38.

43 See B. L. Hutchins and A. Harrison, *A History of Factory Legislation* (London, 1903).

44 'No matter in what state of exhaustion persons may be ... not one can get so much as a drop of water ... until one of these *"written certificates"* is produced to the door-keeper' (1833, p. vii a & b): note the language's undertone of Dives and Lazarus, a parable that offered John Barton revengeful consolation.

45 *Poor Man's Advocate* waged a campaign against night-working, printing names and addresses; their chief objections were noise, greed of the mill-owners, and (unstated, but clear to us) that wages were the same night as day.

46 Charlotte Elizabeth, *Helen Fleetwood* (London, 1841); all references are to this edition.

47 In *Mary Barton*, the widowed Mrs Davenport wonders 'how she might best cheat the factory inspector, and persuade him that her strong, big, hungry Ben was above thirteen' (p. 82); the value of large families appears in the story of a widow asked at her husband's graveside to marry again by a man who saw profit in her children; she refused, having accepted another before she set out for the funeral (E. Royston Pike (ed.), *Human Documents of the Industrial Revolution in Britain* (London, 1966), p. 168).

48 For the dust see Lewald, ii, p. 569; *Michael Armstrong*, p. 25; *Hard Times*, 'Reaping', ch. 1; and it kills Bessy Higgins in *North and South*.

49 In *Hard Times* she is killed by sickly air; Dickens originally intended she should be killed by having her arm torn off by unfenced machinery.

50 For 'silver-fork' see Kathleen Tillotson, *Novels of the 1840s* (1956) (London, 1961), pp. 73–5 (she includes the best known parody of this school, from Dickens's *Nicholas Nickleby*) and M. W. Rosa, *The Silver-Fork School* (New York, 1936).

51 Elizabeth Stone, *William Langshaw, The Cotton Lord*, 2 vols (London, 1842), i, p. 186; called 'Scotch Song', perhaps a cover for Stone's own authorship. There may be a note of irony in this epigraph, but I think not.

52 *Blackwood's Monthly Magazine,* xli (1837) pp. 48-50. Despite the title, no further were published; the quotation is from Knutsford (i, p. xxv).

53 J. G. Sharps, *Mrs Gaskell's Observation and Invention* (Fontwell, Sussex, 1970), p. 60.

54 That Gaskell believed, or came to believe, *John Barton* was her original title is shown by her note to that effect in a presentation copy of 1861 (Manchester Central Public Library).

55 Sharps, pp. 554-7 and Gill (in his edition) pp. 467-8 reproduce the outline; Sharps, pp. 559-61 reproduces the conclusion.

56 Sharps, p. 561.

57 She says the situation makes men 'sore and irritable against the rich, the even tenor of whose seemingly happy lives appeared to increase the anguish', while the belief of injustice and unkindness 'taints what might be resignation to God's will' (pp. lxxiii, lxxiv).

58 The point is made again (the coincidence is too neat) when Barton, desperate for food for his dying son, sees Mrs Hunter come out of the loaded grocer's shop (p. 25).

59 Whatever Gaskell's sympathy with his actions, as Barton becomes 'all that is commonly called wild and visionary', she insists, 'Ay! but being visionary is something. It shows a soul, a being not altogether sensual' (p. 196).

60 I deliberately echo the wording of Wordsworth's 1800 Preface to *Lyrical Ballads:* 'I have said that each of these poems has a purpose ... to follow the fluxes and refluxes of the mind when agitated by the great and simple affections of our nature' (ed. R. L. Brett and A. R. Jones (1963) (London, 1965), p. 247).

61 It was reviewed e.g. adversely in *British Quarterly Review,* ix (1849) pp. 117-36, favourably in *Westminster Review,* ii (1849) pp. 48-63; for Greg, see *Edinburgh Review,* lxxxix (1849) pp. 402-35.

62 Carlyle had so little time for novels that he could call *Bleak House,* Dickens's 'new dud of a Book', though he had read none of it (*New Letters,* 2 vols, ed. Alexander Carlyle (London, 1904), ii, p. 127).

63 E.g. French, 1849, 1856 (8 printings in Bibliothèque Nationale catalogue), 1865; Russian, 1861; Spanish, 1879.

64 Geraldine Jewsbury, *Marian Withers,* 3 vols (London, 1851). All references are to this edition by volume and page.

65 See Gaskell's important retrospective statement of what she attempted in *Mary Barton, Letters,* p. 119.

66 The claim is made by S. Howe, *Geraldine Jewsbury, Her Life and Errors* (London, 1935), p. 111.

67 Jewsbury, *Letters,* pp. 210-11.

68 Quoted in Howe, p. 94. Compare Mrs Langshawe in Stone, whose sister is married to an artisan.

69 Jewsbury, *Letters*, pp. 14–15.

70 Quoted in Howe, p. 97, from the *Athenaeum*; Jewsbury was reviewing Charles Kingsley's *Alton Locke* (1850), a 'condition of England' novel.

71 Dickens, *Letters*, ed. Walter Dexter, 3 vols (London, 1938), ii, p. 202 (31 January 1850).

72 Dickens, *Letters*, ii, p. 457.

73 Dickens, *Letters*, ii, p. 561 (15 June 1854).

74 Dickens, *Letters*, ii, p. 554. There is a general working on this theme by Dickens, personally and through other contributors, in *Household Words* about this time: e.g. [James Lowe], 'Locked Out', viii (December 1853); [Dickens], 'On Strike', viii (February 1854); [Henry Morley], 'Ground in the Mill', ix (April 1854).

75 From Tennyson's 'Will Waterproof's Lyrical Monologue', 11.49–56; omitted in volume issue.

76 Dickens, *Letters*, ii, p. 571.

77 Reference by Charlotte Brontë makes it clear that Gaskell did not wish to publish in serial form but felt an obligation to Dickens; this may have coloured Gaskell's feelings through the problems (see *The Brontës: Lives and Letters*, ed. T. J. Wise and J. A. Symington, 4 vols (London, 1932), iv, pp. 135, 153). *Cranford*, though published serially before this, was conceived as one short story and developed in a series of self-contained 'papers' (see chapter 3).

78 A. B. Hopkins, *Elizabeth Gaskell: Her Life and Work* (London, 1952), p. 143; and see: Winifred Gérin, *Elizabeth Gaskell, a biography* (Oxford, 1976) ch. 14, particularly pp. 153 ff.

79 Dickens, *Letters*, ii, pp. 562, 571 (15 June and 26 July 1854); and see ii, p. 542 (18 February 1854).

80 Dickens, *Letters*, ii, p. 582.

81 Dickens, *Letters*, ii, p. 571.

82 Three chapters were expanded and two entirely new added: chs. 44, 45, 46 in *Household Words* became vol. ii, chs. 19, 22–26 (chs. 44, 47–51 in Knutsford) and vol. ii, chs. 20, 21 (chs. 45, 46 in Knutsford) were added.

83 Dickens, *Letters*, ii, p. 618.

84 See Hopkins, p. 149.

85 For further discussion see F. R. Leavis in *The Great Tradition* (London, 1947), and *Dickens the Novelist* (London, 1970); and my *Hard Times: Commentary and Notes* (London, 1973).

86 Changed at Dickens's suggestion, though it is not clear who originated the present title.

87 When she had read to the end of chapter 9, Charlotte Brontë seems to have felt Mr Hale's doubts to be a leading theme (Wise and Symington, iv, p. 153, 30 September 1854). This was already the fifth episode. Even given Mr Hale's problem, it is no novel of religious

doubt; Mr Hale becomes not an infidel (a term reserved for Higgins), but a Dissenter; he moves from Anglican to Unitarian, accomplishing in little the Presbyterians' historical process: Gaskell's model was the life of Theophilus Lindsey (see p. 17 above and my forthcoming note, 'Mr Hale's Doubts in *North and South*').

CHAPTER 3 *Cranford* (1853)

1 *Household Words*, ix (May 1854); *Fraser's Magazine*, lxix (April-June 1864).

2 Elizabeth Gaskell, *Cranford*, ed. Elizabeth Porges Watson (London, 1972), p. 161: references in text to 'The Last Generation in England' are to this edition; references to *Cranford* to Knutsford. See Southey's letter of 8 January 1833: 'I want to write ... [England's] Domestic History, that is, of manners in the widest acceptation of the word' (Robert Southey, *Letters: A Selection*, ed. M. H. Fitzgerald (London, 1912), p. 475).

3 *Cranford*, ed. Watson, p. 161; Drumble is Manchester, as Cranford is Knutsford.

4 See the comparable violence in George Eliot's related sketches, *Scenes of Clerical Life* (London, 1858), ed. David Lodge (Harmondsworth, 1973), particularly 'Janet's Repentance'.

5 Compare Augustus J. C. Hare's anecdote of Lady Penrhyn's pugs, *Memorials of a Quiet Life*, 2 vols (2nd edn, London, 1872), i, p. 10.

6 Originally serialized, then published 1824-32 in 5 vols. The surface similarity of *Cranford* and *Our Village* is emphasized by uniform editions (London, 1891; 1893), introductions by Anne Thackeray Ritchie, illustrations by Hugh Thomson.

7 George Eliot, *Letters*, 7 vols, ed. Gordon S. Haight (London/New Haven, 1954-6), iii (1954), pp. 198-9.

8 *Cranford*, intro. Ritchie, pp. vi-vii, xix.

9 'Women without Men at Cranford', *Essays in Criticism*, xiii (1963); the quotation is from p. 133.

10 For details of publication and division into chapters when gathered, see *Cranford*, ed. Watson, pp. 179-83.

11 To Ruskin [?Late February 1865]. A contemporary letter (December 1861) stresses the continuity of composition: 'I've written a couple of tales about Cranford in Household Words' (174); she speaks as though Cranford had a real and already known existence, while 'a couple of tales' suggests the vein once opened ran freely.

12 There is a disturbing suggestion retrospectively that Peter's dressing up with the 'baby' was not only a jibe at Deborah for having no suitor (unlike Matty), but played its part in the rejection of Holbrook by Mr Jenkyns and Deborah: enforced by Peter's later comment on Matty's single state.

13 For a common variant see 'The Long Pack' in Katherine M. Briggs, *A Dictionary of British Folk-Tales*, 4 vols (London, 1970-71), B:2, pp. 254-6.

14 Dickens's successor to *Household Words;* reprinted in *Cranford,* ed. Watson.

15 Kate O'Meara, *Madame Mohl: Her Salon and Her Friends* (London, 1885), pp. 110-13.

16 Jane Welsh Carlyle, *Letters and Memorials,* ed. James Anthony Froude, 3 vols (London, 1883), iii, pp. 231-2 (31 October 1864).

CHAPTER 4 *Ruth* (1853): 'An Unfit Subject for Fiction'

1 See Guinevere L. Griest, *Mudie's Circulating Library and the Victorian Novel* (Newton Abbott, 1970), especially chs 3 and (for *Ruth*), 6.

2 See David Skilton, *Anthony Trollope and his Contemporaries* (London, 1972), pp. 92 ff, and Hazel Mews, *Frail Vessels* (London, 1969), p. 186.

3 Anthony Trollope, *Letters,* ed. Bradford Allen Booth (London, 1951), p. 272; and see the section on *The Vicar* in Trollope, *Autobiography* (1883), ed. Frederick Page (London, 1950), ch. 18.

4 Quoted A. W. Ward, introduction to Knutsford, p. xiii.

5 See William Shaen, who accepted female chastity, but insisted its logical consequence was absolute male chastity; M. J. Shaen, *William Shaen: A Brief Sketch,* (London, 1912), p. 33.

6 From *Recollections of George Butler,* 1892, quoted in Patricia Thomson, *The Victoran Heroine* (London, 1956), p. 134.

7 Dickens, *Letters,* ed. Walter Dexter, 3 vols (London, 1938), ii, p. 457; George Eliot, *Letters,* ed. Gordon Haight (London/New Haven, 1954-6), ii, p. 86; Henry Crabb Robinson, *On Books and Their Writers,* ed. Edith J. Morley, 3 vols (London, 1938), ii, p. 722.

8 John Blackmore, *The London by Moonlight Mission* (London, 1860), p. 18.

9 Blackmore, p. 32. Dickens also stressed the idea of a home (see Clara Burdett Patterson, *Angela Burdett-Coutts and the Victorians* (London, 1953), ch. 5 and p. 161 in particular).

10 Trollope, *Letters,* p. 78; I owe the reference to Griest, p. 133.

11 *Autobiography,* p. 329.

12 15 June 1850; quoted in *Hawthorne: The Critical Heritage,* ed. Donald J. Crowley (London, 1970), pp. 163-4.

13 *Hawthorne* (English Men of Letters Series) (London, 1879; 1883), p. 110.

14 Samuel Richardson, *Clarissa* (London, 1748), letters 34, 70, 72; Choderlos de Laclos, *Les Liaisons Dangereuses* (1782), letters 21, 23.

15 Mews, p. 86.
16 See the epigraph she wrote for *Mary Barton*, ch. 14; and Esther's and Mary's awareness of what sexuality involves (though both are older than Ruth).
17 Robinson, ii, p. 722.
18 Eliot, *Letters*, ii, p. 86.
19 'False Morality of Lady Novelists', reprinted in *Literary and Social Judgements* (London, 1868), p. 133.
20 See e.g. Mrs [Mary] Sherwood, *The History of the Fairchild Family* (London, 1818), a children's fiction, or Blackmore's stress on personal conversion: 'God had been pleased to reveal Himself to her, and she believed in, and confessed the name of Jesus' (p. 80).
21 Compare Hawthorne who in a professed Romance has Hesther as nurse, but she lives to change the A for Adultery to A for Able (see *The Scarlet Letter*, ch. 13).
22 *Life of Charlotte Brontë*, pp. 474-5.

CHAPTER 5 *The Life of Charlotte Brontë* (1857)

1 *Life of Charlotte Brontë*, ed. Shelston, hereafter *Life* in the notes; all references in the text to this edition. The article by Elizabeth Rigby is in *Quarterly Review*, lxxxiv (1849); Gaskell speaks as though the reviewer were a man, though it is clear she knew sex and identity of the writer (*Letters*, pp. 404, 418).
2 Manuscript of the *Life* now in the John Rylands University Library of Manchester: I would like to thank them for generous permission to refer to and quote from this manuscript, and record the kindness and courtesy I have received at the Library over a considerable period. Southey is of particular importance in this context because of his kindness in giving advice to Charlotte (*Life*, pp. 166-7, 171-6).
3 The account was added to the 3rd ed; see *Life*, p. 610.
4 See e.g. her comments upon Ruskin (*Letters*, p. 288) and upon George Eliot (e.g. *Letters*, pp. 566, 586, 594).
5 *Life*, p. 305.
6 Gérin, *Charlotte Brontë: The Evolution of Genius* (Oxford, 1967), p. 528; and see her introduction to the *Life* (Everyman), 1971.
7 To Mary Taylor, 4 September 1848, MS John Rylands University Library of Manchester; reproduced in Joan Stevens, *Mary Taylor: Friend of Charlotte Brontë* (Auckland/London, 1972), pp. 176-81.
8 T. J. Wise and J. A. Symington (eds), *The Brontës; Lives and Letters*, 4 vols (London 1932), iv, p. 116.
9 Geraldine Jewsbury, *Letters*, ed. Mrs Alexander Ireland (London 1892), p. 347.
10 Wise and Symington, iv, pp. 112-13.

11 An interesting fictional treatment of the theme is Emily Jolly's *A Wife's Story* (1875; originally serialized, *Household Words*, xii (September 1855)); see my article, 'Dickens, *Household Words*, and a Double Standard', *Dickensian*, lx (May 1964).

12 M. J. Shaen, (ed.), *Memorials of Two Sisters* (London, 1908), p. 111; quoted in full, Gérin, *Charlotte Brontë*, pp. 535–8.

13 Shaen, p. 114.

14 Wise and Symington, iv, p. 84.

15 Correcting 'study' to 'steady' and 'described' to 'discussed' from MS; see my note, 'Substantive Misprints and a Deletion in Elizabeth Gaskell's "Life of Charlotte Brontë"', *Notes and Queries*, ccxxi (February 1976).

16 Wise and Symington, iv, p. 190 (there incorrectly dated July).

17 Wise and Symington, iv, p. 184.

18 Wise and Symington, iv, p. 185; and see Gaskell, *Letters*, p. 347.

19 See J. G. Sharps, *Mrs Gaskell's Observations and Invention* (Fontwell, Sussex, 1970), pp. 575–8, and Dennis Robinson, 'Elizabeth Gaskell and "A Few Words about 'Jane Eyre'"', *Notes and Queries*, ccxxi (September 1976).

20 Wise and Symington, iv, p. 189; for Nicholls's response to Nussey, see iv, p. 196.

21 It was to be published in 1857, shortly after the *Life*.

22 'Conclusion', *The Life of Sterling*, 1902 (Edinburgh edn), pp. 235–6.

23 Wise and Symington, iv, p. 191.

24 For the family tablets, see Gérin, *Charlotte Brontë*, p. 599; Wise and Symington, iv, p. 241. See also Clement Shorter, *The Brontës: Life and Letters*, 2 vols (London, 1908), i, p. 19.

25 See Wise and Symington, iv, pp. 239–42 for Meta's splendid letter (6 November 1860) of the visit with her mother to Haworth and Patrick Brontë; and Gaskell, *Letters*, pp. 641–2.

26 See *Life*, p. 113; present location unknown, being part of the material acquired through Clement Shorter from Nicholls by T. J. Wise, bibliographer and forger, and dispersed to his financial gain and scholarship's loss.

27 Gaskell perhaps did not know and does not mention that much of the material she saw was written by Branwell.

28 Ellen Nussey, *Reminiscences of Charlotte Brontë* in Shorter, i, pp. 84f; quoted from Gérin, *Charlotte Brontë*, pp. 61–2.

29 Shorter, ii, pp. 103; quoted (in part) Gérin, *Charlotte Brontë*, pp. 62–3.

30 See her letter (29 June 1883), Wise and Symington, iv, p. 246.

31 MS ff. 158, 160 – Ellen's name deleted; MS f. 205 (*Life*, p. 217) – 'my dear Nell' allowed to stand.

32 Complete in Stevens, pp. 176–81; Wise and Symington, ii, pp. 250ff – their corrupt 'snow-storm' for 'thunderstorm' misled Gérin,

Charlotte Brontë, p. 360; Gaskell (*Life*, p. 345) correctly gives 'thunderstorm.

33 John Rylands University Library of Manchester.

34 Stevens, p. 162; she reconstructs Mary's letter, pp. 157-67.

35 MS f.288. See Stevens, pp. 161-2.

36 See Stephen Gill, 'A Manuscript of Branwell Brontë, with Letters of Mrs Gaskell', *Brontë Society Transactions* (1970), pp. 408-11.

37 MS f.16; *Life*, pp. 64-5: 'We were driving ... either sympathy or sorrow.'

38 MS f.124; transferred to *Life*, p. 110.

39 There is similar treatment of Branwell; the anecdote of amazing knowledge of London is shifted from the point of his departure to the Royal Academy school (MS f.135; *Life*, pp. 155-6) – though fascination of the city stays – to the beginning of ch.9 (p. 196), chronologically better and underscoring Branwell's fantasy world.

40 *Letters*, pp. 407, 410. The diary fragment quoted in Mildred G. Christian, 'Census of Brontë Manuscripts in the United States: Part One', *Trollopian* (now *Nineteenth-Century Fiction*), ii (1947), p. 192.

41 For what Taylor actually wrote (to Ellen Nussey, 19 April 1856) see Stevens, p. 126.

42 *Charles Kingsley: His Letters and Memoirs of his Life, edited by his Wife*, 2 vols (London, 1888) (16th abridged edn), ii, p. 49.

43 Wise and Symington, iv, p. 226.

44 On 'gibbeting', see *Letters*, pp. 428-9.

45 Wise and Symington, iv, 223 (26 May 1857).

46 In his edition, Shelston prints the whole revised ch. 4 of the 3rd edn (*Life*, pp. 529-43); the Rev. H. Shepheard, Wilson's son-in-law, published *A Vindication of the Clergy Daughter's School, and of the Rev. W. Carus Wilson*.

47 See my articles 'Thackeray, Elizabeth Gaskell, and *The Life of Charlotte Brontë*', *Victorian Studies Newsletter* (forthcoming) and 'Two Suppressed Opinions in Mrs. Gaskell's *Life of Charlotte Brontë*', *Brontë Society Transactions*, 1974.

48 Stevens, p. 134; Wise and Symington, iv, p. 229.

49 Gérin (intro., Everyman) speaks of 'the third (expurgated) edition', p. xi.

50 Is Jameson's letter possibly the one Gaskell replies to 8 September 1856 (*Letters*, pp. 407-08)? The *Quarterly* quotation is xcviii (1856) p. 297, in a review of family histories.

51 MS f.450; *Life*, p. 390 refers only to 'the family into which she was now received'. See *Letters*, pp. 429-30.

52 Shelston's claim that this painting was destroyed except for the fragment depicting Emily (*Life*, p. 579) is incorrect. That fragment is from a separate painting, and the picture Gaskell describes survived

and is the group in the Gallery (see Richard Ormond, *Early Victorian Portraits*, 2 vols (London 1973), i, pp. 57ff for identification and evidence; it is reproduced in vol. ii as no. 98, where the other known portraits of the Brontës also appear).

53 The ban fairly common in the period: both Thackeray and Mrs Oliphant expressed the same wish – see *Letters and Private Papers of William Makepeace Thackeray*, ed. Gordon N. Ray, 4 vols (London 1945-6), i, p. lxvii; Mrs Margaret Oliphant, *Autobiography and Letters*, ed. Mrs Harry Coghill (London, 1899) (facsimile reprint, Leicester, 1974), p. ix.

CHAPTER 6 *Sylvia's Lovers* (1863): Tragical History

1 *Mary Barton*, p. lxxiii.
2 S. Bamford, *Passages in the Life of a Radical* 2 vols (London, 1844), i, 136; see the whale-jaws at the novel's opening, p. 5.
3 J. G. Sharps, *Mrs Gaskell's Observations and Invention* (Fontwell, Sussex, 1970), pp. 374-5.
4 S. Bamford, *Passages*, ii, 112ff. For Tennyson, see Christopher Ricks's edition (London, 1969), p. 1129, which gives possible sources.
5 P. 1; George Young, *A History of Whitby*, 2 vols (Whitby, 1817), has no hint of such a tradition.
6 *Annual Register for 1795*, 'Chronicle', p. 37.
7 Vol. ii, pp. 878ff. Sharps, p. 375 claims Gaskell had been lent Young's work; W. Gérin, *Elizabeth Gaskell: A Biography* (Oxford, 1976), p. 215, makes it her evening reading; I can find no evidence for either case.
8 See Graham Handley, 'The Chronology of "Sylvia's Lovers"', *Notes and Queries*, ccx (August 1965).
9 These details are noted but not quoted by Sharps, pp. 387ff.
10 Quoted by A. W. Ward, Knutsford, pp. xxiii ff.
11 For the episode, but not the description of landscape, see John Barrow, *The Life and Correspondence of Admiral Sir William Sidney Smith*, 2 vols (London 1848), i, pp. 274-94.
12 M38/4 2/25; about sixteen lines on blue paper from the 'Wedding Raiment' chapter (p. 347), given by William Gaskell to C. Rowley.
13 Brooke Herford, *Travers Madge: A Memoir* (London/Manchester/Norwich, 1867), pp. 170, 175.
14 George Eliot, 'Janet's Repentance', *Scenes of Clerical Life* (1858), ed. David Lodge (Harmondsworth, 1973), p. 320.

CHAPTER 7 *Wives and Daughters* (1866): The Echoing Grove

1 Episodes did not even have to be of equal length; the first three episodes of *Wives and Daughters* in the *Cornhill* show a variation from

twenty-five to thirty-six pages.
2 P. 36; clumsily corrected in later editions to conform with the story's later politics, so losing the wordplay on 'liberal-talking'.
3 MS f. 104; p. 77. Manuscript in John Rylands University Library of Manchester; again I should like to express my thanks for generous permission to use and quote from this.
4 The text of *Wives and Daughters* has been badly corrupted in successive editions and reprints; the claim of the Penguin English Library edition to return to the *Cornhill* is untrue (ed. Frank Glover Smith, Harmondsworth, 1969, p. 29).
5 Roger's expedition was already associated with Darwin's in the *Beagle*; Roger and Osborne were to have been more separated in age, Roger 'four or five years younger' (MS f.61), but the published version makes him only two years younger and so allows them to overlap at Cambridge.
6 One page is misnumbered, so f. 609 does not exist, but there is an extra sheet, f.430A; a small number of sheets have extra material on the back.
7 MS f.515; p. 395.
8 Some of the editorial divisions might be omitted, without disturbance; only once in the serial issue did the division fall oddly, at the end of ch. 51, which ran on into the dialogue between Molly and her father, though when Molly is left to cry 'and so ease her heart' (p. 644) there is a natural pause and the alteration was made in the first volume issue.
9 This kind of excision, of course, would disappear in any fair copy, whatever further correction of detail there might be.
10 MS ff.369, 370v; p. 277.
11 Again, Preston is kept in view at the end of ch. 25 ('Hollingford in a Bustle'), where Gaskell added the final section (from p. 323: 'The two girls were dressed ...' to the end), with the arrival of his nosegay and note, angrily cast by Cynthia into 'the very middle of the embers, which she immediately stirred down upon the beautiful shining (MS shrivelling) petals as if she wished to annihilate them as soon as possible' (p. 324). The presence of Preston at 'The Charity Ball' (ch. 26) obviously took Gaskell back to introduce this gift and its destruction, the printer being asked to 'See other side of page' (MS f.430) and the verso with the extra MS f.430A carried the account to the end of ch. 25.
12 MS f.724; p. 588.
13 In the scrapped section, Mrs Gibson's maid had a new dress to answer the door and the Miss Brownings brought their best silver teapot and cream-jug out of their green-baize bag (MS f.378v; compare pp. 314-16).

253

14 *Letters*, p. 748; MS f.437, where blank is left; p. 330.

15 MS f.220; p. 163. MS f.644; p. 515. 'Mr Smith' (p. 165) was the result of the gap: 'with Mr Goodenough or M^r—' (MS f.222): being filled up with the least offensive possibility.

16 MS f.10; p. 8. MS f.594; p. 465. MS f.122; p. 90. MS f.95; p. 71.

17 MS f.114; p. 84. MS f.70; p. 53. MS f.106; p. 79.

18 MS f.14; p.10. MS f.259; p. 194.

19 *Notes and Reviews* (London, 1921; facsimile reprint 1968), p. 156.

20 A point emphasized in MS by a shift from present to past tense: 'he is' becomes 'he was a very immoral poet' (MS f.212; p. 157).

21 On *Vanity Fair*'s chronology see J. A. Sutherland, *Thackeray at Work* (London, 1974), pp. 35-44.

22 Thackeray was doubly aware, since he illustrated his novel as well, deliberately *not* showing dress historically accurate, not having 'the heart to disfigure my heroes and heroines by costume so hideous' (*Vanity Fair*, 1848, ch. 6, p. 35fn. - omitted in subsequent edns.). Gaskell says Cynthia's dress to our ideas 'would be considered ugly and disfiguring' (p. 250).

23 James Orchard Halliwell, *The Nursery Rhymes of England* (2nd edn., London, 1842) p. 140.

24 Originally Cynthia was to be at the Towers with her mother in the opening chapters, but this was dropped almost at once; the idea of Cynthia's separation from her mother is important (MS f.13; *Cornhill* has this reference, but it was cut in the first vol. edn).

25 Despite the well-argued claims of Marilyn Butler, 'The Uniqueness of Cynthia Kirkpatrick: Elizabeth Gaskell's *Wives and Daughters* and Maria Edgeworth's *Helen*', *Review of English Studies*, xxiii (1972).

26 'Dickens and the Passions', *Dickens Centennial Studies*, ed. Ada Nisbet and Blake Nevius (Berkeley/Los Angeles/London, 1971), p. 75.

27 Charlotte Brontë raised a similar question in July 1853: 'are you never tempted to make your characters more amiable than the Life, by the inclination to assimilate your thoughts to the thoughts of those who always *feel* kindly, but sometimes fail to *see* justly?' (T. J. Wise and J. A. Symington (eds), *The Brontës: Lives and Letters*, 4 vols (London, 1932), iv, pp. 76-7).

28 See e.g. Margaret Ganz's remarks on 'the static nature of the relationships' in this novel (*Elizabeth Gaskell: The Artist in Conflict* (New York, 1969), p. 26).

29 In August 1850 Gaskell was hoping to read *The Prelude* soon (*Letters*, p. 130); and see my suggestion, ch. 8 note 9 below.

CHAPTER 8   The Short Stories

1 MS in Berg Collection, New York Public Library; I owe this

information to J. G. Sharps, *Mrs. Gaskell's Observation and Invention* (Fontwell, Sussex, 1970), p. 670. Gaskell's versions are variants of an established folk-narrative; see Briggs, 'The Guardian', B:2, p. 531.

2 I.e. *Lizzie Leigh and other tales*, 1855; *Round the Sofa*, 1859; *Right at Last and other tales*, 1860; *Cousin Phillis and other tales*, 1865; *The Grey Woman and other tales*, 1865 (the two collections of 1865 could be part of the house-buying effort). There was also the Tauchnitz (1861) *Lois the Witch and other tales*, a selection from earlier gatherings (Tauchnitz produced English language editions for sale only on the Continent).

3 Details of payment from Lohrli.

4 Vols 1, 2 and 3; for detailed references of original publication, see Sharps. Except where otherwise indicated, references in text and notes are to Knutsford, by volume and page.

5 Other tales of hers, already published in England, were reprinted in *Harper's*; e.g. 'Lizzie Leigh' (*Household Words*, 1850). See Sharps, bibliography.

6 *Mabel Vaughan*, by the Author of the 'Lamplighter'. [i.e. Maria Cummins] Edited ... By Mrs Gaskell, 1857, p. vi; see my note 'Elizabeth Gaskell, 'An Incident at Niagara Falls' and the editing of *Mabel Vaughan*' (1979). For attribution of 'The Siege' see Sharps, p. 261.

7 For a discreet account, see John Forster, *Life of Charles Dickens* (1872-4), ed. J. W. T. Ley (London, 1928), pp. 670ff. Dickens complicated matters by making his separation unnecessarily public. Gaskell was not very happy about this (see *Letters*, p. 535).

8 See Francisque-Michel, *Histoire des races maudits de la France et de l'Espagne*, 2 vols (Paris, 1847), i, p. 85: 'ceau-ci furent massacrés, et que leur têtes séparées des troncs servirent de boules pour jouer aux quilles sur la place de Saint-Pé'.

9 Evidence perhaps of Gaskell's reading by now of *The Prelude*; see robbing the raven's nest, bk 1, 11.326-39.

10 First published in the *Dublin University Magazine*, November 1858.

11 For the haunting/ghost theme, see Deborah A. Thomas, 'Contributions to the Christmas Numbers of *Household Words* and *All the Year Round*, 1850-1867', pt 2, *Dickensian*, lxx (January 1974), p. 21 and Harry Stone, 'The Unknown Dickens', *Dickens Studies Annual*, ed. Robert B. Partlow (Carbondale/Edwardsville/London/Amsterdam, 1970), i, pp. 8-12.

12 'The Manchester Marriage' appeared later, in the Christmas number, December 1858.

13 For well-argued adverse criticism of this see Margaret Ganz, *Elizabeth Gaskell: The Artist in Conflict* (New York, 1969), p. 220.

14 Charles W. Upham, *Lectures on Witchcraft* (Boston, 1831), pp. 11, 12,

111, 74; see 'Lois the Witch', vii, pp. 118, 114, 182-4, 195. Sharps (p. 316) identifies Upham but seems to leave his undoubted status as source open to question. Upham was a Unitarian.

15 See the versions in Halliwell ('Bluebeard'; 'Mr. Fox') and in Briggs, A:2, pp. 446-9 ('Mr Fox'; 'Mr. Fox's Courtship'). The popularity of the mysterious or suspected husband is shown by Thackeray's 'Miss Shum's Husband' (*Memoirs of Mr. Charles J. Yellowplush* (1837) 1856), Rokesmith's marriage to Bella in *Our Mutual Friend* (1865), and the story of Captain Murderer in Dickens's 'Nurse's Stories' (*The Uncommercial Traveller*, 1861).

16 Dickens, *Letters*, ed. Walter Dexter, 3 vols (London, 1938), iii, p. 320.

17 The first separate Christmas number of *Household Words* and the first to which Gaskell contributed is entitled 'A Round of Stories by the Christmas Fire'.

18 Two fragments of ghost stories, published by Ward (vii, pp. 721-7), have similarly rational openings, the first breaking off at the effective manifestation of a mother and child.

19 Originally 'How the First Floor went to Crowley Castle' in the sequence *Mrs. Lirriper's Lodgings*.

20 Letter to Lady Cowley, 13 December 1863, quoted *Dickensian*, lxx (May 1974), p. 96.

21 See Charles Perrault, *Fairy Tales* (1697), trans. Geoffrey Brereton (Harmondsworth, 1957) and Iona and Peter Opie, *The Classic Fairy Tales* (London, 1974), pp. 21-4, 81-136.

CHAPTER 9 Miscellaneous Writings and the Letters

1 i, pp. xxvi-vii; p. 34 above. Except where otherwise indicated, references in text and notes are to Knutsford, by volume and page.

2 *Blackwood's Magazine*, xli (January 1837).

3 See J. G. Sharps, *Mrs Gaskell's Observation and Invention* (Fontwell, Sussex, 1970), for evidence.

4 'Ginevra', *Italy*, 1830, pp. 92-6; strictly, given the poem's date, Ginevra cannot be the schoolgirl's memory, but a frisson added by the mature Gaskell.

5 The final anecdote of 'Disappearances' was provided with two (different) solutions (*Household Words*, iii, p. 305 and iv, pp. 513-14) and resuscitated by Henry Morley (xix, pp. 139-40) in a brief article, 'Character-Murder' (1859), to Gaskell's distress (*Letters*, p. 534).

6 iii, p. 478; Felicia Hemans, *Poetical Works* (London, 1914), p. 305. At least two other poems, 'Greek Funeral Chant' and 'The Parting Song' (pp. 152, 154) are drawn by Hemans from Fauriel; the original of the latter is in Gaskell, though without mention of Hemans.

7 Charles Brinsley Sheridan published a translation with additions in 1825.
8 See *Letters*, pp. 933, 703, 712.
9 For the unveiling see e.g. Leon Edel, *Henry James: The Untried Years* (London, 1953), p. 189; my quotation from Robert Lowell's 'For the Union Dead'.
10 Sharps, pp. 527-9.
11 To his wife, 14 October 1805; Robert Southey, *Letters: A Selection*, ed. M. H. Fitzgerald (London, 1912), p. 101.
12 See e.g. To Thomas Manning (5 December 1806) and to Baron Field (31 August 1817), Lamb, *Letters* (1950 edn), i, pp. 287ff., 389f., developed into 'Distant Correspondents'; and To Sarah Hazlitt (?10 November 1823), ii, pp. 101f., an earlier draft of 'Amicus Redivivus'.

Select Bibliography

Manuscript Material

Three manuscript music-books of Elizabeth Gaskell (Manchester Central Public Library).

Gaskell, E., *The Life of Charlotte Brontë* (1856-7) (John Rylands University Library of Manchester).

Gaskell, E., *The Life of Charlotte Brontë* (1 page) (Manchester Central Public Library).

Gaskell, E., *Sylvia's Lovers* (fragment of 1 page) (Manchester Central Public Library).

Gaskell, E., *Wives and Daughters* (1864-5) (John Rylands University Library of Manchester).

Brontë, Charlotte, Letter to Mary Taylor, 4 September 1848 (John Rylands University Library of Manchester).

Gaskell, William, Letters (from Unitarian College, Manchester; in keeping of John Rylands University Library of Manchester).

Manchester and Salford Sanitary Association: Visiting Committee's Reports: Deansgate District [1853-4] (Manchester Central Public Library).

Rev Wm Gaskell Memorial Fund: Minutes of Proceedings 1878 (Manchester Central Public Library).

Elizabeth Gaskell's Writings (*HW = Household Words*; *AYR = All the Year Round*)

'Sketches among the Poor – No. I' [with William Gaskell] (*Blackwood's Edinburgh Magazine*, xli, 1837).

'Clopton Hall' [in William Howitt's *Visits to Remarkable Places*], 1840.

'Libbie Marsh's Three Eras' (*Howitt's Journal*, i, 1847).

259

'The Sexton's Hero' (*Howitt's Journal*, ii, 1847).

'Our Manchester Correspondent; Emerson's Lectures' (*Howitt's Journal*, ii, 1847) [dubious attribution].

'Letter of Enquiry' (*Howitt's Journal*, ii, 1847) [dubious attribution].

'Christmas Storms and Sunshine' (*Howitt's Journal*, iii, 1848).

Mary Barton, 2 vols, 1848.

'The Last Generation in England' (*Sartain's Union Magazine*, 1849) [later expanded as *Cranford*].

'Hand and Heart' (*Sunday School Penny Magazine*, ii, 1849).

'Martha Preston' (*Sartain's Union Magazine*, vi, 1850) [rewritten as 'Half a Lifetime Ago'].

'Lizzie Leigh' (*HW*, i, 1850).

'The Well of Pen-Morfa' (*HW*, ii, 1850).

'The Heart of John Middleton' (*HW*, ii, 1850).

'The Moorland Cottage', 1850.

'Mr Harrison's Confessions' (*The Ladies' Companion*, iii, 1851).

'Disappearances' (*HW*, iii, 1851).

'Bessy's Troubles at Home' (*Sunday School Penny Magazine*, n.s.ii, 1852).

'The Schah's English Gardener' (*HW*, v, 1852).

'The Old Nurse's Story' (*HW*, Xmas 1852 in 'A Round of Stories by the Christmas Fire').

'Cumberland Sheep Shearers' (*HW*, vi, 1853).

Ruth, 3 vols, 1853.

Cranford, 1853 (serialized *HW*, iv-vii, 1851-3).

'Morton Hall' (*HW*, viii, 1853).

'My French Master' (*HW*, viii, 1853).

'Traits and Stories of the Huguenots' (*HW*, viii, 1853).

'The Squire's Story' (*HW*, Xmas 1853 in 'Another Round of Stories by the Christmas Fire').

'Modern Greek Songs' (*HW*, ix, 1854).

'Company Manners' (*HW*, ix, 1854).

Lizzie Leigh and other Tales, 1855 (contents: 'Lizzie Leigh'; 'The Well of Pen-Morfa'; 'The Heart of John Middleton'; 'The Old Nurse's Story'; 'Traits and Stories of the Huguenots'; 'Morton Hall'; 'My French Master'; 'The Squire's Story'; 'Libbie Marsh's Three Eras'; 'Christmas Storms and Sunshine'; 'Hand and Heart'; 'Bessy's Troubles at Home'; 'Disappearances').

North and South, 2 vols, 1855 (serialized *HW*, x, 1854-5).

'A Few Words about "Jane Eyre"' (*Sharp's London Magazine*, n.s.vi, 1855) [part of this article seems to reproduce or draw on a letter of Gaskell's].

'An Accursed Race' (*HW*, xii, 1855).

'Half a Lifetime Ago' (*HW*, xii, 1855) [reworked version of 'Martha Preston'].

'The Poor Clare' (*HW*, xiv, 1856).

'The Siege of the Black Cottage' (*Harper's New Monthly Magazine*, xiv, 1857) [uncertain attribution; see Sharps].

Mabel Vaughan, by the Author of the "Lamplighter" [i.e. Maria Cummins]. Edited . . . By Mrs. Gaskell, 1857 [Gaskell provided preface, some annotation, and interpolated material].

The Life of Charlotte Brontë, 2 vols, 1857.

'The Doom of the Griffiths' (*Harper's New Monthly Magazine*, xvi, 1858).

'My Lady Ludlow' (*HW*, xviii, 1858).

'An Incident at Niagara Falls' (*Harper's New Monthly Magazine*, xvii, 1858) [almost certainly Gaskell's; an interpolated episode in Cummins's *Mabel Vaughan* listed above].

'The Sin of a Father' (*HW*, xviii, 1858) [republished as 'Right at Last'].

'The Half-Brothers' (*Dublin University Magazine*, Nov, 1858).

'The Manchester Marriage' (*HW*, Xmas 1858 in 'A House to Let').

Round the Sofa, 2 vols, 1859 (contents: frame narrative; 'My Lady Ludlow'; 'An Accursed Race'; 'The Doom of the Griffiths'; 'Half a Lifetime Ago'; 'The Poor Clare'; 'The Half-Brothers').

'Lois the Witch' (*AYR*, i, 1859).

'The Ghost in the Garden Room' (*AYR*, Xmas 1859 in 'The Haunted House') [republished as 'The Crooked Branch'].

Right at Last and other tales, 1860 (contents: 'Right at Last' [originally 'The Sin of a Father']; 'A Manchester Marriage'; 'Lois the Witch'; 'The Crooked Branch' [originally 'The Ghost in the Garden Room']).

'Curious if True' (*Cornhill Magazine*, i, 1860).

'The Grey Woman' (*AYR*, iv, 1861).

'Six Weeks at Heppenheim' (*Cornhill Magazine*, v, 1862).

Preface to Vecchi, C. Augusto, *Garibaldi at Caprera*, 1862.

'A Dark Night's Work' (*AYR*, viii–ix, 1863).

'Shams' (*Fraser's Magazine*, lxvii, 1863).

'An Italian Institution' (*AYR*, ix, 1863).

Sylvia's Lovers, 3 vols, 1863.

'The Cage at Cranford' (*AYR*, x, 1863).

'Robert Gould Shaw' (*Macmillan's Magazine*, ix, 1863).

'Cousin Phillis' (*Cornhill Magazine*, viii, 1863).

'How the First Floor went to Crowley Castle' (*AYR*, Xmas 1863 in 'Mrs Lirriper's Lodgings') [republished as 'Crowley Castle'].

'French Life' (*Fraser's Magazine*, lxix, 1864).

Review of Torrens, W. T. M., *Lancashire's Lesson* (*The Reader*, v, 1865) [uncertain attribution].

'A Column of Gossip from Paris' (*Pall Mall Gazette*, 25 March 1865) [This and two following items identified by Sharps, q.v.].

'A Column of Gossip from Paris' (*Pall Mall Gazette*, 28 March 1865).

'A Letter of Gossip from Paris' (*Pall Mall Gazette*, 25 April 1865).

Cousin Phillis and other tales, 1865 (contents: 'Cousin Phillis'; 'Company

Manners'; 'Mr Harrison's Confessions'; 'The Sexton's Hero').

The Grey Woman and other tales, 1865 (contents: 'The Grey Woman'; 'Curious if True'; 'Six Weeks at Heppenheim'; 'Libbie Marsh's Three Eras'; 'Christmas Storms and Sunshine'; 'Hand and Heart'; 'Bessy's Troubles at Home'; 'Disappearances')

Wives and Daughters, 2 vols, 1866 (serialized *Cornhill Magazine*, x-xiii, 1864-6).

'On Visiting the Grave of My Stillborn Little Girl' (sonnet, 1836) [printed by Ward, i, xxvi-xxvii].

Two Fragments of Ghost Stories [printed by Ward, vii, 721-7].

My Diary, ed. Clement Shorter, 1923 (privately printed).

Collected Editions

There is no complete edition: the most comprehensive are

The Works of Mrs. Gaskell, ed. A. W. Ward, 8 vols (London, The Knutsford edition, 1906), [excludes *The Life of Charlotte Brontë*].

The Novels and Tales of Mrs. Gaskell, ed. Clement Shorter, 11 vols (London, World's Classics, 1906-19) [includes *The Life of Charlotte Brontë*].

Single Editions

The novels and some stories are currently available in the Everyman Library. Individual editions of value, which offer good texts, introductions, notes, and further reading include:

Cranford, intro by Anne Thackeray Ritchie (London, 1891).

Cranford, ed. Elizabeth Porges Watson (London, 1972 [includes 'The Last Generation in England' and 'The Cage at Cranford']; paperback, 1977).

Cranford/Cousin Phillis, ed. Peter Keating (Harmondsworth, 1976) [includes 'The Last Generation in England' and 'The Cage at Cranford'].

The Life of Charlotte Brontë, intro. Winifred Gérin (Oxford, 1971).

The Life of Charlotte Brontë, ed. Alan Shelston (Harmondsworth, 1975) [text of 1st edn].

Mary Barton, ed. Stephen Gill (Harmondsworth, 1970).

North and South, ed. Dorothy Collin (Harmondsworth, 1970).

North and South, ed. Angus Easson (London, 1973; paperback, 1977).

Letters, Biographies and General Studies

Letters of Mrs. Gaskell and Charles Eliot Norton 1855-1865, ed. Jane Whitehill (London, 1932).

Letters of Mrs. Gaskell, ed. J. A. V. Chapple and Arthur Pollard (Manchester, 1966).

Gérin, Winifred, *Elizabeth Gaskell: A Biography* (Oxford, 1976).

Hopkins, A. B., *Elizabeth Gaskell: Her Life and Work* (London, 1952).

Craik, W. A., *Elizabeth Gaskell and the English Provincial Novel* (London, 1975).

Ganz, Margaret, *Elizabeth Gaskell: The Artist in Conflict* (New York, 1969).

Lansbury, Coral, *Elizabeth Gaskell: The Novel of Social Crisis* (London, 1975).

Pollard, Arthur, *Mrs. Gaskell: Novelist and Biographer* (Manchester, 1965).

Sharps, J. G., *Mrs. Gaskell's Observation and Invention* (Fontwell, Sussex, 1970).

Wright, Edgar, *Mrs. Gaskell: The Basis for Reassessment* (London, 1965).

For further studies see the bibliographies in single editions above; Miriam Allott's contribution to *New Cambridge Bibliography of English Literature* (vol. 3), ed. George Watson (Cambridge, 1969); *Year's Work in English Studies; Annual Bibliography of English Literature*; and General Bibliography below.

General Bibliography

Adams, W. E., *Memoirs of a Social Atom*, 2 vols (London, 1903).

Annual Register for 1795.

Annual Register for 1796.

Arnold, Matthew, *The Function of Criticism at the Present Time*, (London, 1864).

Ashton, T. S., *The Industrial Revolution 1760-1830* (London, 1948; revised edn 1968).

Baines, Edward, *History, Directory and Gazatteer* [sic] *of the County Palatine of Lancaster*, 2 vols (Liverpool, 1824-5; facsimile reprint, 2 vols, Newton Abbot, 1968).

Baines, Edward, *History of the Cotton Manufacture in Great Britain ... and a View of the Present State of the Manufacture, and the Conditions of the Classes Engaged in its Several Departments*, n.d. [London, 1835].

Bamford, Samuel, *Passages in the Life of a Radical*, 2 vols (London, 1844).

Bamford, Samuel, *Early Days* (1848), 2 vols (Manchester and London, 1859).

Barbauld, A. L., *Lessons for Children* (London, 1808).

Barbauld, A. L., *A Legacy for Young Ladies* (London, 1826).

Barrow, John, *The Life and Correspondence of Admiral Sir William Sidney Smith*, 2 vols (London, 1848).

Blackmore, John, *The London by Moonlight Mission* (London, 1860).

Boase, T. S. R., *English Art 1800-1870* (Oxford, 1959).

Boswell, James, *Life of Samuel Johnson* (London, 1791).

Boucicault, Dion, *The Long Strike* (New York, n.d.) [performed 1866].

Brantlinger, Patrick, 'The Case Against Trade Unions in Early Victorian Fiction', *Victorian Studies*, xii (1969).

Briggs, Asa, *Victorian Cities* (London, 1963; Harmondsworth, 1968).

Briggs, Katherine, M., *A Dictionary of British Folk-Tales*, 4 vols (London, 1970-1).

British Quarterly Review, ix (1849) (review of *Mary Barton*).

Brontë, Charlotte, *Jane Eyre* (London, 1847).

Brontë, Charlotte, *Shirley* (London, 1849).

Brontë, Charlotte, *Villette* (London, 1853).

Brontë, Charlotte, *The Professor* (London, 1857).

The Brontës: Their Lives, Friendships and Correspondence, ed. T. J. Wise and J. A. Symington, 4 vols (London, 1932) [in the Shakespeare Head Brontë, 19 vols, London, 1931-8].

Burnett, John, *Plenty and Want*, (London, 1966; Harmondsworth, 1968).

Butler, Marilyn, 'The Uniqueness of Cynthia Kirkpatrick: Elizabeth Gaskell's *Wives and Daughters* and Maria Edgeworth's *Helen*', *Review of English Studies*, xxiii (1972).

Carlyle, Jane Welsh, *Letters and Memorials*, ed. James Anthony Froude, 3 vols (London, 1883).

Carlyle, Thomas, *Past and Present* (London, 1843; Ashburton edn, vol 2 1885).

Carlyle, Thomas, *The Life of Sterling* (London, 1851; Edinburgh edn) 1902.

Carlyle, Thomas, *New Letters*, ed. Alexander Carlyle, 2 vols (London, 1904).

Catalogue of the Art Treasures of the United Kingdom. Collected at Manchester in 1857, n.d. [1857] or place.

Chadwick, Edwin, *Poor Law Commission Report* (London, 1842).

Chadwick, Owen, *The Victorian Church* pt. 1 (London, 1966; 3rd edn, 1971).

Character, Object, and Effects of Trades' Unions; with Some Remarks on the Law Concerning Them (London, 1834).

Christian, Mildred G., 'Census of Brontë Manuscripts in the United States: Part One', *Trollopian* (now *Nineteenth-Century Fiction*), ii (1947).

Clare, John, *Sketches in the Life*, ed. Edmund Blunden (London, 1931).

Coleridge, S. T., *Biographia Literaria* (1817), ed J. Shawcross, 2 vols (London, 1907; 1969).

Coleridge, S. T., *Notebooks*, ed. Kathleen Coburn, vol. 1 (London, 1957).

Dickens, Charles, *The Old Curiosity Shop* (1841), ed. Angus Easson (Harmondsworth, 1972).

Dickens, Charles, *David Copperfield* (London, 1850).

[Dickens, Charles], 'On Strike', *Household Words*, viii (1854).

Dickens, Charles, *The Uncommercial Traveller* (London, 1861).

Dickens, Charles, *Our Mutual Friend* (London, 1865).

Dickens, Charles, *Letters*, ed. Walter Dexter, 3 vols (London, 1938).

Dickens, Charles, *Speeches*, ed. K. J. Fielding (Oxford, 1960).

Dickens, Charles, [Letter to Lady Cowley], *Dickensian*, lxx (1974).

Dickens, Charles, *Selected Short Fiction*, ed. Deborah A. Thomas (Harmondsworth, 1976).

Disraeli, Benjamin, *Sybil, or The Two Nations* (London, 1845).

Dodderidge, Philip, *Family Expositor*, 6 vols (London, 1739).

Dodsworth, Martin, 'Women without Men at Cranford', *Essays in Criticism*, xiii (1963).

Drummond, James and Upton, C. B., *The Life and Letters of James Martineau*, 2 vols (London, 1902).

Dubois, E-T., 'Madame de Sévigné et l'Angleterre', *XVIIe Siècle* (1971).

Easson, Angus, 'Dickens, *Household Words*, and a Double Standard', *Dickensian*, lx (1964).

Easson, Angus, *Hard Times: Commentary and Notes* (London, 1973).

Easson, Angus, 'Two Suppressed Opinions in Mrs. Gaskell's *Life of Charlotte Brontë*', *Brontë Society Transactions*, xvi (1974).

Easson, Angus, 'Substantive Misprints and a Deletion in Elizabeth Gaskell's "Life of Charlotte Brontë"', *Notes and Queries*, ccxxi (1976).

Easson, Angus, 'Thackeray, Elizabeth Gaskell, and *The Life of Charlotte Brontë*', *Victorian Studies Newsletter* (1979).

Easson, Angus, 'Elizabeth Gaskell, 'An Incident at Niagara Falls' and the editing of *Mabel Vaughan*', (1979).

Edel, Leon, *Henry James: The Untried Years* (London, 1953).

Eliot, George, *Scenes of Clerical Life* (1858), ed. David Lodge (Harmondsworth, 1973).

Eliot, George, *Adam Bede* (London, 1860).

Eliot, George, *Silas Marner* (London, 1861).

Eliot, George, *Felix Holt the Radical* (London, 1866).

Eliot, George, *Middlemarch* (London, 1871).

Eliot, George, *Letters*, ed. Gordon S. Haight, 7 vols (London/New Haven, 1954-6).

'Charlotte Elizabeth' [Mrs Tonna], *Helen Fleetwood* (London, 1841).

Engels, Frederick, *The Condition of the Working Class in England* (1845; London, 1969).

Faucher, Leon, *Manchester in 1844: Its Present Condition and Future Prospects* (London and Manchester, 1844; facsimile reprint 1969).

Fauriel, Claude, *Chantes populaires de la Grèce moderne* (Paris, 1824-5).

Flinn, M. W., 'Social Theory and the Industrial Revolution', in Tom Burns and S. B. Saul (eds), *Social Theory and Economic Change* (London, 1967):

Forster, John, *Life of Charles Dickens* (1872-4), ed. J. W. T. Ley (London, 1928).

Francisque-Michel, *Histoire des races maudits de la France et de l'Espagne*, 2 vols (Paris, 1847).

Gaskell, William, *Two Lectures on the Lancashire Dialect* (London, 1854).

Gaskell, William, *Sermon for Milton's Death-Day* (London, 1857).

Gaskell, William, 'The Person of Christ', in *The Religion and Theology of Unitarians* (London, 1906).

Gérin, Winifred, *Charlotte Brontë: The Evolution of Genius* (London, 1967).

Gill, Stephen, 'A Manuscript of Branwell Brontë, with Letters of Mrs. Gaskell', *Brontë Society Transactions*, xii (1970).

Gombrich, E. H., *Norm and Form* (London, 1966).

[Greg, W. R.], [Review of *Mary Barton*], *Edinburgh Review*, lxxxix (1849).

Greg, W. R., *Literary and Social Judgements* (London, 1868).

Griest, Guinevere L., *Mudie's Circulating Library and the Victorian Novel* (Newton Abbot, 1970).

Haight, Gordon, *George Eliot: A Biography* (Oxford, 1968).

Hallé, Charles, *The Autobiography*, (1896; ed. Michael Kennedy, London, 1972).

Halliwell [later Halliwell-Phillips], James Orchard, *The Nursery Rhymes of England* (London, 1842, 2nd edn).

Hammond, J. L. and Barbara, *The Town Labourer* (London 1925, 2nd edn).

Handley, Graham, 'The Chronology of "Sylvia's Lovers"', *Notes and Queries*, ccx (1965).

Hardy, Barbara, 'Mrs. Gaskell and George Eliot', *Sphere History of Literature in English* (vol. 6), ed. Arthur Pollard (London, 1970).

Hardy, Barbara, 'Dickens and the Passions', *Dickens Centennial Essays*, ed. Ada Nisbet and Blake Nevius (Berkeley/Los Angeles/London, 1971).

Hare, Augustus J. C., *Memorials of a Quiet Life*, 2 vols (London, 1872, 2nd edn).

Hawthorne, Nathaniel, 'The May Pole of Merrymount' (1835; reprinted in *Twice-Told Tales*, 1837).

Hawthorne, Nathaniel, *The Scarlet Letter* (London, 1850).

Hawthorne, Nathaniel, *French and Italian Notebooks* (Boston/New York, 1896).

Hawthorne: The Critical Heritage, ed. Donald J. Crowley (London, 1970).

Head, George, *A Home Tour through the Manufacturing Districts of England in the Summer of 1835* (London, 1836; facsimile reprint 1968).

Hemans, Felicia, *Poetical Works* (London, Oxford edn, 1914).

Herford, Brooke, *Travers Madge: A Memoir* (London/Manchester/Norwich, 1867).

Hicks, Phyllis D., *A Quest of Ladies: The Story of a Warwickshire School* (Birmingham, n.d.) [1949] (privately printed).

Hobsbawm, E. J., *Industry and Empire* (Harmondsworth, 1969).

Holland, Bernard, *The Lancashire Hollands* (London, 1917).
Holland, Edgar, *A History of the Family of Holland*, ed. W. F. Irvine (Edinburgh, 1902).
Holland, Henry, *Recollections of Past Life* (London, 1872).
Holme, Thea, *The Carlyles at Home* (London, 1965).
Holyoake, George Jacob, *Bygones Worth Remembering* (London, 1905; 2 vols, 1915).
Howe, Susanna, *Geraldine Jewsbury: Her Life and Errors* (London, 1935).
Hutchins, B. L. and Harrison, A., *A History of Factory Legislation* (London, 1903).
James, Henry, *Hawthorne* (English Men of Letters Series) (London, 1879; 1883).
James, Henry, *William Whetmore Story and His Friends*, 2 vols (London, 1903; facsimile reprint n.d. [1957]).
James, Henry, *Notes and Reviews* (London, 1921; facsimile reprint 1968).
Jameson, Anna, *Letters and Friendships (1812-1860)*, ed. Mrs Steuart Erskine (London, 1915).
Jewsbury, Geraldine, *Zoë* (London, 1845).
Jewsbury, Geraldine, *Marian Withers*, 3 vols (London, 1851).
Jewsbury, Geraldine, *Letters*, ed. Mrs Alexander Ireland (London, 1892).
Kingsley, Charles, *Alton Locke* (London, 1850).
Kingsley, Charles, *Yeast* (London, 1851).
Kingsley, Charles, *His Letters and Memoirs of his Life, edited by his Wife*, 2 vols (London, 1888; 16th abridged edn).
Laclos, Choderlos de, *Les Liaisons Dangereuses* (1782).
Lamb, Charles, *Letters*, 2 vols (London, 1950).
[Lamb, R.], *Free Thoughts on Many Subjects by a Manchester Man*, 2 vols (London, 1866).
Leavis, F. R., *The Great Tradition* (London, 1947).
Leavis, F. R. and Q. D., *Dickens the Novelist* (London, 1970).
Lewald, Fanny, *England und Schottland*, 2 vols (Brunswick, 1851-2).
Lohrli, Anne, *Household Words* (Toronto, 1973).
[Lowe, James], 'Locked Out', *Household Words*, viii (1853).
[McDermid, T. W.], *The Life of Thomas Wright, The Prison Philanthropist* (Manchester, n.d.) [1876].
McLachlan, H., *The Unitarian Home Missionary College 1854-1914* (Manchester/London, 1915).
McLachlan, H., 'Cross Street Chapel in the Life of Manchester', *Memoirs and Proceedings of the Manchester Literary and Philosophical Society*, lxxxiv (Manchester, 1942).
Manchester as It Is (Manchester, 1839; facsimile reprint, 1971).
Marlow, Joyce, *The Peterloo Massacre* (London, 1969).
Martineau, James, *Endeavours after the Christian Life* (London, 1843).

Mason, William, 'Memoir of Thomas Gray' [prefixed to *Poems*] (London, 1775).

Maurice, F. D., *The Kingdom of Christ*, 2 vols (London, 1837).

Mews, Hazel, *Frail Vessels* (London, 1969).

Mitford, Mary Russell, *Our Village* (1824–32), intro. Anne Thackeray Ritchie (London, 1893).

The Monitor, compiled Mrs H. Gregg (Liverpool, 1804).

Moorman, Mary, *William Wordsworth: The Early Years 1770-1803* (Oxford, 1957).

Moorman, Mary, *William Wordsworth: The Later Years 1803-1850* (Oxford, 1965).

[Morley, Henry], 'An Unpaid Servant of the State', *Household Words*, iv (1852).

[Morley, Henry], 'Ground in the Mill', *Household Words*, ix (1854).

National Gallery: Descriptive and Historical Catalogue of the British and Foreign Pictures ... (London, 1913, 81st edn).

Newman, F. W., *The Soul* (London, 1849).

Newman, F. W., *Phases of Faith* (London, 1850; 1860; facsimile reprint, Leicester, 1970, intro U. C. Knoepflmacher).

Newman, F. W., *Personal Narrative in Letters* (London, 1856).

[Nightingale, Florence], *Letters from Egypt* (1854, privately printed).

Norton, C. E., *Notes of Travel and Study in Italy* (1859; Boston, 1881).

Oliphant, Mrs Margaret, *Autobiography and Letters*, ed. Mrs Harry Coghill (London, 1899; facsimile reprint, Leicester, 1974, intro. Q. D. Leavis).

O'Meara, Kate, *Madame Mohl: Her Salon and Her Friends* (London, 1885).

Opie, Iona and Peter, *The Classic Fairy Tales* (London, 1974).

Ormond, Richard, *Early Victorian Portraits*, 2 vols (London, 1973).

Pardon, G. F., *The Manchester Conductor* (Manchester, 1857).

Parkes, Mrs William, *Domestic Duties: or, Introduction to Young Married Ladies on the Management of their Households* (London, 1825).

Patterson, Clara Burdett, *Angela Burdett-Coutts and the Victorians* (London, 1953).

Perrault, Charles, *Fairy Tales* (1697), trans Geoffrey Brereton (Harmondsworth, 1957).

Perrin, Joseph, *The Manchester Handbook* (Manchester, n.d.) [1859].

Pike, E. Royston (ed), *Human Documents of the Industrial Revolution in Britain* (London, 1966).

Playfair, Lyon, *Report on the State of Large Towns in Lancashire* (Health of Towns Commission) (London, 1845).

The Poor Man's Advocate (1832–3; facsimile reprint, New York, 1969).

[Priestley, Joseph], *An Appeal to the Serious and Candid Professors of Christianity* (London, 1771, 3rd edn).

Priestley, Joseph, *Autobiography* (1805), ed. Jack Lindsay (Bath, 1970).

268

Quarterley Review, xcviii (1856) [review of *Memorials of the Bagot Family*, etc].

Ratchford, Fanny E., *The Brontës' Web of Childhood* (New York, 1941).

Report of the Committee of the Manchester and Salford Sanitary Association for the Year 1861 (Manchester, n.d.) [1861].

Report of the Road and Street Cleansing Company (Manchester, 1843).

Richardson, Samuel, *Clarissa* (London, 1748).

[Ribgy, Elizabeth] [review of *Vanity Fair, Jane Eyre*, etc.], *Quarterly Review*, lxxxiv (1849).

Robinson, Dennis, 'Elizabeth Gaskell and "A Few Words about 'Jane Eyre'"', *Notes and Queries*, ccxxi (1976).

Robinson, Henry Crabb, *On Books and Their Writers*, ed. Edith J. Morley, 3 vols (London, 1938).

[Rogers, Samuel], *Recollections of the Table Talk of Samuel Rogers*, ed. Alexander Dyce (London, 1856, 2nd ed).

Rosa, M. W., *The Silver-Fork School* (New York, 1936).

A Schoolmaster's Notebook, ed. Edith and Thomas Kelly (Manchester, Chetham Society, 3rd series, vol. 8, 1957).

Scoresby, William, *An Account of the Arctic Regions, with a History and Description of the Northern Whale Fishery*, 2 vols (Edinburgh/London, 1820).

Shaen, M. J., (ed.), *Memorials of Two Sisters* (London, 1908).

Shaen, M. J., *William Shaen: A Brief Sketch* (London, 1912).

Shepheard, H., *A Vindication of the Clergy Daughters' School, and of the Rev. W. Carus Wilson* ... (Kirby Lonsdale/London, 1857).

Sherwood, Mrs [Mary], *The History of the Fairchild Family* (3 pts) (London, 1818-47).

Shorter, Clement, *The Brontës: Life and Letters*, 2 vols (London, 1908).

Sieveking, I. Giberne, *Memoir and Letters of Francis W. Newman* (London, 1909).

Simpson, M. C. M., *Letters and Recollections of Julius and Mary Mohl* (London, 1887).

Skilton, David, *Anthony Trollope and his Contemporaries* (London, 1972).

[Southey, Robert] [review of Cottle's *Reminiscences of Coleridge*, etc.], *Edinburgh Review*, clxxvi (1848).

Southey, Robert, *Letters: A Selection*, ed. Maurice H. Fitzgerald (London, 1912).

Stevens, Joan, *Mary Taylor: Friend of Charlotte Brontë* (Auckland/London, 1972).

Stone, Elizabeth, *William Langshawe, The Cotton Lord*, 2 vols (London, 1842).

Stone, Harry, 'The Unknown Dickens', *Dickens Studies Annual*, ed. Robert B. Partlow (Carbondale/Edwardsville/London/Amsterdam, 1970), i.

Sutherland, J. A., *Thackeray at Work* (London, 1974).

Taylor, Arthur J. (ed). *The Standard of Living in Britain in the Industrial Revolution* (London, 1976).

Tennyson, Alfred, *Poems,* ed. Christopher Ricks (London, 1969).

Thackeray, W. M., *Memoirs of Mr Charles J. Yellowplush* (1837; London, 1856).

Thackeray, W. M., *Vanity Fair* (London, 1848).

Thackeray, W. M., *Letters and Private Papers,* ed. Gordon N. Ray, 4 vols (London, 1945-6).

Thomas, Deborah A., 'Contributors to the Christmas Numbers of *Household Words* and *All the Year Round, 1850-1867',* pt II, *Dickensian,* lxx (1974).

Thompson, E. P., *The Making of the English Working Class* (Harmondsworth, 1968).

Thompson, Patricia, *The Victorian Heroine* (London, 1956).

Tilley, Arthur, *Madame de Sévigné* (Cambridge, 1936).

Tillotson, Kathleen, *Novels of the 1840s* (1956; London, 1961).

Trimmer, Mrs [Sarah], *Fabulous Histories, or The Story of the Robin* (London, 1786).

Trollope, Anthony, *The Vicar of Bullhampton* (London, 1870).

Trollope, Anthony, *Autobiography* (1883), ed. Frederick Page (London, 1950).

Trollope, Anthony, *Letters,* ed. Bradford Allen Booth (London, 1951).

Trollope, Frances, *The Life and Adventures of Michael Armstrong the Factory Boy* (London, 1840), serialized 1839-40; facsimile reprint 1968).

Tyerman, L., *The Life and Times of the Rev. John Wesley,* 3 vols (London, 1871).

Upham, Charles W., *Lectures on Witchcraft* (Boston, 1831).

Waters, A. T. H., *Report on the Sanitary Condition of Certain Parts of Manchester* (Manchester and Salford Sanitary Association) (Manchester, 1853).

Westminster Review, ii (1849) [review of *Mary Barton*].

White, Gilbert, *The Natural History of Selborne* (London, 1789).

White, R. J., *Waterloo to Peterloo* (London, 1957).

Wilbur, Earl Morse, *A History of Unitarianism* (Cambridge, Mass., 1952).

Willey, Basil, *The Eighteenth-Century Background* (London, 1940; Harmondsworth, 1972).

Willey, Basil, *Nineteenth-Century Studies* (London, 1949; Harmondsworth, 1973).

Willey, Basil, *More Nineteenth-Century Studies* (London, 1956).

Williams, Raymond, *Culture and Society 1780-1950* (London, 1958).

Winkworth, Catherine, *Lyra Germanica* (London, 1855).

Winkworth, Catherine, *Christian Singers of Germany* (London, 1869).

Winnifrith, T. J., *The Brontës and Their Background: Romance and Reality* (London, 1973).

Wordsworth, William and Coleridge, S. T., *Lyrical Ballads* (London, 1800, 2nd edn), ed. R. L. Brett and A. R. Jones (London, 1963; 1965).

Young, George, *A History of Whitby*, 2 vols (Whitby, 1817).

Index

Index

Index

Index